The San Francisco V-J Day
Peace Riots

ALSO BY GENE ERIC SALECKER
AND FROM MCFARLAND

*Typhoon Louise vs. the United States Navy:
Catastrophe at Okinawa, October 9–10, 1945* (2023)

# The San Francisco V-J Day Peace Riots
## Celebration Turned Deadly, August 13–15, 1945

GENE ERIC SALECKER

McFarland & Company, Inc., Publishers
*Jefferson, North Carolina*

ISBN (print) 978-1-4766-9889-2
ISBN (ebook) 978-1-4766-5802-5

Library of Congress cataloging data are available

© 2026 Gene Eric Salecker. All rights reserved

*No part of this book may be reproduced or transmitted in any form or by any means, electronic or mechanical, including photocopying or recording, or by any information storage and retrieval system, without permission in writing from the publisher.*

Front cover image: The crowded intersection of Market and Mason Streets on V-J Day, August 14, 1945 (San Francisco History Center, San Francisco Public Library).

Printed in the United States of America

*McFarland & Company, Inc., Publishers*
*Box 611, Jefferson, North Carolina 28640*
*www.mcfarlandpub.com*

To my brothers, Alan, Gary, Paul, and Greg.
And to Scott, Chris, Noah, and Adian,
who call San Francisco their home.

# Table of Contents

*Introduction*   1

1. Hope and Preparation   3
2. A False Flash   13
3. Another False Alarm   18
4. Celebrate   29
5. It Begins   37
6. Wild Night   48
7. The Darker Side   55
8. Quiet   62
9. Renewal   67
10. The Aftermath   76
11. The Blame Game   84
12. Liquor Wars   94
13. The Grand Jury   99
14. Support and Planning   103
15. Passing the Buck   108
16. The Quiet Holiday Weekend   114
17. Celebration Done Right   119
18. Compare and Contrast   129

*Conclusion*   140
*Chapter Notes*   145
*Bibliography*   162
*Index*   167

# Introduction

While reading a book about V-J Day (Victory Over Japan Day) and the end of World War II in the Pacific, I came across a mention of a riot in San Francisco. Beginning on the evening of August 13, 1945, when a news flash announced that Japan was going to accept the official surrender documents, the people of the City by the Bay rushed into the streets to celebrate. Many, mostly teenagers and people in their early 20s, crowded the downtown area, flooding Market Street, the main thoroughfare in San Francisco. Soon, they were joined by thousands of young service personnel, mostly sailors, from the nearby army and naval bases. At first the celebration was all fun, with the men kissing the girls, people dancing in the street, and everybody having a grand time. However, with alcohol flowing freely, the situation soon got out of hand. People started bonfires in the street and damaged trolley cars and automobiles. Both civilian and armed forces police did little to stop the unruly celebration. The celebrating would pause during the morning hours and then begin anew in the late afternoon, eventually turning into a riot. The destruction went on for three straight nights, resulting in the deaths of 13 people, the rape of at least six women, the breaking of more than 100 plate glass storefront windows, and more than 1,000 people injured.

I have read literally hundreds of books on World War II and have written five books on the war in the Pacific, yet I had never heard of the San Francisco V-J Day "Peace Riots." In the book I had been reading, *VJ Day: The End of WWII in the Pacific*, author Kim Lockwood wrote, "The VJ Day riots in San Francisco became something of an unspoken secret in the city.... [I]t seems people wanted to forget that night [sic] and move on. Later generations didn't even know it had happened."[1] Too true.

Immediately after the three nights of disturbance, the San Francisco district attorney swore to find the cause of the rioting and bring the guilty parties to justice. A grand jury began interviewing dozens of individuals, but in the end, it became a giant whitewash. In August 1945, with the war

## Introduction

finally behind it, San Francisco just wanted everybody to forget about the riot. In fact, maybe it still does.

Occasionally, near the anniversary dates of the riot, a San Francisco journalist might run an article describing those wild nights in August 1945, and a few authors who have written books about the history of San Francisco have included some lines about the riot. But generally, the story has been overlooked and brushed aside. Whether this is through a concerted effort or simply out of ignorance is unknown. Today, many San Franciscans have probably never even heard of the V-J Day Riots. As a whole, San Francisco has risen high above those dark nights in August 1945 and can hold her head up high among the wonderful cities of the United States, even the world. Still, the rioting took place and is a part of history. It cannot be swept aside or overlooked.

In gathering research for this book, I sent several letters to the San Francisco district attorney's office, simply asking where I could go to obtain a copy of the 1945 grand jury information and transcripts. All the letters went unanswered, including the certified letter. When I finally called the district attorney's office, a young man informed me that he had never heard of the Peace Riots and told me that the DA's office did not keep any records from events that happened 80 years ago. He directed me to the San Francisco History Center of the San Francisco Public Library.

Andrea Grimes, program manager for the library's Book Arts & Special Collections, went out of her way to find "the full (or excerpts) of the Grand Jury transcript for the 'peace riot' reports." Unfortunately, she could find nothing. "I am disappointedly letting you know that the Library does not have a copy of the report," she wrote to me. Grimes added, "Although our Government Information Center does hold grand jury reports from this time-period (prior to 1995), they are the final reports, not specific reports of grand jury investigations such as the 'victory riot'/ 'peace riot.'" Since there was never any further action taken on the findings of the August 1945 grand jury investigation, there may not be a copy of the report in existence anywhere. There may never have been one.

In 1953, the San Francisco grand jury published the "Report of the Grand Jury, San Francisco" covering the year 1945. While the report makes offhand reference to the Peace Riots, there is no specific coverage of the event. Not even one paragraph. No matter. I found enough information in other sources, mainly in the contemporary newspaper accounts of the affair, to complete this book. It is time to bring the San Francisco Peace Riots back into the light.

CHAPTER 1

# Hope and Preparation

In early August 1945, the citizens of the United States, and almost all people throughout the world, had been anticipating the official surrender of the Japanese Empire and the end of World War II. The war had been raging since September 1, 1939, when Germany invaded Poland, and for the United States since December 7, 1941, when the Japanese staged a surprise attack on the American fleet at Pearl Harbor in the Territory of Hawaii. Now, after almost six years of terrible warfare, in August 1945, the world held its collective breath and waited.

In July 1945, the leaders of the United States, Great Britain, China, and the Soviet Union had met in Potsdam, Germany, to work out an ultimatum to be issued to Japan for the cessation of hostilities. Author John C. McManus explained in the third book of his three-volume work on the U.S. Army in the Pacific in World War II, "The Allied powers issued the Potsdam Declaration on July 26 stipulating unconditional surrender, postwar occupation, transformation of the Japanese government, and the punishment of war criminals, and hinting at but not guaranteeing the perpetuation of the emperor." Japan ignored a response to the declaration as both civilian and military personnel debated the effects of the acceptance of the pronouncement. Then, on August 6, the Americans dropped an atomic bomb on Hiroshima, killing an estimated 80,000 people instantly. When Japan still failed to accept the terms of the Potsdam Declaration, a second atomic bomb was dropped on Nagasaki on August 9, obliterating another 20,000 people. Since then, the world had waited for the Japanese to capitulate. Although it seemed like an easy, and sensible, thing to do, there was still much wrangling and haggling among the Japanese military and civilian authorities. Japan wanted a conditional surrender whereby Emperor Hirohito would remain on his throne.[1] Finally, by the middle of August, there were strong indications that the official surrender would come at any time.

In San Francisco, the City by the Bay, hundreds of newly recruited and trained service men and women, mostly sailors, along with the almost

## The San Francisco V-J Day Peace Riots

650,000 inhabitants of the city, eagerly awaited the surrender announcement.[2] During World War II, San Francisco had been turned into "Fortress San Francisco." Three coastal defense structures, Forts Baker, Barry, and Cronkhite, protected the northern end of the Golden Gate Bridge and the entrance into San Francisco Bay, which was also protected by a submarine net. Guarding the southern end of the bay entrance was Fort Point, built prior to the Civil War in the Presidio, the site of the first Spanish settlement and fortress. Along the Pacific shores, both north and south of the all-important entrance to the bay, were numerous concrete gun emplacements. "Mobile antiaircraft guns, searchlights and radars were positioned on virtually every hill and knoll overlooking the Golden Gate," noted National Park Ranger John A. Martini in a pamphlet created for the National Park Service. All these forts, gun emplacements, and various installations were manned by hundreds of young recruits, both volunteers and draftees.[3]

Inside the Bay, on the north end of San Francisco, between Fisherman's Wharf and the Golden Gate Bridge, sat Fort Mason, an old Civil War–era facility that had become a major point of embarkation for troops. "During World War II, Liberty ships built in Bay Area shipyards were constantly ferrying troops to the immense pier and dock system at Lower Fort Mason," says a National Park Service brochure on the fort. Because of the importance of San Francisco within a protected bay, the port of embarkation was expanded so that by the middle of 1945, there were a total of 13 facilities along the waterfront, which included 20 piers with 43 berths and millions of square feet of warehouse space, being operated and used by the United States government to send troops and supplies to the Pacific theater. Noted *New York Times Magazine*, "[San Francisco's Port of Embarkation] has one main commodity to send abroad. It is exporting war." Second only to New York City on the East Coast, which sent over three million service men and women and over 33 million tons of supplies to the European and Mediterranean theaters, the entire San Francisco Bay area, under the control of the commander of the San Francisco Port of Embarkation, sent 1,657,509 combatants and over 22 million tons of supplies off to support the war in the Pacific between 1941 and 1945.[4]

In addition to the numerous military points of embarkation, San Francisco Bay also contained a large naval training base on Treasure Island, an artificial island that had been constructed between San Francisco and Oakland in 1937 for the 1939 Golden Gate International Exposition. Composed of 400 acres of land, Treasure Island, connected by a

## Chapter 1. Hope and Preparation

**U.S. Naval Training and Distribution Center, Treasure Island. The Oakland–San Francisco Bridge and the city of San Francisco are in the background (San Francisco History Center, San Francisco Public Library).**

six-lane causeway to nearby tiny Yerba Buena Island, which itself was connected to both Oakland and San Francisco by a major highway, was known as the U.S. Naval Training and Distribution Center, San Francisco. By August 1945, nearly 4.5 million "of the world's finest fighting men" had been trained at Treasure Island.[5]

However, as author Wayne Bonnett wrote in his work *Build Ships! San Francisco Bay Wartime Shipbuilding Photographs*, "The San Francisco Bay Area's major contribution to victory during World War II was shipbuilding. Over 30 shipyards, large and small, and scores of machine shops, and metal and wood fabricators joined together to create the world's largest combined shipbuilding complex." Added a National Park Service pamphlet on the San Francisco shipyards, "Proximity to the Pacific war made the Bay Area a logical ship production site. Victory in the Pacific depended on ships; all men and material had to reach the war zone by ship."[6]

On the east coast of San Fransico itself was Hunters Point Naval Shipyard, a shipyard and repair facility. North of the city, at Sausalito, was Marinship Corporation, which built cargo ships and tankers. Across the Bay, northeast of San Francisco, at Richmond, was Henry J. Kaiser's Richmond Shipyard Number Three, which built approximately 1,400 ships during the war, averaging one ship a day. Also at Richmond was the Ford Motor Company Assembly Plant, which during the war had converted from making automobiles to making armored tanks. Twenty-three miles north of San Francisco, at Vallejo on San Pablo Bay, was Mare Island Naval Shipyard, and just east of there, at Benicia, was the Benicia Arsenal and nearby Camp Stoneman, an army processing area. These several facilities employed tens of thousands of workers, both male and female, adding to the wartime increase in the population of the San Francisco Bay area. Noted author Bonnett, "Tens of thousands of unskilled men and women were recruited to meet demands of new emergency shipyards."[7]

For the thousands of men and women who came to San Francisco, either as new recruits of the army or navy or to work in the numerous war plants and shipbuilding facilities, the City by the Bay was a sight to behold. In September 1942, Sergeant Major Cedric Soper, Jr., from Newport, Maine, arrived at San Francisco by train and wrote, "It is really great here. Wish I could stay the rest of the war." That same year, Private John Skinner, a soldier stationed on Angel Island in San Francisco Bay, wrote to his parents, "San Francisco is a nice city and you always can enjoy yourself very much, especially down in Chinatown.... I have been across the Golden Gate bridge several times, and also the Oakland–San Francisco bridge and I declare they both are beautiful bridges."[8]

A year later, Electricians Mate 3rd Class (EM3c) Marvin Mouw, from Sioux Center, Iowa, commented on the large number of enlisted personnel he encountered on the streets of the Bay City. "If I see all the service men here in Frisco alone," he wrote home, "I wonder who is fighting this war anyway." As one resident of the city later recalled, "San Francisco had, throughout the war, been so invariably hospitable to the men in service." Bud Simmons, a 12-year-old San Francisco resident with a newspaper delivery route in 1945, recalled years later, "During that time San Francisco was an extremely patriotic town, on Market Street you would always see several members of each branch of the service."[9]

For the men and women recruits who earned liberty to visit the Bay City, or sailors back from the fighting in the Pacific who received shore leave while their ships were being refitted or repaired, the citizens of San Francisco treated them kindly. Hospital Corpsman First Class (HA1c) David S. Greene, who had been on the hospital ship USS *Repose* (AH-16),

## Chapter 1. Hope and Preparation

recalled, "Predominantly a Navy town, San Francisco was considered one of the best liberty ports. Not many talked about San Francisco the way they talked of other port cities." To most sailors who steamed into San Francisco, the city offered numerous bars and canteens, theaters, civic centers, and a first-class USO (United Service Organization) facility. Perhaps the sailors liked San Francisco so much because the other ports lacked, as Corpsman Greene put it, "places to go to celebrate."[10]

While most military personnel saw the outward charms of San Francisco, behind the scenes, the citizens of the fair city had been working hard to do their part to bring the war to a successful conclusion. In many instances, this meant doing without. "San Francisco was transformed in many ways," wrote author John Garvey in *San Francisco in World War II*. "Books, tires, stoves, hot-water bottles, magazines, stretchers, cots, splints, and jams/jellies were collected at the Columbia Park Boys Club.... Shortages of the times affected the availability of bread, butter, eggs, candy, fuel, and hosiery."[11] As in every other city in America, San Franciscans had done their part to bring the war to a speedy, and victorious, end.

On May 7, 1945, when Hitler's Germany surrendered to the Allied forces in Europe, the citizens of San Francisco and the military personnel within and around the city took the news calmly. There was still a war being waged in the Pacific and San Franciscans knew that they still had a huge part to play in Japan's defeat. On May 8, the *San Francisco Examiner* reported, "San Francisco took in stride yesterday the news that the war had ended in Europe and gave every indication that the formal proclamation of V-E [Victory in Europe] Day today would not produce any spontaneous outbursts of celebration." As the *Examiner* noted, the service personnel and citizens were well aware of the "grim task yet unfinished in the Pacific."[12]

Although San Francisco's chief of police, Charles Dullea, had backup plans to call out every regular and auxiliary police officer upon the official announcement of V-E Day if need be, he anticipated no unruly celebration. "What have we got to celebrate, anyway, with kids being killed every hour in the Pacific," he was quoted as saying. When the announcement by Pres. Harry S Truman finally came on May 8 and no wild carousing erupted, Chief Dullea canceled the "general alert." As a precaution, however, he sent a few inspectors to strategic locations around the city to keep a watchful eye on things.[13]

As planned, and in compliance with a request by the State Board of Equalization, which was responsible for the oversight of California's

## The San Francisco V-J Day Peace Riots

Alcoholic Beverage Tax, when the official announcement of the end of the war in Europe was made by President Truman at 6:00 a.m. Pacific War Time (PWT) on May 8, all the bars and taverns in San Francisco closed for 24 hours. The *San Francisco Examiner* stated, "Nearly everyone expressed this conviction: V-J [Victory over Japan] Day had to come before the shouting, confetti throwing, [and] the convivial drinking could be justified." Stated San Francisco Mayor Roger D. Lapham, "To recognize German surrender by any widespread celebration at this time when there is still a job to do against Japan would be an affront to our Allied fighters in the Pacific. Keep on the job!"[14]

On May 9, a reporter for the *San Francisco Examiner* stated, "Churches of all denominations conducted special services, taverns were closed ... otherwise VE Day in San Francisco was just another day.... There was no outburst of hilarious celebration—the whole tone of the city's behavior was one of thanksgiving and the realization that Japan remains to be conquered." Added a reporter from the United Press, "In San Francisco, it was business as usual—not the feared hilarity. Bars were closed. Streets held their normal flow of traffic, in contrast to eastern cities where crowds shouted and sang."[15]

Instead of wild celebrations, most of the people of San Francisco went to church to pray for a speedy end to the war in the Pacific. On Treasure Island, it was reported that 10,000 sailors, marines, and navy WAVES (Women Accepted for Voluntary Emergency Services) came together and heard an address by Commander Robert Webster Cary, Jr., the commanding officer of the Naval Training and Redistribution Center. "[A]ll of us at this station ... on this day of rejoicing ... resolutely turn our thoughts and energies westward and dedicate ourselves to staying in the fight—all out to the finish." At the same time, Major General Clarence Howard Kells, in command of the San Francisco Port of Embarkation, warned that the continuing war against Japan "is going to take more of everything, carried more miles, in more ships ... most of [which] will move through San Francisco Port of Embarkation and the other Pacific ports.... Let us keep before us the thought that every second we save here will shorten the war, save the lives of our boys. Let's stay in there pitching, with all we have, until the whole job is done."[16]

On May 10, the *San Francisco Examiner* ran a small article titled "V-E Day a Sober Occasion in S.F." While a few people took the opportunity to celebrate the end of the war in Europe, the police reported that, for the most part, the celebrants were very disciplined. Police records showed that only 11 people—nine men and two women—were arrested

## Chapter 1. Hope and Preparation

for public intoxication, an all-time low when "compared to the daily average of eighty." Noted the *Examiner*, "There was not a single drunk driving arrest, which usually run to about five a day."[17]

Having come through VE Day with glowing reports, the citizens of San Francisco and the service men and women stationed at the surrounding naval and army bases settled down to finishing the job in the Pacific. At the same time, Mayor Lapham and Chief of Police Dullea prepared for what they knew would be a more enthusiastic celebration with the surrender of Japan.

Undoubtedly, Mayor Lapham and Chief Dullea had read in the California papers about the V-E Day celebrations in Halifax, Nova Scotia, Canada, that had gotten out of hand. A navy town like San Francisco, the port city had seen thousands of Canadian sailors flood the streets to celebrate the victory over Hitler's Nazi Germany. As the *Oakland Tribune* reported on May 9, 1945, "A sudden outburst of 'victory riots' in Halifax and two other Nova Scotia towns last night caused damage of more than $1,000,000.... Scarcely a window was intact in the business section. Thousands of dollars' worth of goods and an unaccounted amount of liquor and beer were looted." As the *Oakland Tribune* reported the next day, both military and civilian authorities blamed the other side for the damage and riot. As the newspaper stated, "Rear Admiral L.W. Murray, officer commanding the Canadian Northwest Atlantic area, declared 'civilians led the assault and encouraged service personnel to take part.'" At the same time, the newspaper reported that Halifax Mayor Alan Butler was claiming that "the trouble arose because 8000 sailors were given leave ... and allowed to be at large on the streets."[18]

In all, 564 Halifax businesses suffered damage and 207 shops were looted during the two-day riot. Three rioters were killed and dozens more were injured. Only a few dozen rioters were arrested.[19] Undoubtedly familiar with what had happened almost 4,000 miles to the northeast, Mayor Lapham and Chief Dullea began thinking of ways to prevent a similar "celebration" from occurring in their city.

Roger D. Lapham had become mayor of San Francisco on January 8, 1944, after serving as the industry representative of the National Labor Relations Board. It was his first run at public office, and he had campaigned on the stipulation that he would serve only one four-year term. Born in New York City in 1883, Lapham had served as a captain of infantry in World War I and had then gone on to become president of the American-Hawaiian Steamship Company, which brought him to San Francisco. In August 1945, with the war against Japan winding down, the mayor was undoubtedly hoping that his remaining time in office would be productive but quiet, with a celebration of joy and peace.[20]

Charles W. Dullea, the San Francisco chief of police, was born in San Francisco in 1889 and had joined its police force in 1914 after a stint in the United States Marine Corps. After rising through the ranks, he was appointed chief of police in February 1940. When the United States entered World War II in December 1941, many of Dullea's regular police officers had rushed out to enlist. Over the next few years, the draft had taken many more of his trained officers. In response, Chief Dullea had created an auxiliary police force of about 2,500 men. Noted the Museum of the City of San Francisco, "Chief Dullea quickly organized an auxiliary police force and used these men, mostly 4-Fs [a person not qualified for military service] and grandfathers, on traffic details, freeing what was left of the regular force for more urgent work."[21] Short of regular officers, Chief Dullea, like Mayor Lapham, was hoping that the celebrations following the end of the war against Japan would be docile and joyful.

For four more months, from May to August 1945, navy ships left San Francisco for the Pacific loaded with new recruits while injured ships returned for repair after facing the incredible kamikaze attacks of a desperate enemy. The young civilian men in San Francisco and throughout the United States continued to be drafted into the service while the commissioned and noncommissioned officers on Treasure Island and at Camp Stoneman continued to train new recruits to replace those men and women who had been killed or injured in the war in the Pacific. "We were 'on hold'—a term that hadn't as yet been coined," remembered Lynn Hartsell, a copygirl working for Acme-Newspaper Enterprise Association Syndicate in downtown San Francisco. "We were waiting without knowing what we were waiting for. The invasion of Japan, probably, and the long casualty lists that would certainly follow."[22] Then, on August 7, and again on August 9, 1945, when San Francisco and the world learned that atomic bombs had been dropped on Hiroshima and Nagasaki, Japan, the people around the Bay City knew that it was only a matter of time before the Empire of Japan accepted the surrender terms drawn up by the Allied leaders at Potsdam, Germany, between July 17 and August 2. With V-J Day within sight, city leaders in San Francisco prepared for the expected day of jubilation.

Again, hoping to prevent an unruly celebration, Chief Dullea placed the entire San Francisco police force on "standby" for an emergency call. Because of the loss of 186 police officers to the draft or as volunteers to

## Chapter 1. Hope and Preparation

the service, the entire force numbered only 1,116 men, while the population of San Francisco had grown between 1941 and 1945 by about 100,000. Despite the lack of numbers, when the "V-J Day plan" went into effect, the officers were expected to go to the downtown hotels and cafés and concentrate along Market Street. As Chief Dullea's order stipulated, "it is anticipated large gatherings of people will congregate [on Market Street]." Accordingly, auto and streetcar traffic was to be prohibited along the thoroughfare, although parked cars already on the street would be allowed to remain where they were.[23]

Sergeant Sidney Georgeson, an army veteran of the European conflict, who had lost his right arm in the fighting north of Rome, remembered, "[O]n August 10, authorities had feared that celebrations might get a little out of hand. That day, San Francisco Police Chief Charles Dullea had issued 'stand-by' orders to all his men, regular and special, who guard the peace of a city that had been traditionally lively in its joys since the Gold Rush of 1849. That same day, liquor boss George Reilly also asked bars and liquor stores to close when victory was announced. He admittedly had no power to enforce his request. Compliance had to be voluntary."[24]

George R. Reilly was the longtime representative of the San Francisco district of the California Board of Equalization, a government organization established in 1879 to make sure that assessment of property taxes was equal across the state. Although the board was responsible for issuing liquor licenses and collecting taxes on alcoholic beverages throughout California, Reilly had no real power over any of the establishments in his district other than forcing them to pay their taxes. He could, however, and did, make a request for liquor stores and bars to shut down for a period of 24 hours after the official announcement of the end of the Pacific conflict, fearing that thousands of people would want to celebrate by getting drunk and possibly unruly. According to Reilly, the army provost marshal had made the request for the San Francisco liquor dealers to close after the official announcement, "In the interest of public welfare and morals."[25]

However, in the state capital of Sacramento, the chairperson of the Board of Equalization, Richard E. Collins, suggested a "hands off" policy toward the liquor establishments. After a meeting of the board, Collins told the press that there would be no special liquor regulations asked of the liquor stores and bar owners. "It looks like a day for justifiable celebration," he said.[26] He apparently saw no need to curb liquor sales throughout the state. Any shutdowns of bars and liquor stores would be up to the discretion of the owners.

### The San Francisco V-J Day Peace Riots

With San Francisco, and the entire world, gearing up for the long-awaited celebration of the surrender of the Japanese Empire and the end of World War II, the authorities in the Bay City felt that they had done everything within their power to prevent undo mayhem in their beloved city. All they could do now was wait for the expected news flash to come across the airwaves and hope for the best.

## Chapter 2

# A False Flash

On Friday, August 10, San Franciscans awoke to an article by the International News Service and the Associated Press advising readers that "Japan's conditional offer to surrender—'If the Emperor's prerogatives as a sovereign ruler are not prejudiced'—sent the Governments of the United States, Great Britain, Russia, and China into a long-distance huddle yesterday to decide whether they will accept or reject the Japanese proposal." As it turned out, the United States and Great Britain were willing to accept that the Japanese emperor would remain on his throne as a condition for surrender, while Russia and China still wanted the "unconditional surrender" demanded by the Potsdam Declaration. The Allied powers were at a stalemate.[1]

While some people turned out in towns across America, particularly in New York City, to celebrate what they knew was the beginning of the end, the civilians and military personnel in San Francisco decided to wait. "There was no celebration in the great Pacific port city of San Francisco over the Japanese conditional surrender offer," wrote a United Press correspondent stationed in the Bay City. "Most sailors, soldiers, Marines and civilians in San Francisco hope the Allies keep fighting until Japan is forced to accept a total surrender ousting the emperor."[2] August 10 passed as the "big four" worked out whether to accept or reject the Japanese condition of allowing their emperor to stay in place after the formal surrender of Japan.

Saturday, August 11, 1945, came and went with still no word of the official surrender. "A palpable air of expectation overhung San Francisco yesterday as the city which has stood at the crossroads of the Pacific war since Pearl Harbor cocked its ears for official word that peace had returned after three years and eight months," noted the *San Francisco Examiner*. On that date, San Francisco military authorities reiterated their desire to have a peaceful celebration. Once again Mayor Lapham and Chief of Police Dullea requested that George R. Reilly, the California Board of Equalization representative, try his hardest "to shut off the flow of liquor." Again, while Reilly admitted that he had no power to enforce such an order, he reiterated that he had made the request to the local liquor dealers and bartenders' union and that they had all agreed to "voluntarily obey" the request and shut down two hours after the official announcement by President Truman. All the bars and liquor stores had also agreed to remain closed for the next 24 hours. It was hoped that restaurants "and other establishments that handle liquor" would abide by Reilly's request.[3]

Sunday, August 12, started out as just another lazy Sunday for most residents of San Francisco and the surrounding Bay communities. People went to church and prayed that the official announcement for the end of the war would come soon, while others did leisurely activities in their homes with an ear cocked toward their radios. As A.E. Anderson, a columnist with the *Oakland Post-Enquirer* wrote, "By Sunday noon the suspense was like that of an expectant dad in the corridor outside the maternity ward. Was it or wasn't it." In the afternoon, people listened to station KLX, which broadcast a double-header baseball game between the rival San Francisco Seals and the Oakland Oaks of the Pacific Coast League. By 6:00 p.m. Pacific War Time, the contests were over, with the teams splitting the games. At 6:15, KLX switched to its *Dinner Concert* program. At the same time, other stations began broadcasting similar programs.[4] Then, suddenly, at 6:34 p.m., United Press cut in with breaking news: "Flash—Washington—Japan accepts surrender terms of Allies."[5] The news that the world had been waiting for had finally arrived.

Almost immediately, people at home, people in the bars and nightclubs, and people anywhere within earshot of the radio broadcast began to celebrate. People driving their cars while listening to the radio began blowing their horns and shouting the news to everyone they passed. Ships in the harbor began sounding their whistles while the whistles at the shipyards and factories across the bay in Oakland chimed in. Church bells were rung throughout San Francisco, and in the Chinatown area residents began clanging cymbals, blowing off firecrackers, and tossing confetti into the air. In downtown San Francisco, along Market Street and elsewhere, it was reported, "Soldiers and sailors crowding downtown streets showered girls with kisses." In nearby San Mateo, people rushed out of the San Mateo Theater in the middle of the Cary Grant/Jean Arthur movie *Only Angels Have Wings* and began to celebrate in the streets.[6]

At the many San Francisco fire stations, however, the sirens remained silent. The fire chiefs had been instructed to hold off on blowing their sirens until they heard the official announcement from President Truman

## Chapter 2. A False Flash

himself. Although a news flash had gone out, an official presidential announcement had yet to be made. The fire sirens remained quiet.[7]

The lack of an official presidential announcement confused many of the Bay-area tavern owners. In both San Francisco and Oakland, the owners had agreed to shut down their businesses two hours after the official announcement of the surrender of Japan came. But, had the 6:34 p.m. news flash been "official"? In a near panic, many of the tavern owners called their local police stations, wanting to know if they should stay open or start the two-hour countdown before they closed their doors. Since the news flash was not considered official, the police told the owners to stay open. Within minutes, the taverns along Fisherman's Wharf on San Francisco Bay, on the northeastern edge of the city, were "packed with people anxious to drink a victory toast."[8] It was almost too much for people to believe. At long last, World War II had come to an end. Or had it?

One minute after the initial news flash, radio stations were flooding the airwaves with the news that the breaking flash had been in error. Embarrassed announcers were forced to proclaim, "Hold up that flash." At 6:37 p.m. Pacific War Time, three minutes after the monumental news had swept across the airwaves, United Press explained to everyone that the earlier news flash had been false and that it was investigating the fabricated report. Four minutes later, at 6:41 p.m., United Press from New York sent the following message to all radio stations: "Washington bureau advises they did not send flash just transmitted on leased wires. We are investigating to ascertain the origin." And minutes later, United Press declared, "We are still checking on the (Washington) flash, but as yet have not been able to determine its origin. We will carry an explanatory story as soon as possible." An hour after the false news flash, United Press reported to the many radio stations that it had asked the Federal Bureau of Investigation and the Federal Communications Commission to determine who "could have cut in on the United Press's wire system with the intent to disseminate false information."[9] The long-awaited news of the surrender of Japan had finally been broadcast, but it had been in error. An official surrender had not been agreed upon. But the news had already gone out, and San Francisco was beginning to celebrate.

It was almost an hour before the people celebrating in the streets of San Francisco learned that the surrender news flash had been retracted. Wrote an Associated Press correspondent, "The boisterousness was short-lived. Word soon circulated that the news was false." For those still listening to their radios, announcers quickly tried to explain what had happened and encouraged their listeners not to celebrate. The news flash had been a sick joke. The war was not officially over. The Japanese had not agreed to a surrender. Noted the Associated Press reporter, "Most persons who let off pent-up 'steam' agreed their observance of genuine peace will be milder than it would have been but for the mistaken report."[10] Slowly, the news of the false flash spread through the streets and the disappointed crowds began to disperse, trickling back to their homes or apartments or back to their naval or army barracks buildings.

The next morning, Monday, August 13, the *San Mateo Times* stated, "Climaxing a day of tension, the false report of peace carried by radio stations last night at 6:34 o'clock sent thousands of [people] cheering into the streets only to trail disappointedly back into their homes within a few minutes [sic] after the erroneous news flash had been corrected." The newspaper continued, "Service men and women were the most enthusiastic in the brief celebration that ended on a sober note of disappointment. Faces of soldiers, sailors, WACS [Women's Army Corps], and WAVES changed visibly from wild elation to expressions of deep disappointment." For a moment, the servicemen and servicewomen had believed that the war had ended and the possibility of going to fight in the Pacific had come to an end. Their celebrations of joy and a long life were unexpectedly dashed when the retraction announcement came and the possibility of death or injury in the Pacific returned.

While the whole world waited for the Allied Powers to accept Japan's requested modified Potsdam surrender terms, which would allow Emperor Hirohito to remain on his throne, Hugh Baillie, the president of United Press, offered a reward of $5,000 for the "identification and conviction of the person who fed into the UP-wire system … a false alarm saying that Japan had accepted the allies' surrender terms."[11] The reward was never collected. Nobody was ever arrested or convicted for the prank.

That Monday, August 13, San Francisco tried to return to the normal workday routine of a city still at war. Although a Navy spokesman said that "the Navy continues on a wartime basis and has not postponed the departure from this port of any war vessel," and the War Shipping Administration said that it was "sticking to its schedule on all departing vessels carrying the goods of war," there was a certain feeling in the air. While the *San Francisco Examiner* reported that "San Francisco awaited calmly … for word that the war is over" and that "most citizens went about their daily tasks quietly," the newspaper had to admit that there was a "mood of tense expectancy which [had] held the city over the weekend."[12]

"Radios were turned on early in homes this morning for latest developments and the prospect of news that for thousands would mean

## Chapter 2. A False Flash

a holiday from their jobs," noted one Bay-area reporter. Throughout the day of Monday, people all over San Francisco and the United States were champing at the bit. In the Bay City, Hospital Corpsman Greene recalled, "For days there were rumors the Japanese were to surrender, and this day just about everyone felt it was true. It was a day of waiting and hoping." Sergeant Georgeson, the army veteran with the missing right arm, said, "Since the premature victory flash of August 12, a palpable air of expectancy had hung over the city."[13]

"San Francisco was crowded with so many [Navy] men," Corpsman Greene went on, "many who had been overseas and expectant of getting 'shipped' again at any time. We made every 'liberty,' trying to store up good times against the bad that might follow." Although two atomic bombs had been dropped on Japan, those combat veterans who had seen the enemy up close, who had witnessed their last-ditch banzai charges or suffered through the harrowing kamikaze air attacks, felt that the Japanese might never give up. "We knew—or rather felt," Greene stated, "the next big campaign would be the invasion of Japan, and only those who had not seen war seemed anxious to get into combat. It had been a long time since most had felt that way."[14]

To reiterate what had long been planned, the *San Francisco Examiner* ran an article on August 13 that explained, "The Army announced that every available military policeman will go on duty at the moment the flash comes, and the Navy said it will not grant special liberty to men in port." As the paper indicated, all previous plans remained intact. "Bars will close within two hours after word comes. Most kinds of retail stores will close. Restaurants will stay open. The day following the announcement will be a State holiday."[15] As the expected surrender announcement drew closer, the San Francisco city and military authorities appeared to be ready.

# Chapter 3

# Another False Alarm

On the evening of Monday, August 13, San Franciscans went to their favorite restaurants or bars, went out to movie theaters, or simply stayed home reading their books and newspapers or listening to their favorite shows on the radio. Around 8:00 p.m. PWT, the radio announcers suddenly reported that Japanese radio had alerted its listeners to be ready to receive a broadcast of "unprecedented importance." Although there were no specifics, everyone in America hoped that it would be the announcement of the official acceptance of the Allied surrender terms drawn up at Potsdam that would ensure peace for the world.[1] For the next two hours, however, as the world waited, Tokyo radio remained silent. Finally, near 10:00 p.m., when the announcement was still not forthcoming, many families retired for the evening and went to bed.

Then, at 10:49 p.m. PWT, with some people still crowded into many San Francisco taverns, restaurants, and movie houses, all of which generally stayed open until midnight, the United Press listening post near San Francisco picked up an official announcement from the Japanese Domei news agency. In the middle of a discussion on the cures for chilblains, Domei radio broke in: "Flash—Tokyo—14/8 [14 August Japan time]- Learned Imperial message accepting Potsdam declaration forthcoming soon." Although still unofficial, the first word of Japan's acceptance of the Potsdam Ultimatum had been received. As historian John C. McManus wrote, "the Japanese government ... accepted Allied surrender terms, with the mutual agreement that the institution of the emperor would continue, subject to the authority of the Allied occupation forces."[2]

An Associated Press reporter wrote, "It was a nerve-tingling climax to long, suspenseful waiting—marked by premature celebrations last Friday, when the Japanese offered to quit if they could keep their Emperor, and Sunday night, when a quickly killed false surrender flash moved on wires of the United Press." Noted Joe W. Morgan, a United Press staff correspondent, "The news of the Tokyo surrender broadcast hit [the] Pacific embarkation port at 10:49 p.m. while the streets, restaurants, night clubs

*Chapter 3. Another False Alarm*

and movies were still filled." This time, to make certain that it was real, strangers were heard asking strangers, "Is this the real McCoy?"³ Although San Franciscans had resisted a celebration on Friday night and had rushed out after the false news flash for an impromptu, albeit short, celebration on Sunday evening, they grabbed onto the latest "flash" with a relish and would not let go.

Within seconds of the report of the Domei broadcast, people in various nightspots rushed outside to celebrate. "The news spread like wildfire through the crowds in both [San Francisco and Oakland] shortly before midnight as people spilled out of theaters, bars, restaurants, and hotels," noted one newspaper. In Oakland, it was reported, "The news that Japan was ready to surrender unconditionally to the United States brought people tumbling sleepy-eyed out of their bed in the early morning hours.... People from the outlying districts poured into the downtown section by auto, streetcar and bus when the first flash came through from Tokyo that acceptance of unconditional surrender terms was on the way." In San Francisco, a confused sailor who had missed the Domei broadcast ran up to one of the celebrants and excitedly asked, "Won't somebody please tell me what's going on? What's all the excitement about?"⁴

**Postcard aerial view of Market Street. To rear right is the Oakland–San Francisco Bridge. Rear left is Treasure Island, site of the U.S. Naval Training and Distribution Center (author's collection).**

## The San Francisco V-J Day Peace Riots

Market Street, the wide, busy thoroughfare that reportedly is "the only street in the nation where street cars run four abreast," and which runs at a southwest-to-northeast angle through the very heart of San Francisco, became the main site of celebration. Reporter Joe Morgan wrote, "Thousands of servicemen waiting for ships to take them into battle went wild with joy." For the first half hour, a United States Army jeep, sporting a couple of American flags, "serpentined up and down Market Street" followed by dozens of happy, boisterous people until the celebrants became bored with that activity and ventured off for other things to do. "Everyone was on Market Street, all the way from the Ferry Building at the waterfront Embarcadero all the way up Market Street past the big USO [at 989 Market Street] where you could get your uniform pressed while you waited," noted navy Corpsman David S. Greene. "The celebrations began with just a lot of milling around, slaps on the back and kissing the girls." Wrote San Francisco historian Charles Fracchia, who was only eight years old on August 13, 1945, "[T]here was a spontaneous howl of delight that went throughout the city, people hugging each other, you know, laughing, singing."[5]

Kissing girls seemed to be the number one entertainment at the beginning of the festivities. "Girls on the streets were kissed constantly as they were spun from arm to arm," noted an Associated Press correspondent. Another reporter wrote, "Men in uniform kissed civilian girls. Civilian men kissed WACS and WAVES." Bill Bodenweck, who was only 14 years old at the time, remembered, "Kissing was epidemic, and any woman on the street was fair game." In Oakland, it was reported that "shouting, kissing throngs jammed Broadway," the main site of revelry. The next morning, as the crowd began breaking up, Associated Press reporter Eugene Burns wrote about the girls who had been kissed so often. "Most of the girls on Market Street this morning had lost their lipstick and rouge," he wrote jokingly. "That morning they did not have time to put it on."[6]

Second behind kissing was the stealing, or swapping, of hats, both military and civilian. Wrote one reporter, "Favorite sport of enlisted servicemen during the hilarious melee was snatching caps from the heads of officers, few of whom escaped unscathed." Eugene Burns, the Associated Press correspondent, recorded, "On Market Street sailors were swapping uniforms prematurely with civilians and enlisted men were snatching officer's caps." One navy ensign was seen marching down Market Street wearing the headgear of an army colonel while an army private was spotted walking around with a navy officer's cap perched on top of his own cap. In Oakland, police Sergeant William Plummer had his cap stolen twice but got it back both times. When a civilian rushed up to Officer Plummer and

## Chapter 3. Another False Alarm

**A U.S. Marine lieutenant and a young lady share a celebratory kiss after hearing the news of Japan's surrender (San Francisco History Center, San Francisco Public Library).**

complained that his $15 hat had just been stolen, Plummer pointed to a sailor wearing the confiscated $25 cap of a navy officer and said, "What are you complaining about?"[7]

Adding to the playful mood of the crowd, two young women decided to go skinny-dipping in one of the large ponds in front of the San Francisco Civic Center, a block and a half north of Market Street. "Two nude beauties

## The San Francisco V-J Day Peace Riots

**Intersection of Market, Fourth, Ellis, and Stockton streets crowded with happy revelers on Victory Over Japan Day (V-J Day), August 14, 1945 (San Francisco Railway Museum).**

late last night stopped a taxi near the Civic Center Servicemen's dormitory, stepped out—a bit unsteadily—and plunged into the center's lily pond," a reporter wrote. "Servicemen ... lined the pond, applauding the cavorting nudes. When the girls emerged, some of the men offered towels which were gratefully accepted. The nocturnal Godivas then entered the taxi and were seen no more." As Corpsman Greene noted, "A rumor that two girls were swimming nude in the goldfish pond at the government center set some sort of record as it raced through the crowd." Added a San Francisco resident, "Two ... girls stripped nude and went bathing in the lily pond at the Civic Center, the boys in the barracks nearby supplying them with towels. Then they got back in their cab, where they dressed and drove off."[8]

As the clock ticked closer to midnight and Tuesday, August 14, some in the crowd, fueled by alcohol, became rowdy. "Servicemen climbed to the top of marquees where they whooped and shouted," wrote an Associated Press correspondent. Teenager Bill Bodenweck added, "Along the street, people, mostly GIs, were shinnying up onto marquees and most of the statues were draped with sailors." At one movie theater, a sailor climbed up

## Chapter 3. Another False Alarm

onto the marquee and started tossing down the letters that announced what movie was playing. Other marquees were equally assaulted. "Roos Bros. store at Stockton and Market went under heavy attack," commented a newspaper reporter. "Sailors climbed to the top of the marquee, seized United Nations flags still up from the conference and pitched them ... into the street." Between April 25 and June 26, 1945, San Francisco had been host to the first conference of the newly formed United Nations. Delegates from 50 different countries had come to the Bay City to draw up the Charter of the United Nations and establish an International Court of Justice. As late as this mid-August night, the flags of many of those nations were still being flown atop the entranceway marquee at Roos Brothers. On this momentous night, sailors stole the flags and tossed them down to the cheering mob below. Stated one newsman, "Impromptu parades sprang up periodically, with gangs of servicemen and girls singing and shouting through the downtown streets, waving looted flags and signs."9

In addition to pitching down the flags of the different nations, the sailors who climbed atop the Roos Brothers marquee also threw down the "shrubs and plants" that lined the edge of the canopy. Wrote one eyewitness, "The large concrete potted plants, which were also arranged above Roos Brothers' entrance with the flags, were knocked off the ledge causing a huge hole in the pavement below." As people watched, a drunken

Sailors, soldiers, and civilians celebrate the surrender of Japan near a bonfire ignited in the middle of Market Street. The sailor at left wears a confiscated fireman's hat from Engine Company Number 2 (San Francisco History Center, San Francisco Public Library).

serviceman stood over one hole, imagining it to be a cave entrance occupied by Japanese soldiers. "Come out of there, ya dirty Japs!" he kept repeating.[10] There seemed to be no concern for anyone below as the potted plants continued to rain down from above.

On wide Market Street, bonfires suddenly sprang up to light the darkness. Jack Dailey, a staff correspondent for United Press, commented, "Five bonfires fed by the remains of war bond booths blazed on Market Street, where crowds [were] estimated up to 50,000 persons." Noted another reporter, "Bond booths, flower stands and everything inflammable was piled on bonfires lighted in the middle of the street." When firefighters responded to the fires, throngs of people flooded the fire trucks. "The fire department finally gave up [on their] futile effort to quench Market Street bonfires and let the asphalt melt amid the cheers of the mob," noticed one eyewitness. "Sailors aided the firemen but then refused to get off trucks and rode back to the fire stations." As Virginia Hennigan, a young girl visiting San Francisco with her parents and older brother, a former lieutenant in the U.S. Navy, witnessed, if a false fire alarm was sounded, the revelers quickly set fire to piles of trash, so "the firemen wouldn't be disappointed."[11]

While the fires continued to burn, reportedly reaching as high as 30 feet into the air,[12] the revelers turned their attention to the San Francisco trolley cars, which moved along the trolley tracks by electricity from overhead wires. The electric current flowed to the electric motors through trolley poles attached to the roof of each car. "The city's famed cable cars were claimed by servicemen as their own," said one newspaper correspondent. Noted an Associated Press reporter, "Street cars were unable to proceed as their trolleys [poles] were pulled from the wires. Cable cars were spun 'round and 'round on their turntables." Wrote one eyewitness, "[A] car was captured on its turntable at the foot of Powell Street and spun around like a top." Some of the frenzied partiers, undoubtedly fueled by alcohol, tried to steal some of the cable cars despite their weight and size. "Sailors commandeered one of the 'Toonerville trolleys' and partially lifted it off its tracks," wrote one newspaperman. Another noted, "One whooping crowd of soldiers, sailors and Marines appeared to be trying to take another away as a souvenir." It was recorded that the dispatcher at the home trolley barn was "afraid to call a wrecking car—he feared it would be wrecked, too." Streetcar service on Market Street and the adjoining streets was discontinued at 1:00 a.m. because of the destruction and because the cable cars were "barely able to inch through the throngs."[13]

In addition to attacking the stalled trolley cars, the crowd also

## Chapter 3. Another False Alarm

A riotous crowd of civilians and servicemen, mostly sailors, overturn a delivery truck on Market Street (San Francisco History Center, San Francisco Public Library).

began targeting automobiles. Jack Dailey, a United Press staff correspondent, admitted, "Several automobiles venturing out onto Market Street were wrecked. Soldiers and sailors commandeered a truck and rolled it over and over, ripping off tires and tearing out wiring." Another reporter commented, "Some motorists made the mistake of venturing onto Market. Their autos were mobbed, weighed down until springs creaked, and many were commandeered by merrymakers." It was later reported that "three taxis were overturned." No vehicle, or even stationary objects, were spared. Correspondent Dailey was amazed at what was attacked by the mob. "'No Parking' standards," he wrote, "were torn from their apparently solid sidewalk moorings."[14]

Although a crowd estimated between 20,000 and 50,000 people filed into downtown San Francisco to celebrate, thousands more San Franciscans went to church to pray for the quick official announcement of the end of the war. "Instead of snake dancing in the streets," wrote United Press

## The San Francisco V-J Day Peace Riots

staff correspondent Joe W. Morgan, "thousands knelt in prayer at church." As Morgan noted, many of the churchgoers were held back from celebrating "by a caution that said wait until President Truman makes the peace official."[15] Until President Truman got on the airwaves and made the surrender announcement official, many San Francisco residents were content to pray and wait before breaking into wild celebration.

At 5:00 a.m., the celebration along Market Street was still going strong. During the first few hours, the city and armed forces police had done little to stop the rowdiness, even if they could have. One Navy Shore Patrol (SP) officer was heard to say, "This is the boys' night and they're doing it right." Three hours later, near 8:00 a.m., after most of the civilian celebrants had gone home and almost all the military personnel had gone back to their barracks buildings, the different police forces decided that enough was enough and began to "round up [the remaining] over-exuberant sailors and civilians." Behind them they left a "shambles of confetti, broken glass, and debris." Throughout the celebration, no special call had been issued by Chief of Police Dullea. The city authorities had determined that "the crowd was good natured for the most part."[16]

Although termed a "good natured" crowd, 24 liquor stores had been looted within the first five hours of celebration, amounting to the loss of about $10,000 worth of alcohol. Noted one police officer, "They must have enough for a week." Additionally, six other stores, including two jewelry stores, had their windows smashed. The two owners of the jewelry stores reported that "only novelty jewelry" had been taken, since the expensive items had all been locked in their safes. In Oakland, seven storefront windows were broken and civilian police made only "a normal number of arrests for drunkenness." In Chinatown, the Shore Patrol officers had arrested an inebriated "lone sailor [clinging] to a lamppost there shouting 'Merry Christmas.'" Army Military Police or MPs reportedly picked up only two soldiers and Shore Patrol officers took custody of "an untabulated number [of sailors] ... apparently for their own good." Later, it would be determined that 262 sailors had been arrested. By midmorning, apparently after sobering up, all the detained revelers had been released.[17]

Despite the broken windows and downright unruly behavior of some of the celebrants, San Francisco hospitals reported that they had "a very average evening," with preliminary reports showing that only 28 civilians had been injured, none seriously. At army and navy aid stations, medical personnel treated close to 100 servicemen for cuts and bruises, mostly from broken glass. However, they admitted that they spent most of the early morning hours of August 14 "trying to sober up celebrants brought

## Chapter 3. Another False Alarm

in by [military] police and shore patrolmen." Said one police officer, "It was a miracle that no one was killed...."[18]

While it was said that the late night/early morning celebration of August 13–14, 1945, was the "biggest mass celebration in the history of San Francisco," other cities had also celebrated the news that Japan was ready to surrender. New York City received the Domei radio news flash at 1:49 a.m. Eastern War Time on August 14. Because of the early morning hour, a United Press correspondent noted, "Crowds gathered slowly in Times Square, and the revelry was confined during the first hours to the blowing of automobile horns." Washington, D.C., received the news at the same time and date. It was reported that "a small crowd gathered before 4:00 a.m. in Lafayette park across from the White House. That little gathering of about 200 persons grew hourly."[19]

In Chicago, the Domei flash was heard at 12:49 a.m. Central War Time (CWT), Tuesday, August 14, while some of the bars and nightspots were still open. "Thousands of merrymakers packed [downtown] Chicago," reported the United Press. "Motorists leaned on horns and backfired their engines. Girls planted kisses on the cheeks of service men and civilians alike." Added the Associated Press, "Bands of revelers stopped automobiles, climbed on fenders and tops and cruised through the district. A false fire alarm was rung ... and six pieces of apparatus had difficulty breaking through the jam." In St. Louis, also in CWT, "Automobiles were paraded through the streets, their horns blowing, some of them dragging tin cans noisily over the pavements."[20]

Albuquerque, New Mexico, in Mountain War Time, received the news at 11:49 p.m. on August 13. "Night club celebrations were set off here early today by announcements of a Tokyo radio report saying Japanese acceptance of the Potsdam proclamation was expected," stated the Associated Press on August 14. "Soldiers threw tables over when the news was told.... Folks started kissing each other." In Salt Lake City, Utah, also in Mountain Time, it was reported, "Bottles passed freely from hand to hand as total strangers became friends."[21]

In Los Angeles, in PWT, the radio announcement came at 10:49 p.m., August 13, same as in San Francisco. "The news, while received with jubilation, touched off no demonstration worthy of the name," wrote one reporter. "Biggest celebration was staged by students at the University of Southern California. They set off three bonfires and put on a snake dance." However, as it was noted, "the great majority of residents were in their homes, and it is possible that a city-wide celebration will get under way when official announcement of the war's end was made." From the state capital of Sacramento, Governor Earl Warren released the following comment: "I think the people of California are entitled to a holiday."[22]

As Tuesday, August 14, progressed, the celebrations in New York City, Washington, D.C., Chicago, St. Louis, Salt Lake City, and in thousands of other cities grew until they rivaled the one in San Francisco. However, after a few hours, most of the celebrants in all those cities ceased and decided to await the official announcement from President Truman. "Peace hopes soared to the celebration point today (Tuesday) from the Far Pacific to the Atlantic seaboard as indications multiplied that Japan's surrender was near," wrote an Associated Press reporter. "Wild, spontaneous demonstrations—touched off by an early morning Japanese broadcast that an imperial surrender message was forthcoming—subsided in most cities [while people] … awaited official word from the White House."[23] The celebration would come, but not right now.

In San Francisco, Mayor Lapham and Chief of Police Dullea readied the city for the time to come. They had gotten a taste of the wild celebrations during the late night and early morning hours of August 13/14. As the *Oakland Tribune* noted, "[I]t took only unconfirmed news that Japan is ready to surrender to touch off a celebration … that lasted all night and continued into the morning hours."[24] Mayor Lapham and Chief Dullea had better be ready.

## Chapter 4

# Celebrate

On Tuesday morning, August 14, 1945, the San Francisco newspapers hit the street with early "extras" proclaiming that Tokyo radio had admitted that Japan had surrendered. However, the official announcement from President Truman had yet to be given. Despite the newspaper headlines, the celebrations of late Monday night/early Tuesday morning had quieted down and the people in San Francisco and elsewhere had dutifully gone to their wartime jobs, though all the time keeping a cocked ear toward the radio. No news was forthcoming until 3:45 p.m., when radio listeners were apprised that President Truman would be making an announcement at 4:00 p.m. Immediately word spread throughout workplaces to those who had not been near a radio. Likewise, people at home or in the street who had heard the news passed the word to neighbors, friends, and anyone else who might have missed the notice. Then, for the next few minutes, the different radio announcers ad-libbed while the nation collectively held its breath and excitedly awaited the president's pronouncement.[1]

Finally, after 16 minutes of breathless waiting, at 4:01 p.m. San Francisco time, 7:01 p.m. Washington, D.C., time, President Truman came on the radio from the White House. "I have received this afternoon a message from the Japanese government—," he began, and then abruptly stopped to address the reporters in the room. "Before I go any further," the listening audience heard, "this will be in the form of releases, so you don't have to copy it unless you want to." He then continued with the words that everybody had been waiting to hear. "—in reply to the message forwarded to that government by the Secretary of State on August 11. I deem this reply a full acceptance of the Potsdam declaration which specifies the unconditional surrender of Japan." President Truman went on for another 476 words but few people heard them.[2] Most people had latched onto the four words "unconditional surrender of Japan." World War II was finally over! Few people waited to hear the rest of the president's announcement as they rushed into the streets to celebrate.

## The San Francisco V-J Day Peace Riots

"Peace hopes soared to the celebration point today from the far Pacific to the Atlantic seaboard," noted the Associated Press after the 7:01 p.m. Washington time announcement by President Truman. Spontaneous celebrations spread from the East Coast to the West Coast, and from north to south, and every point in between. In most cities, towns, and villages it was dancing, singing, kissing, and drinking. Large metropolises such as New York City and Chicago overflowed with tumultuous crowds. Years later, National Public Radio host Robert Siegel reminded his audience, "The iconic image of V-J Day in this country was the one captured by *Life* magazine photographer Alfred Eisenstaedt: a sailor kissing a woman in Times Square, a joyous celebration."[3] Like the rest of the country, and even the rest of the world, San Franciscans flooded into the streets to celebrate. Noted one journalist, "As the primary port of embarkation for US troops headed to the Pacific, San Francisco's revelry was especially intense."[4]

"The Japanese surrender did not come as a surprise," said San Francisco resident Dave Heagerty, a 17-year-old student at the time. "In fact, we expected the Japanese warlords would have capitulated between the dropping of the two atomic bombs, Hiroshima (August 6th) and Nagasaki (August 9th)." Immediately after President Truman uttered the immortal words, the air was filled with the sounds of celebration. "The ships in the Bay all whistled, and the sirens and auto horns created a din beyond thinking," wrote one San Francisco woman. Virginia Hennigan, the young girl visiting San Francisco with her family, remembered, "We had just gone into our hotel when the bells and whistles started and we knew that peace had been declared." Josette Dermody Wingo, a 21-year-old San Franciscan at the time, recalled years later, "Anyone on Market Street on V-J Day, as I was, will probably never forget. The noise, ship's whistles shrieking incessantly, church bells booming a cacophony of *te deums* [praise to God], car horns honking without stop, cable car bells clanging, every siren of any sort going off. It made the bricks vibrate." Added army veteran Georgeson, "By the time the sirens howled Tuesday, the crowd was ready to burst out of its wartime bondage."[5]

San Francisco air raid sirens, installed in 1942 to warn against expected Japanese air attacks, joined in the on the clamor. Alvin D. Hyman, a reporter with the *San Francisco Examiner*, recalled, "[T]hirty air raid sirens split the stiff ocean breezes with their combined wail and sent the population into a demonstration that far outstripped the premature [Monday night] effort." Wrote a United Press reporter, "[T]he city's great air raid siren thundered an ear-piercing shriek for the first time since it was tested for the Japanese bombers that never came." For dozens of miles

## Chapter 4. Celebrate

along the coast, air raid sirens added their shrill notes to the wild jubilation. "From Pigeon Point to Sharp Park along the coast," noted one chronicler, "the air raid sirens wailed for hours."[6]

Navy recruits at Point Montara Anti-Aircraft Training Center, a few miles south of San Francisco, quickly raced to their 40mm guns and began sending noisy "salvo after salvo" out over the Pacific Ocean while other recruits manned .50-caliber machine guns and "fill[ed] the air with a screaming hail of red-gleaming tracer bullets." As a San Mateo newspaper reported, "Similar scenes were enacted at other coast service garrison and firing range points." One sailor, realizing that the cessation of war meant that he would soon be discharged and going home, responded sort of tongue-in-cheek when a middle-aged motorist pulled up beside him and said, "Hop in, sailor, where can I take you?" With a smile on his face, the sailor replied, "Home, sir. Right back to Burlington, Washington."[7]

At the American Women's Voluntary Services Canteen at 406 Geary Street, several blocks southeast of Market Street, a Victory Bell, which had been "installed long ago against the great day," began to peal loudly, joining the noise that was already flooding the air. Wrote San Francisco reporter Bernardine Snyder, "[T]he sound [was] very small against the din of sirens, shouts, auto horns and general hullaballoo." On the other side of Market Street, the Stage Door Canteen at 420 Mason Street, five blocks north of Market, distributed "2,000 horns and other noise makers" that the proprietors had been aching to hand out for the longest time.[8]

Another person making a lot of noise on August 14 was the newborn baby of Walter and Evelyn Foehr. The firstborn child of the new parents was christened Caroline Mary but was instantly nicknamed Vicky, in honor of victory. She was born at 4:20 p.m., the first baby born in San Francisco after President Truman's momentous announcement.[9]

"On the whole the crowd held up pretty well," recalled Virginia Hennigan, who was visiting San Francisco with her parents and brother. She predicted, "San Francisco, with its wild jubilation, will make August 14 a day to remember." Although only 14 years old, Bill Bodenweck was already working for the Recorder Printing and Publishing Company, at 99 South Van Ness, at the corner of Market Street and South Van Ness Avenue, but was at City Hall, picking up some court filings, when the city suddenly exploded. "It was about 4 in the afternoon, give or take," he said. "Clerks started jumping up and down and shouting and hugging and kissing each other." Instead of going the three blocks back to the Recorder office, Bill decided to travel the 12 or so blocks to the White House Department Store

## The San Francisco V-J Day Peace Riots

at Grant Avenue and Post, where his mother worked. One block from the store, Bill passed Union Square and noticed "a lot of hollering, and laughing, and there was a lot of kissing." Later, he admitted, "[I] didn't get back to the Recorder for three days but it was OK because everything stopped anyhow."[10]

Hoping to prevent any broken windows and play to the patriotic heartstrings of the merrymakers, the employees in the White House Department Store quickly covered their windows with red, white, and blue bunting. In anticipation of the careless nature of happy revelers, in hotels up and down Market Street, managers, clerks, bellhops, maids, and every other available employee quickly began removing everything breakable from the lobbies and storing them in safer places.[11]

Acme-Newspaper Enterprise Association Syndicate copygirl Lynn Hartsell remembered the reaction to the president's words. "The city exploded," she said. "Market Street instantly filled with curb-to-curb people. Department stores closed. Office buildings emptied. Sailors in uniform were everywhere. They were young, exuberant and ready to celebrate." She continued, "The news came through the Associated Press teletype in our office a few minutes after 4 p.m. One of the secretaries and I were sent out to stock up for the party that would continue far into the night." As Lynn and the other lady pushed through the crowds to get to a liquor store before it closed, they noticed that some office personnel in other buildings had been expecting the long-anticipated news. "Large gunny sacks of bottles dangled out of many an office window," she said, "away from bosses' official eyes."[12]

An unknown office woman also witnessed the hoarded bottles of alcohol and the beginning of the merrymaking. "Our office was a very gay party," she proclaimed. "Employees and bosses dragged out cherished bottles of beverages saved for years for this occasion. Also, sacks of confetti, serpentine firecrackers, etc., were in abundance. And when this gave out, adding machine tape, shredded newspapers, ticker tape, toilet paper and everything else went fluttering through the air. Everybody kissed everybody else, but we all watched the wild demonstration on the streets from our windows and exchanged our kisses between ourselves in the office. It was too rough down on the street." The unknown office woman admitted later, "I celebrated until I got so plastered I passed out in my office."[13]

Bud Simmons, the newspaper delivery boy, was at home with his family celebrating his 13th birthday on August 14 when the glorious news broke. "We initially heard the news over the radio," he wrote, "and neighbors were out in the streets on the avenues. My reaction was one

## Chapter 4. Celebrate

of great joy and [I] thought of how great our country is, after following the advancement of our troops in the Pacific on a daily basis through the delivery of our newspapers." Simmons and his family headed down to the center of the city to be a part of the downtown celebration. He recalled, "Market Street was a joyous place to be on VJ Day and one which I will never forget."[14]

Among the uniformed personnel celebrating the surrender of Japan was Florence Boyd, a 23-year-old navy recruiter for the WAVES. "I heard the war was finally over when someone in the office received a phone call," she said. "Thousands of people were suddenly filling Market Street, pouring out of all the buildings. It was a solid crowd of people, a really exciting time. People were kissing and dancing and celebrating in the street.... It was absolutely wonderful to know it was over. I had lots to do to close down the offices, but those were good times. It was a wonderful time of transition."[15]

Another uniformed person in downtown San Francisco on that date was Photographer's Mate 1st Class Petty Officer (PHOM1c) Anthony Ficalora. "On August 14, 1945, the surrender of Imperial Japan, was announced," he said. "I was in San Francisco on Market Street, celebrating, there were church bells ringing, car horns beeping, sirens going off. Everyone was hilarious, kissing each other, dancing and whooping it up. At the Pepsi-Cola Center for Service Men and Women [948 Market Street], sailors climbed up the statue's pole, waving American flags. [It was] the greatest of time." Also witnessing people climbing poles was Bill Payne, a 24-year-old equipment operator. "I couldn't believe it, everybody was going crazy," he wrote. "We went and changed into our best clothes and went to Market Street and it was packed. There was people everywhere, climbing light poles, drinking and everything."[16]

Reporter Alvin Hyman with the *San Francisco Examiner* was in the joyous crowd and wrote, "At once, Market Street and the financial district teemed with grinning, cheering, aimlessly milling throngs, erupting from offices and stores which closed shop to mark the arrival of peace." Commenting on one of the sights that struck his eye, Hyman noted, "Serpentine ticker tape and shredded telephone books wafted from a thousand windows, and sifted earthward in a blizzard of paper."[17]

At the southeast corner of Union Square, teenager Bill Bodenweck, who was still trying to get to his mother at the White House Department Store, witnessed a strange encounter between a drunken sailor and an automobile. He wrote, "A Navy officer, driving with a young woman, was stopped on Geary for the old birdcage stop signal at Powell. A sailor in white staggered in front of his car and leaned on the hood to keep the officer from going on. While the signal kept changing and traffic backed up, the sailor leaned on the radiator, but slipped down. The officer tried to talk him out of it, but he wouldn't give up, and the last [I] saw of him he'd crawled under the car and was hanging onto something there while the officer and another sailor tried to pull him out."[18]

All up and down San Francisco Bay, people were celebrating the exciting news. Betty Rule had married her army veteran husband two days earlier and the two were driving up to San Francisco from his base near Los Angeles to take a train ride to Betty's hometown of St. Louis. She wrote:

> We stopped in a nice, small, friendly appearing roadside bar and grill as we were approaching Palo Alto [about 30 miles south of San Francisco].... We were sitting at the bar having a cold beer after a hot car ride awaiting our order to arrive when all heck broke loose. The radio was playing when there came an announcement of Japan's surrender and the war was over!! Horns blew, music was playing, red, white and blue streamers were everywhere. The bartender locked the door, passed out free drinks and a wonderful gift of a pair of nylons for the women as we hadn't been able to buy them anywhere for months. Under the bar he dug up several cartons of cigarettes that had not been seen in ages— real brands we had been used to before the war, Camel, Chesterfield, Pall Mall. We'd become used to seeing unknown and not-so-good brands like Kools and Fatima....[19]

Betty went on, "Everything was all on the house since most of the fellows there were in uniform and were for the moment 'royalty.' Instead of an hour's break for a meal, we enjoyed a room full of laughter, fun, lots of new friends and enjoyed the ... repast party to the fullest for a couple hours."[20]

Within a matter of minutes after President Truman's historic announcement, the city of San Francisco was flooded with young soldiers and sailors from the nearby army and navy bases who suddenly realized that they were not going to die or get maimed in the Pacific war. "Sudden peace came like a thunderclap to the Pacific's largest port of embarkation," noted a United Press correspondent stationed in the Bay City. "Thousands of ... servicemen who realized they wouldn't have to fight their way to Tokyo topped even yesterday's celebration in noise and chaos." One navy recruit was heard to say, "I'm so excited I can't stand it!" while another young sailor, standing among a group of his friends, was heard to say, "Just six more months and we'll be out of these silly suits." At another street corner, three young seamen were seen kissing a "white-haired old lady." As one of the young men withdrew from his planted kiss, he exclaimed, "You're exactly like the little old lady we're going home to."[21]

## Chapter 4. Celebrate

Perhaps seeing the quickly growing crowd, and reacting to the enthusiasm, several liquor stores and taverns immediately shut and locked their doors, ignoring the Board of Equalization request to stay open for two hours after the official announcement of peace. Noted Corpsman Greene, "Anticipating trouble at war's end, many of the bars and clubs closed up with the official announcement of the surrender." At Third and Market Streets, across from the *San Francisco Examiner*'s main office, the tavern owner took the added precaution of boarding up the front windows of his establishment. Another liquor store owner, hoping to appeal to the patriotic side of the crowd and stop them from breaking his windows, filled "each huge show window with an American flag."[22]

Still, most of the liquor establishments abided by their earlier agreement with the California Board of Equalization to stay open, meaning that they would not shutter their doors until 6:00 p.m. They were asked to reopen at 10:00 a.m. Thursday morning, August 16. However, the bartenders' union and the Liquor Dealers Association, both realizing the amount of money that would be lost if they shut down for 40 hours, hinted that they might open for business as early as 6:00 p.m. the next day, only 24 hours after shutting their doors.[23] In the meantime, between 4:01 p.m., when the official announcement of the Japanese surrender was made, and 6:00 p.m., when the liquor stores and bars were due to close, the alcohol flowed freely.

Reporter Hyman noted, "Far-sighted service men and civilians alike, warned that liquor stores must close within two hours, rushed for the nearest package goods store and queued up to acquire a stock for the night's work ahead." Bob Caredio, a resident of San Francisco who had recently been discharged from the army, was one who partook of the early sales of refreshments. "I was discharged before the war ended," he recalled years later. "I remembered when I heard the news that the war had ended. I felt happy and satisfied. I celebrated in San Francisco, California, in the streets and buildings with a group of people including [another] Bob, one of my closest friends. We drank good wine (i.e., Vino) and champagne."[24]

Upon receiving the word that President Truman had made the official announcement that Japan had surrendered, Police Chief Dullea was quoted as saying, "I'm damn glad—enough said." Anticipating heavy drinking and boisterous crowds before the closing of the bars and liquor stores, Chief Dullea sent the "Signal 400" blast to his entire police force of 1,116 officers and an additional 2,000 auxiliary policemen. Later, as thousands of military personnel flooded into the downtown area, the city officers were joined by roughly 500 Shore Patrol officers and 15 SP

## The San Francisco V-J Day Peace Riots

patrol cars. Additionally, 450 Military Police officers were sent out, with another 660 standing by if needed. Realizing that most of the celebrants had been holding on to their emotions for four long years, and were expected to go a little wild, instructions went out to both civilian and armed forces police officers alike to let the people celebrate as long as there was no wanton destruction.[25] Similar to the night before, authorities were willing to let the people have a little fun, as long as things did not get too out of hand.

## Chapter 5

# It Begins

For perhaps the first two hours of celebration, the atmosphere in downtown San Francisco was one of genuine euphoria. "We poured into the streets in a frenzy of relief and joy," said Josette Dermody Wingo. "Kissing, crying, dancing, bonfires and firecrackers. The noise reverberated until it became solid." Navy Corpsman David S. Greene added, "Sailors, soldiers, Marines, girls and a few elderly civilians surged first one way and then the other." Almost immediately, the sound of popping firecrackers could be heard up and down Market Street and throughout the nearby Chinatown area. Two people seen blowing off firecrackers on Market Street were a couple of Soviet naval officers whose ship was tied up to a San Francisco dock. As they lit the crackers and watched them explode, the two tipsy Soviets kept repeating in English, "Okay, okay, Russians and Americans good friends."[1]

In Chinatown itself, the residents let loose with a wild celebration. China had been fighting the Japanese since 1931, when Japan invaded the Chinese province of Manchuria and had set it up as the puppet state of Manchukuo. Now, 14 years later, Japan had been brought to her knees. "Strings of firecrackers were hurtled from every window and balcony, creating a terrific din and suffusing the entire district with a pall of smoke," it was reported. "Cymbals clanged and reed instruments emitted their nasal squeals." Wrote a United Press correspondent, "Firecrackers, hoarded for eight years [sic] in America's largest Chinatown, rattled like a battery of machine guns along Grant avenue. They were tossed from doorways by poker-faced Chinese who had been waiting for this moment since arrogant Japanese stormed the Marco Polo bridge outside Peking nine years ago." The next morning, an Associated Press correspondent wrote, "This city's famous old Chinatown, a din of noisy merrymaking and a blaze of color in last night's peace celebration, was littered today with the black and red remains of millions of firecrackers." It was later revealed that nearly $50,000 worth of fireworks had been fired off during the joyous celebration.[2]

## The San Francisco V-J Day Peace Riots

While most of the younger people rushed out into the streets to celebrate, many older individuals and elderly couples elected to go to their house of worship and thank God for the cessation of hostilities. "There was a solemn side to the celebration, too," wrote one reporter. "Wives and mothers and fathers of loved ones went to church last night to offer prayers of thanksgiving." At the Cathedral of Saint Mary of the Assumption, several blocks north of Market Street, a spokesperson invoked, "It is singular that the Japanese attack occurred December 7, 1941, the day of the Vigil of the Feast of the Immaculate Conception. We are observing peace today, [August 14] which is the occasion of the Vigil of the Feast of the Assumption. Throughout the war we have been praying to the Blessed Virgin for Divine Intercession to end Hostilities." At Saint Ignatius Church, Lieutenant Commander Joseph T. O'Callahan, a Jesuit priest and navy chaplain, who would eventually be presented with the Medal of Honor for his selfless actions in helping the wounded and dying on March 19, 1945, aboard the aircraft carrier USS *Franklin* after that vessel had been severely damaged by Japanese aircraft, offered "a prayer of Thanksgiving at a Solemn High Mass."[3] It seemed as though finally, everyone's prayers had been answered.

As the revelry went on, 40 or 50 people, "whooping and bursting into brief snatches of songs," lined up shoulder to shoulder and arm in arm across wide Market Street and began marching down the middle of the street, heading toward the Embarcadero along the Bay shore. Before they got to the waterfront, however, the revelers met a band marching up Market Street from the Ferry Building at the Embarcadero. The band was headed in the opposite direction, toward the Civic Center Plaza near Market Street and Larkin Street. Almost immediately, the street-wide set of merrymakers opened their file, let the band pass through, and then simply turned around and headed back the way they had come, this time following the band. As they marched and sang, hundreds joined in behind them.[4]

Eventually, the Market Street trolley cars, which had continued to run, could not get through the burgeoning crowd. Teenager Dave Heagerty was trying to get home to Oakland by taking a K Line streetcar. He explained, "[The trolley] would normally drop us off at First and Market Street for a block's walk down First Street to Mission Street." He would then catch a train at Mission Street to Oakland. "Celebrating the war's end quickly and wildly got underway on Market Street in downtown San Francisco," he continued, "so Market Street car lines were directed to Mission Street."[5] Located only one block southeast of Market, in time even the redirected cars were suspended as the revelers began to spill out from

## Chapter 5. It Begins

the main thoroughfare and onto the neighboring streets. Unfortunately, dozens of trolleys were already stuck inside the growing mass on Market Street.

While Heagerty was trying to get on a train to Oakland, some San Franciscans who worked in Oakland were trying to get back to the City by the Bay. "I had been working in Oakland, but after hearing the news ... [I] decided to head back to the city and go home," one reveler recalled. "I rode across the bridge on a Key System train and caught a K car [trolley]. Our motorman was able to get through the growing crowd on Market Street." Years later he asked, "Was that the last car to get through, I wonder?"[6]

People were enjoying themselves immensely, doing crazy, silly things. Having fun. A sailor ringing a tiny dinner bell was spotted "sashaying right and left up Market Street with a line of girls behind him." At the intersection of Market, Turk, and Mason Streets, an already drunken soldier with a beer bottle in hand climbed up onto the Admission Day Monument, commemorating the September 9, 1850, date when California became the 31st state to be admitted to the Union. Another monument to be assaulted was Lotta's Fountain at Third and Market Streets. "[T]wo sailors and one girl, the girl brandishing a bottle," noted reporter Hyman, "scaled the base of Lotta's fountain and began shinnying up the shaft." He added, "The girl got kissed."[7]

Crowded intersection of Market and Mason streets on V-J Day, August 14, 1945 (San Francisco History Center, San Francisco Public Library).

## The San Francisco V-J Day Peace Riots

**Happy celebrants climb all over the base of the Admission Day Monument near the intersection of Market, Turk, and Mason streets, August 14, 1945 (West Virginia & Regional History Center).**

In a repeat of the early morning revelry, both civilians and servicemen, predominantly sailors, began grabbing the headgear off passing revelers, military and civilian alike, many throwing them into the air in celebration. Bernard A. Harris, an African American navy steward's mate second class (STM2/c), went into downtown San Francisco with some of his buddies to join in on the tumultuous celebration. "They were throwing up hats and caps and everything," he stated. "Some of the girls took my cap. I never did get it back." Only 19 years old at the time, Harris worried about the loss of his white "Dixie cup" sailor's cap. "I thought they'd put me on report when I got back to base, but they didn't," he recalled. "Everybody was out of uniform."[8]

Linda Smutko's mother, who had joined the Marine Corps Women's Reserve when the war began, also lost her cap. Daughter Linda wrote, "Mom was a Marine in WWII.... She was on leave in San Francisco when V-J day came. She and her girlfriends ... went out to celebrate.... She had

## Chapter 5. It Begins

lost her uniform hat in the revelry, but came back with a sailor's hat—after all she couldn't report back to [base] without a hat!" With the same light attitude, the staff at the *San Francisco Examiner* delighted over the fact that wire operator Jimmy Hampton had his "green homburg" hat stolen from him. "[F]or years," his colleagues wrote delightedly, "[it] has been an office eyesore." And, while many service personnel were taking hats from civilian revelers, a few civilians turned the tables and snatched the service caps from the soldiers and sailors. Bernadine Snyder, a reporter with the *San Francisco Examiner*, remembered seeing a "Civilian girl ... [with] an armful stacked THIS high of sailor's caps."[9]

Across San Francisco Bay, in Oakland and other East Bay communities, people were celebrating as elsewhere. Having caught the train to Oakland and after returning home, teenager Dave Heagerty and his parents joined in the celebration. "After a quick dinner at home," he remembered, "I would join my parents for a ride downtown to participate in a spontaneous celebration of the war's end that would take place at Oakland's 14th and Broadway." Akin to what was happening along Market Street in San Francisco, enlisted men on liberty in Oakland began snatching the hats off both civilians and service personnel alike. However, the nonrated sailors seemed to go a step further with commissioned officers. "Enlisted men observed their belief in democracy," wrote one reporter, "by stripping commissioned officers of their headgear, sleeve stripes and other ornaments." All done in a joyful mood, "the officers responded by sharing quaffs from the bottles of high proof potables carried by the men."[10]

In San Francisco, one-armed army veteran Sergeant Georgeson noticed a change in the crowd after a short time of friendly celebration. "It started off harmlessly enough," he recounted. He had exited his hotel on Market Street when the news first broke about the end of the war. He wrote, "Sailors snatched civilian hats and patriotic kisses. Soon, however, the sailors formed into street-blocking gangs that didn't just snatch kisses but grabbed them. They passed the girls from hand to hand, for fondling and kissing, before they let them go. But this was only the beginning." As Hospital Corpsman Greene realized, "suddenly, it became a riot in San Francisco."[11] The crowd was fast becoming inebriated and beginning to get a little out of hand.

One of the first victims of the overexuberant crowd were the streetcars. Phil Hoffman was only a youngster at the time and wrote, "My mother must not have been paying attention, because I was 14 years old and said, 'Can I go down and see the celebration?' and in a moment of

## The San Francisco V-J Day Peace Riots

**Celebrants perched atop a San Francisco trolley car at Market and Stockton streets (Karl R. Youst, West Virginia & Regional History Center).**

weakness she said yes." Rushing down to Market Street, Hoffman was soon swept up in the euphoria. "I began to see people on the roofs of the streetcars," he remembered. "'Ha. This is my golden opportunity.' So I climbed on the roof of Car 86, all the way up Market, until finally the inspector at Van Ness told me to come down, so off I went. I was '86'd' [i.e., ejected] from Car 86."[12]

Soon, however, as the crowd thickened, the streetcars could no longer move. They then became targets of opportunity for the quickly inebriating crowd. "Street cars were unable to proceed as their trolleys were pulled from the wires," stated a United Press reporter. "A few windows were broken." On at least one occasion, homeward-bound riders engaged in fisticuffs with the drunken crowd, trying to prevent them from destroying their ride home. The next morning, Larry Marshall, division superintendent of the Market Street Railway, reported that 25 out of 52 streetcars had to be removed from service for the next few days because of bent trolley poles, missing fenders, broken windows, and other damage.[13]

## Chapter 5. It Begins

*San Francisco Examiner* reporter Hyman was in the crowd and felt that the liquor that had been flowing freely since 4:00 p.m. began to have bad effects about an hour or two later. "Liquor began taking hold and fights began breaking out," wrote Hyman. "Servicemen ripped fenders off street cars and left debris lying on the streets." A drunken soldier was spotted on a corner shouting to anyone that would listen, "I'm drunk and I'm going to get drunker. This war cost me two brothers." Josette Dermody Wingo commented on the change in atmosphere among the revelers. "It was wonderful for a while, everybody caught up in the same euphoria," she said. "Then things started to get out of hand. The liquor stores were looted. Alcohol and abandon made men mad."[14]

Gladys Hanson was 20 years old in August 1945 and arrived downtown near Mason and Market Streets, at the eight-story Pepsi-Cola Center for Service Men and Women. "My mother said I was too young to go down there, but a couple of aunts took me down there with them," she stated. "It was great fun and I'm glad I went, but pretty soon we decided we'd better get out of there." Another person who made the decision to retire before the crowd got too out of hand was the young copygirl Lynn Hartsell. "Around 7 p.m., I made my own way up Market Street to the Greyhound bus that would deliver me back to the suburbs," she commented. "Flags and banners waved, girls were kissed and sailors' hats snatched in return. The street lights were turned on for the first time since Dec. 7, 1941. Most of them even worked. At this early hour, it was just one big enthusiastic block party." On the bus ride home, Hartsell remembered the jubilant riders singing several patriotic songs, including "Coming in on a Wing and a Prayer," "Praise the Lord and Pass the Ammunition," "Anchors Aweigh," and the 1917 George M. Cohan melody "Over There," made popular during the last war. Lynn recalled, "'Over There' was resurrected from World War I, but that didn't matter, this one was over over there, and we were all happy." Having been caught up in the gaiety, she admitted, "I had a sailor's hat."[15]

Peggy Leiser, a young war widow whose husband had been killed in the fighting in Europe, was living in San Francisco and went over to Market Street with one of her girlfriends to join the crowd that was celebrating the end of the war that had cost the life of her husband. "It was the worst decision we could have made," she remarked years later. "We thought we'd go see the celebration. And it was awful. We were scared to death. Everybody went crazy, they had a good reason to go crazy, of course, but not that crazy." When the celebrants became too crazy, Peggy and her girlfriend headed for home.[16]

Near 6:00 p.m., the streetcar turntable at Powell and Market Streets drew the attention of the surging mob. "The turntable for the

## The San Francisco V-J Day Peace Riots

little trolley cars (cable cars) at Powell and Market streets was made into a merry-go-round," recalled one Bay City resident.[17] One-armed veteran Sidney Georgeson had returned to his hotel on Market Street when the crowd started to become unruly but returned to the street when he heard "a yell from a thousand throats that filled the night."[18]

As Sergeant Georgeson remembered, "After working myself through a cheering crowd of servicemen and their girls, I saw the focus of their fun." He later wrote it was "enough to turn my stomach." He explained:

> It was a cable car, standing on the turntable where Powell Street joins Market. It was filled with screaming passengers. They were peaceful people who'd made up their minds, too late, to go home.
> Swarming around the car were young sailors. They were trying to topple it. They couldn't. But under the pressure of their bodies, the car started turning on its table. The sailors had discovered a new form of fun. They made it spin. Faster and faster. A few passengers jumped off. Others tumbled off the whirling merry-go-round.[19]

During the war years, many of the typically male-oriented jobs throughout the nation had been filled by capable women. One of those positions was the conductor on the San Francisco trolley cars. Sidney Georgeson continued with his narrative.

> The sailors soon got tired. This was work. And one of them, a yelling youngster, discovered a pretty conductorette on the platform, hanging on for life.
> "Let's get her," the sailor yelled.
> "Let's see if it's a man or a woman," someone shouted.
> "Take it off," several voices howled in advance.
> They yanked her off the car. She stood in their midst, shivering. Two sailors grabbed her. They took off her uniform jacket and blouse. Then they lifted her high in the air and yanked off her trousers.
> "More, more," came a shout.
> The sailors gladly obliged. The conductorette was crying now, tears smudged her mascara, as the punks ripped her short slip to shreds, tore the brassiere off her and grabbed at her panties.
> She finally stood there, pitifully nude except for her shoes and stockings rolled above her knees. She made no effort to hide herself. She sobbed into her hands. Her torn clothing lay scattered on the ground. The crowd screamed.
> A man handed her a coat. He led her away, shielding her with his arm. There were some shouts of derision against the helpful civilian. But nobody tried to stop him.[20]

To Georgeson, it seemed that at this time, all the crowd wanted was to have some fun at the young woman's expense. While the civilian savior was successful in stepping in to help the woman, years later, when recalling

## Chapter 5. It Begins

the incident, the one-armed veteran doubted if such would have happened a few hours later, hinting that the young conductorette would have been sexually assaulted by the inebriated sailors. "The evening was still young," he explained. "Later it would have been different."[21]

Similar to what had occurred in the early morning, the drunken revelers also targeted any automobiles that made the mistake of appearing along Market Street. Additionally, parked cars along the wide thoroughfare were attacked. "Cars were overturned and others had their tops crumpled by stomping feet," noted Navy Corpsman Greene. Another eyewitness reported, "I passed toppled automobiles that lay against the curb, a Yellow cab whose roof was flattened by a load of sailors. Glass from broken bottles crunched all over the place."[22]

At Market and Fifth Streets, the revelers broke the window of a cigar store managed by V.M. Zlokovich and looted the place, taking $1,091 in merchandise. Not far away, people shattered the windows in the Premier Cigar Store and stole all the inventory. At the Sommer & Kaufmann Shoe Store at 838 Market Street and at the S.H. Kress & Co. Department Store at 935 Market Street, revelers broke the windows and took much of the merchandise. Up and down Market Street, people began breaking the windows of cigar, liquor, and many other stores. The once-peaceful, fun-loving celebration had suddenly turned ugly. "I continued along Market Street, hearing yells and the tinkling crash of breaking glass," wrote the ever-observant Sergeant Georgeson. "All along the wide street, big department store windows were crumbling under the pressure of the sidewalk crowds. Glass spilled down on them. People with bleeding faces passed."[23]

Fourteen-year-old Bill Bodenweck, who had finally linked up with his mother at the White House Department Store, noted the change in atmosphere as the two of them joined the celebration on Market Street. "There was a lot of gaiety, but there was an edge of violence," he said. "In front of the old Hub Theater [at 727 Market Street], a sailor with a bottle stood over a yard-wide pool of blood, laughing, and saying over and over, 'Somebody got it right in the schnozzola.'"[24]

As Bill and his mother advanced along Market Street, he noticed that people lining the south side of the thoroughfare "mostly just watched the milling mass" but on the north side, "the windows had begun to shatter." It turned out that there was a distinct line of demarcation along Market Street. Although everybody was there to celebrate the end of World War II, the people on the south side of the street were simply enjoying themselves and having a good time. The people on the north side were more raucous, more rowdy. They were ready to let loose and cause a bit of destruction. The people on the north side of the street were the ones setting off firecrackers, stealing hats, stripping women of their clothing, and breaking bottles. As long as a person stayed on the south side of the street and did not venture over to the other side, the rowdies tended to leave them alone. When the crowd on the north side began to break windows and loot stores, the people on the south side looked on in disapproval but did nothing about it. They seemed to know that they could not stop the now riotous crowd on the north side.[25]

Young Bill later admitted that at first the windows were broken "because they were invitingly filled with rows on rows of liquor bottles, but later clothing store windows began to break and sailors passed out civilian hats and ties to wear on their uniforms." While pressing through the crowd, Bill's mother was suddenly grabbed by a big sailor with a lot of service stripes on his blue uniform sleeve. "[I] grabbed his arm and said, 'Leggo my mother,'" Bill recalled. "The sailor said, 'Kid, kiss your mother for me.' [I] did and the two of [us] decided it was about time to head home. [We] got one of the last cabs."[26]

In addition to targeting cigar stores and liquor establishments, many in the crowd began shattering the big front windows of jewelry stores. "In the shattered show window of a jewelry store," noticed army Sergeant Georgeson, "sailors stood in the light holding a mock auction of articles displayed for sale. Yells of the spectators spurred them on. A little further down, the window of a jewelry store had been similarly smashed. Several sailors and Marines were prowling in the ruins, but there was apparently nothing left for them. All the diamonds, gold, silver, and platinum had already been cleaned out. Through the window I could see other servicemen rummaging in the back of the store." Later, he added, "There was the constant tinkling of broken glasses and broken windows, a cacophony of destruction."[27]

About an hour before the sun began to set, the revelers once again began setting fires in the middle of Market Street, reminding many of the bonfires that had lined the street during the wee hours of the morning when the city had responded to the news that Japan was simply *thinking* of surrendering. "Bonfires started up in the accumulated litter of the confetti," recalled Alvin Hyman. In addition to burning the mountain of confetti that now littered the streets, many in the crowd tore down almost all the remaining wooden war bond booths, concluding that they certainly were no longer needed. Likewise, any sign that was now deemed unnecessary was torn down and burned. "Tattered signs that reminded the city of war," noted a United Press correspondent, "'Magnesium Alloys for

## Chapter 5. It Begins

Wartime Uses' and 'Buy War Bonds'—were used to kindle bonfires for the second straight night."[28]

As the crowd began to turn ugly, the local and armed forces police seemed to remain idle. In defense of the city police officers, Sergeant Georgeson commented, "[D]espite the 'stand-by' emergency, police officers were helpless. There just weren't enough of them that night."[29]

## Chapter 6

# Wild Night

Once again, in response to the big bonfires blazing along Market Street, several fire trucks tried to force their way through the crowds to extinguish the blazes. "Fire apparatus responded to numerous alarms, some false, some brought on by bonfires," wrote reporter Hyman, "and every piece of apparatus which slowed down to a reasonable safe pace was boarded by dozens of soldiers, sailors, Marines—and their girls—who rode cheering through the streets." Recording the exact time of one such incident, reporter Bernadine Snyder noted, "7:10: The Armed Forces take over a fire truck with WAVES, WACS, Marines, sailors atop." In a repeat of the night before, another reporter noted that "when fire trucks arrived, cheering service men helped extinguish the blazes, then swarmed over the engines, insisting on rides back to the fire stations."[1]

Across the Bay in Berkeley, 19-year-old Evelyne G. Endicott, one of the so-called "bobby soxers," was celebrating the news of the Japanese surrender while standing on the back of a truck parked in front of the WAC headquarters building at Shattuck Avenue and Carleton Street. Near 6:40 p.m., when the vehicle unexpectedly surged forward, Endicott toppled to the ground, striking her head. She was immediately taken to Peralta Hospital in Oakland suffering from serious head injuries. Faring a bit better, Albert Toro, a civilian merchant marine, was partying at home when he fell out of a second-story window. He was treated at Oakland's Highland Hospital for a "laceration of the left arm."[2]

In San Francisco, near 6:45 p.m., the American War Community Services (AWCS) Junior Officer's Club, although several blocks north of Market Street at 740 Taylor, closed for the evening due to "too much breakage." However, the United Service Organization (USO) club at 989 Market Street, right in the center of the celebration, remained open.[3] While many movie theaters had shut down almost immediately after their last picture had ended after President Truman's announcement, the State Theater at 787 Market Street remained open. To the

## Chapter 6. Wild Night

dismay of Bonnie Getchell, a diminutive 106-pound assistant manager, dozens of sailors flooded the establishment without stopping to purchase a ticket.[4]

"I got a call on the house phone that the usherette in the balcony was in trouble, and I couldn't find the manager or the stagehand, so I ran up there to try to help," Getchell recalled. "As I got to the top of the ramp, these three big sailors came around the corner and made a grab for me." Despite her small size, she refused to back down. "I just straight-armed the first one and they were so drunk that when he fell over, he took the other two with him," she beamed. "The manager came running up with the stagehand and said, 'We came to help, but I guess you didn't need it.'"[5]

By 7:30 p.m., as twilight settled on San Francisco, the overenthusiastic and overinebriated celebrants really began to get crazy. "Women were pulling off their clothes, people were breaking windows, overturning cars and kissing and hugging," remembered Al Bowen, a San Francisco resident. "I went crazy, too. I was just a kid. I was happy it was over with because it was pretty rough, even for a kid." As shown in the dozens of photographs taken at the time of the rioting by photographers from the many different area newspapers, most of the participants were sailors, dressed in their dark blue uniforms and wearing their distinct white "Dixie cup" caps. Mixed in among the

Crowd celebrating the news of Japan's surrender at the Admission Day Monument on the evening of August 14, 1945 (San Francisco History Center, San Francisco Public Library).

## The San Francisco V-J Day Peace Riots

sailors were a sprinkling of young teenage women, the so-called "bobby soxers."[6]

"There were fistfights for women," wrote one eyewitness. "By that time, kissing girls or undressing them was not enough anymore. Most girls were willing to do most anything to celebrate the victory." Among the women "willing to do most anything" was a young auburn-haired lady who climbed atop the crowded base of the Admission Day monument at the intersection of Market, Turk, and Mason Streets. "A plump redhead danced naked atop the base of San Francisco's Native Sons [i.e., Admission Day] monument ... after hysterical service men tore off her dress and underpinnings," noted the *San Mateo Times*. "After several minutes of nudity, the woman borrowed a coat from a sailor, and the pair disappeared in the yelling crowd."[7]

As it turned out, the young lady who climbed atop the Admission Day monument was not the only female who ended up without her clothes on that night. Robert Frederickson was a high school student working at the beautiful Fox Theater at 1350 Market Street when he suddenly noticed a change in the crowd. Walking up Market Street was a young lady and her marine escort. As the young student recalled, "[the crowd] parted before them like Moses parting the Red Sea." While Frederickson stared at the marine's chest, "covered with the wings of a flier, battle stars and enough decorations to show he had been there and back," others stared at the chest of his companion. Sergeant Georgeson was still among the drunken revelers on Market Street when he also spotted the pair. "Coming up Market Street, smiling happily and completely unconcerned about the looks, cheers and jeers they caused, was a young couple," he wrote. "The man was a Marine sergeant. He wore a blissful smile above his chestful of fruit salad. Which was not the least bit surprising. Walking by his side, her arm through his, was a lovely platinum blond. She had the best figure I'd ever seen. And see it I did. She had absolutely nothing on except a sailor's jacket, and that was open on either side of her perky breasts."[8]

A young lady who decided to forgo a navy coat and bare it all was spotted atop the overhanging canopy over the main entryway into the Pepsi-Cola Center for Service Men and Women. "One girl did a strip tease on top of the Pepsi-Cola center at Market and Mason, tossing off every bit of her clothing down to the boys, including her shoes," recorded an unnamed San Francisco woman. "She had absolutely nothing on. Then a sailor got her down, put his peacoat on her and took her home."[9]

The carefree, drunken night turned ugly when 20-year-old navy Radioman Third Class (RM3c) William James "Sonny" Thompson from

## Chapter 6. Wild Night

Hermitage, Arkansas, was thrown out of a second-story window along Market Street by a couple of drunken marines. Suffering a fractured skull, he was rushed to the base hospital on Treasure Island. Another injured serviceman taken to Treasure Island Hospital was 19-year-old Seaman Second Class (S2c) Hans Herbert Pfister from the attack transport USS *Henrico* (APA-45). While partying on Market Street, he was shoved through a plate glass window. He likewise suffered a fractured skull.[10] Taken to Central Emergency Hospital was Private James W. Prim, 38 years old, married with a seven-year-old daughter. A United States Marine Corps veteran of the 3rd Marine Division, he had gone through the bloody battles of Bougainville, Guam, and Iwo Jima without injury. Prim was seriously injured when he fell, or was shoved, down the stairs of a small hotel at 34 Ellis Street, just a few steps from Market. He died later that morning.[11]

While serious injuries were beginning to occur among the celebrating service personnel, the civilian participants began to suffer as well. Although alcohol consumption was suspected, no one knew for sure what caused 35-year-old Charles David Mooney, a longtime switchman for the Western Pacific Railroad, to be struck by a train and killed instantly at the intersection of 25th and Third Streets, miles from the downtown area. Another railroad employee, 48-year-old Bruce Keith Tarkington, suffered a skull fracture when he apparently fell, or was knocked down, on the sidewalk in front of 151 Sutter Street, only one block north of Market. Suffering a skull fracture, he was taken to Harbor Emergency Hospital at the Embarcadero.[12]

Near 11:00 p.m., with the celebrations showing no sign of slowing down, two celebrants were victims of a hit-and-run accident at Macdonald Avenue and 28th Street in Richmond, California, across the Bay from San Francisco. Daniel Burdette Williams, age 34, was pronounced dead at the scene while his girlfriend, Alice Conrad, age 31, suffered shock and abrasions.[13]

Perhaps the most heart-wrenching incident of the evening also involved a hit-and-run accident. At 4:30 that afternoon, just 29 minutes after President Truman made his announcement that World War II had finally come to an end, 46-year-old Estelle McArdle and 39-year-old Seaman First Class John Morris became husband and wife. Later that evening, after only a few hours of marital bliss, as the newlyweds were partying near Van Ness and Washington Street, far from the downtown area, they were struck by an unknown automobile. Estelle was declared dead at the scene. An ambulance took John to the U.S. Naval Receiving Hospital at

## The San Francisco V-J Day Peace Riots

Geneva Avenue and Moscow Street, where he was admitted with serious injuries.[14]

The most heinous injury of the evening, however, occurred at 12th Street and Market, near the center of the two-mile-long party central. Municipal Railway inspector Joseph Samuel Gyorgy, age 34, was switching trolley cars when he was struck in the head by an unidentified assailant. Suffering a fractured skull, Gyorgy was rushed to Mission Emergency Hospital, where he died early the next morning. Before expiring, however, Gyorgy managed to report that he had been struck by an unidentified marine. It was an unprovoked attack by another overexuberant, and probably intoxicated, serviceman. He was survived by his wife and two young children. His wife would later file a $50,000 lawsuit against the city of San Francisco for "the beating death and her husband."[15]

By 9:00 p.m., hospital emergency rooms all around San Francisco had treated an estimated 240 people, including one individual who had suffered a fractured skull from being hit over the head with a bottle. City hospitals also reported treating "a lady who became hysterical over peace; a drunk who sat down on some broken glass, [and] a shipyard worker who jumped out of a second-story window to 'see if peace had relaxed him.'" As the reporter who broke the story wrote, "It had."[16]

City fire departments had responded to numerous alarms, "some false, some brought on by bonfires" and the city police were reporting that the arrest rate for public drunkenness was "above normal." They also reported an "unparalleled number" of arrests for "riding on [the] roofs of streetcars and disrobing in public," both misdemeanor offenses. Reporter Hyman wrote, "Ambulances and patrol wagons began clanging through the streets collecting celebrants who had overestimated their capacity—collecting them and piling them up like cordwood before delivering them to hospital or station house."[17]

On the military side, Navy Shore Patrol officers had found it necessary to set up a local headquarters at a vacant two-story former garage at 850 Bryant Street across from the Hall of Justice and several blocks south of Market Street. By midnight, the SP "seemed likely to exhaust all floor space available in its two stories for storing 'passed out' sailors." Wrote one-armed Sergeant Georgeson, "All over the downtown area young sailors were reeling under their unaccustomed loads of hard liquor. Some collapsed against buildings, falling into their own vomit; others passed out into the middle of the streets to be trampled mercilessly by their mindless fellow celebrants."[18] The unconscious individuals were slowly being rounded up and taken to the temporary headquarters building.

## Chapter 6. Wild Night

Just before midnight, Jack Krystal, 51 years old, a salesman with President Theater, married and a father of nine children, was pronounced "Dead on arrival" at Park Emergency Hospital. The cause of death was listed as "Multiple fractures of skull. Lacerations & contusions of brain. Simple fracture of right leg." A short time earlier, Krystal had walked out from between two parked cars at Fell and Ashbury Streets, near Panhandle Park, and had been struck by an auto driven by navy Lieutenant Commander Leon Grabowsky. It was determined at the scene that Krystal had been heavily drinking prior to being struck and that the navy commander was not responsible. Commander Grabowsky was not ticketed or held.[19]

Near midnight, delivery drivers tried to work their trucks through the crowds, hoping to quickly drop off their merchandise and just as quickly remove themselves from the area. As expected, however, overanxious crowds swept over the vehicles. "Trucks were looted, right in the midst of delivering their merchandise, and autos were danced upon," commented one San Franciscan. Noted one-armed Sidney Georgeson, "Traffic was at a standstill. There were no taxis, no streetcars, no buses. They'd stopped running in face of the human road blocks."[20]

Although the liquor stores and taverns had closed their doors near 6:00 p.m., enough liquor stores had been broken into and looted to seemingly supply the entire crowd for a week. David S. Greene, the navy corpsman, spotted "a girl with a bottle of whisky in each hand ... perched on a trash can offering a drink to all comers." A photo published the next morning in the *San Francisco Examiner* showed a pretty young woman perched atop a corner mailbox, draped with streamers of toilet paper and holding two bottles in her lap while drinking from a third. The caption stated, "High, but, 'er, not quite dry, this young woman staged a one-woman celebration atop a mail box on a Market Street corner yesterday, oblivious to passersby who smiled at her and perhaps envied her. She was well-stocked for the evening of victory celebrations that swept the city."[21]

Also noticing an individual well stocked for the evening was Sidney Georgeson, who was still on Market Street. He wrote, "From a side street, a soldier in a torn uniform stumbled on the main thoroughfare. He was hugging a wild collection of liquor bottles. Several tumbled out of his grasp. He left a trail of whiskey and splinters." The one-armed Georgeson concluded, "I found out later that the soldier's liquor, like most of the other alcohol that flowed that night and next, must have come from one of the 25 liquor stores that were looted when their owners complied with the request by the State Board of Equalization and closed shop."[22]

### The San Francisco V-J Day Peace Riots

Wrote one reporter, "San Francisco's untrammeled victory revelry of Tuesday night reached 'ugly' proportions, as disorder, chiefly in the 900 block on Market Street, reached a stage of destructive and riotous looting." As midnight slipped by and Tuesday, August 14, changed to Wednesday, August 15, 1945, the celebration unbelievably took a turn for the worse. Noted Sidney Georgeson, "By midnight all hell had broken loose."[23]

CHAPTER 7

# The Darker Side

At Fort McDowell on Angel Island, inside San Francisco Bay and just north of Alcatraz Island, 200 Japanese soldiers were being held as prisoners of war, captured at various posts throughout the Pacific. The reaction of the POWs to the news of Japan's final surrender was far different from that in the cities around the Bay and across the United States. Noted a United Press correspondent, the Japanese POWs "greeted the news with no visible emotion." Since the army guards reported hearing "no discussion among the prisoners," no additional precautions were taken.[1]

Just after midnight, the real destruction of downtown San Francisco began. "Almost as if they had been organized," said one eyewitness, "the boot camp sailors systematically tore down store and theater signs and carried them to large heaps at Market and Fifth. Soon huge bonfires burned, sending up flames many stories high. A stench of holocaust filled the crowded streets." Sergeant Georgeson was present and described what happened next. "From behind me came the sound of fire engines. But the trucks didn't make it. They ran up against living barricades and were commandeered by sailors who kicked the firemen off. From far away, I saw [dark blue] uniforms swarming over the stalled trucks." He continued, "Some rioters had now gained access to office buildings along the street, presumably in search of fuel to feed the fires. Various items of furniture started crashing down on the sidewalks. A huge desk landed not far from me with a terrific thump. Luckily, no one was hit."[2] It seemed providential now that most of the hotel owners and employees along Market Street had taken the precaution of removing most of the furniture from their lobbies.

In a letter to a friend written a couple of days after the rioting, an unnamed San Francisco woman chronicled the destruction that she had witnessed on the night of August 14 and the early morning hours of August 15. "Hardly a window on Market Street remains intact, and all sorts of merchandise, hats, shoes, luggage, cosmetics, lingerie and women's apparel were stolen," she wrote. "Variety stores and liquor stores had their show windows broken and the contents stolen. Awnings were ripped to pieces, and every place was looted and destroyed by hoodlums and also servicemen. The damage was terrific.... Everyone was well fortified, carrying a bottle ... autos [were] overturned, streetcars pushed off tracks. I am telling you, it was *terrible*."³

Many area residents were disgusted with what they witnessed on Tuesday night/early Wednesday morning. They realized that everybody had waited four long years for the war to end but what was transpiring after President Truman's four o'clock announcement was too much. From the San Francisco suburb of Stanford, one irate citizen who had been in the Bay City during the celebrations wrote to the editor of the *Stanton Daily* a few days later, complaining about the breaking of storefront windows despite the attempts by proprietors to ward off the rioters by hanging American flags in their windows. He wrote, "After seeing what both servicemen and civilians were doing to the American flag on Market Street Tuesday night, I can experience no 'spirit of patriotism' when the Stars and Stripes dangle in the breeze."⁴ In spite of the American flags, many of the storefront windows had still been broken and the stores looted.

By midnight, most of the celebrating families, the people with children, had retired for the night and had gone back to their houses or hotel rooms. It was mostly civilians in their late teens and early 20s, and the many service personnel, who continued to crowd the downtown streets and raise a ruckus. Eventually word passed among the revelers that Lieutenant Governor Frederick F. Houser, who was currently the acting governor since California Governor Earl Warren was on his way to Washington, D.C., for a meeting of governors, had declared that Wednesday, August 15, would be a state holiday. All state government buildings would be closed. Wrote reporter Alvin D. Hyman, "As the celebrating thousands whooped it up into the post-midnight hours, they were encouraged that today will be a State holiday, by proclamation of acting–Governor Fred Houser." In accordance with an announcement made earlier on August 14, whereby Mayor Lapham stated that San Francisco would observe a city holiday once the government in Sacramento announced a state holiday, retail stores and other businesses throughout the city would also remain closed on Wednesday.⁵ To those still partying in the streets, the twin announcements added fuel to the fire. They were celebrating an "official holiday." There was no need to quit now.

At both the Golden Gate Bridge and the Oakland Bay Bridge, between San Francisco and Oakland, people continued to come and go into or out of both cities so that each bridge became "clogged with traffic." Shortly after midnight, California Highway Patrol Officer Merton Hart was on

## Chapter 7. The Darker Side

the crowded Bay Bridge directing traffic and investigating an earlier accident when suddenly, an auto driven by 20-year-old Patricia De Lair struck another car, bounced off it, and struck Officer Hart. Thrown 30 feet, Officer Hart sustained "head, back and neck injuries, possible internal injuries, bruises and the loss of three teeth." He was quickly rushed to East Oakland Hospital. Miss Hart was "cited for reckless driving."[6]

Another incident on the Bay Bridge happened when 19-year-old Freida R. Jepson somehow opened the passenger side door of a moving car and fell out onto the pavement. She was subsequently run over by the following automobile. An ambulance took her to Harbor Emergency Hospital in San Francisco, where the slightly intoxicated Jepson was treated for "a broken right leg, cuts, bruises, and contusions."[7]

It was sometime after the midnight hour, after most of the liquor had been consumed and inhibitions had been tossed aside, that incidents of a sexual nature began to take place along Market Street. At Fifth and Market, a young girl did a striptease to the music of an amusement arcade. When she was down to her lace panties, a group of excited sailors grabbed her and carried her off to a darkened corner. As she balanced on the shoulder of one big sailor, she looked at the amazed young men still standing in a crowd and shouted, "Come and get it, boys!" Disgustedly, one eyewitness recalled, "She had a glittering wedding ring on her left hand. I wondered in which corner of the world her husband was, and what he thought she did that night."[8]

Some of the women who had remained with the crowd, many of them teenage "bobby soxers," were not such willing participants. Several women became the victims of sexual assault that morning. Eyewitnesses later testified that they saw young girls fighting and screaming as drunken groups of sailors dragged the girls into nearby storefront doorways and sexually molested them. Disabled veteran Sidney Georgeson, who was still milling about among the celebrants, claimed to have witnessed two such attacks, one inside a looted furniture store and one in the entranceway to a movie theater. He added, "Here and there were groups that tried to keep their sanity. They still had their good, clean, patriotic fun, dancing and singing on the streets, kissing the girls that were with them, forming small impromptu victory parades.... But it wasn't long before these groups were raided by rougher mobs who tore their shrieking girls away, hauling them by brute force into alleys and dark doorways."[9]

In commenting on the lack of police presence when young women were being assaulted, Ellis Levy, the manager of the Telenews Theater at 930 Market Street, told how he had been unable to find a police officer after he spotted "five sailors holding down and criminally attacking a woman

## The San Francisco V-J Day Peace Riots

in a Market Street doorway." Sergeant Georgeson may have witnessed the same incident. He remembered "five punk boots [i.e., new sailors] grabbed a big-chested brunette and started ripping off her clothes. The girl seemed to think it was all in fun, but she started arguing when the sailors pulled her into the dark entrance of a movie house.... In the theater entrance, the sailors were soon surrounded by a cheering multitude who pushed and shoved each other and started fighting for their turn." Georgeson wrote that he recalled one of the original five sailors shout, "Take it easy. There's enough of her for the whole damn Navy."[10]

Before the night was over, the San Francisco hospitals would treat six women for rape.[11] Many people wondered how many more sexual assaults went unreported. In 1945, it was uncommon for a young lady to go to the hospital or to a police station to report being raped. Such an incident was looked upon as a blot or stain against the reputation of the young lady. What had caused the rape? Surely it was something that the young lady had brought on herself. Even parents were reluctant to take their daughter to a hospital after being sexually attacked. They were afraid that such a report might stigmatize their daughter and make her ineligible for future marriage. It was better to just forget about the whole ugly thing and look the other way. As such, no one would ever know how many women were sexually assaulted on the nights of the San Francisco Peace Riots.

One-armed veteran Sidney Georgeson wrote years later about a sexual assault he witnessed on August 14.

> Up the street, hurrying, came a woman and her daughter. I don't know what they were doing out so late that dangerous night. Maybe they'd been to a late show. The girl already had the full figure of maturity, but she sure wasn't over 16.
> 
> Some sailors spotted her. They ran over and tried to pull her away from her mother. The mother looked at the sailors. She started to cry.
> 
> "Please, please," she pleaded. "Leave her alone."
> 
> "Go home, you old bitch," said a sailor. He was possibly 19. "She wants some fun too, don't you babe?"
> 
> "Sure she wants it," another young sailor bawled.
> 
> The girl clung to her mother. The older woman hugged the youngster. The sailors tore the two apart. They pulled the girl over to the store window. The mother ran after them, beating at their backs, trying to pull their hair. One of the men turned. He hit the woman in the face.
> 
> I rushed at the sailor. But I was in no shape to do any good.... He noticed my empty sleeve, and gave me a final shove. "Whyn't you take off," he panted, "before you get hurt?"

Turning from the ugly scene, Georgeson ran down Market Street until he came across a Navy Shore Patrol officer. When he explained what was

## Chapter 7. The Darker Side

going on and asked for help, according to Georgeson, the SP replied, "Are you kidding, soldier?"[12] Knowing that they were heavily outnumbered by the drunken revelers, many of the civilian and armed forces police seemed reluctant or afraid to act.

Commenting on the lack of response by the Navy Shore Patrol officers, Lloyd Taylor, the executive secretary of the Market Street Association, who had a vested interest in what was happening along the main thoroughfare, stated, "Time after time, I would see a shore patrolman standing in one spot looking for drunks, while 10 feet away someone was smashing a window. The shore patrol was left in the hands of petty officers with little police training. I saw very, very few commissioned officers of the shore patrol." Taylor believed that the navy servicemen were out of control because of "the collapse of the shore patrol." However, it was later reported that Shore Patrol officers had arrested 748 sailors that Tuesday night/Wednesday morning.[13]

At times, it seemed as though the small number of available city and armed forces police officers were not even trying to stop the rioting and molestation. United Press reporter Hennen Hackett compared the early Wednesday morning activities with what she had witnessed just the past afternoon. "Looting unequalled during the earlier stages of the victory demonstration was reported by irate Market Street merchants," she wrote. Although dozens of windows had been broken and thousands of dollars of liquor and other goods had been taken by the mob on Tuesday night/Wednesday morning, the San Francisco police would later make the unbelievable statement that the "looting was substantially less than yesterday [Tuesday] morning."[14]

Both the civilian and armed forces police had done little to quell the wild celebration. Instead, they had seemed to stand by and let the revelry die of exhaustion. "All we could do was keep them from taking more stuff out of the stores," said city Police Officer Cahill. "All the windows were broken." As he summarized, Officer Cahill felt that the riot served as "a perfect example of the theory that you can get lost in a mob." In trying to comprehend why only a "meager 150" people were arrested for drunkenness by both the city and armed forces police, one newspaper reasoned, "Two explanations were offered: Police weren't arresting any drunk who didn't demand arrest. And the military authorities weren't talking about their bag of men in uniform who dropped out of the celebration." After most of the partiers had finally gotten tired and gone home, the civilian and armed forces police simply swept the streets for passed-out individuals.[15]

## The San Francisco V-J Day Peace Riots

It was near 4:00 a.m. on Wednesday, August 15, before the partiers finally ran out of steam and the celebration finally neared an end. Navy Corpsman David S. Greene recalled, "Sometime during the night, loudspeakers scared most servicemen back to their bases. Muster would be taken, they said, and any man not present at a certain hour would be counted as absent without leave." Greene and his friends headed back to their base at Alameda Naval Air Station near Oakland, taking with them a heavily inebriated army chaplain. As Greene remembered, "My buddies and I had somehow joined up with an Army chaplain who had been celebrating and was now almost dead weight on our hands. We took him to Alameda Naval Air Station, and left him asleep on a bench in the chapel. He was gone the next day."[16]

In Oakland, police reported that between 4:00 p.m. Tuesday, August 14, when President Truman came out with his surrender announcement, and 6:00 a.m. Wednesday, August 15, normally a quiet time, there were 24 traffic accidents with 13 people injured, though none seriously. Oakland's Highland Hospital officials treated 80 people in the emergency room where normally they would have treated fewer than 40. "There apparently were a lot of fights and a lot of falls," said one hospital attendant. "We were so busy we didn't stop to get much in the way of case histories."[17]

In San Francisco, the many hospital emergency rooms handled over 600 cases during the same 14-hour period, mostly for "firecracker burns, swinging fists, and flying bottles." One of the more serious injuries occurred to Police Officer George Hill, who had been hit over the head with a bottle by an "unidentified assailant," and another serious injury occurred to Antone Zmak, who suffered a "possible skull fracture" when he too was clobbered over the head with a bottle. The "more than 600" number was said to be "a new city record."[18]

Another city record was set when police reported that 95 motorists had reported their parked cars stolen from around the fringes of the celebration. While responding to those reports, police also set a record in answering 1,250 calls during the 13 hours between 4:00 p.m. Tuesday and 5:00 a.m. Wednesday. Not to be outdone, the San Francisco Fire Department recorded that it had responded to an amazing 185 calls during the same period, most of them false alarms. This too was a new city record.[19]

By 8:00 a.m. on Wednesday, August 15, almost all the remaining servicemen and servicewomen on the streets of San Francisco had been rounded up and taken back to their bases or had returned voluntarily. Almost all the civilians had either gone home or were sleeping off their inebriated state in "drunk tanks" in police stations throughout the city.

## *Chapter 7. The Darker Side*

"Market Street woke up to its second day of shattered window panes and littered streets today," wrote a United Press correspondent, "as police reported at least three persons dead and hundreds injured in the wild … victory celebration." Although the festivities had come to an end, police admitted that with Wednesday being declared a state and city holiday, "[I]t could get restarted later today."[20]

CHAPTER 8

# Quiet

In response to the announcements that both the state and the city had declared Wednesday, August 15, a holiday, Rear Admiral Carleton H. Wright, commander of the 12th Naval District, with headquarters on Treasure Island and covering the geographic areas of northern California, Colorado, Utah, and almost all of Nevada, decided to follow suit. According to a United Press correspondent, Admiral Wright stated, "All naval and civilian personnel of the 12th Naval District, with exception of skeleton crews of officers and enlisted men, have been granted a holiday today and tomorrow to observe Japan's surrender." A spokesman for Admiral Wright estimated that the announcement would probably "pour more than 100,000 sailors into the community from neighboring stations."[1]

Born in Iowa in 1892, Carleton Herbert Wright had graduated from the United States Naval Academy at Annapolis, Maryland, in 1912. He saw service in the First World War aboard a destroyer in the South Pacific and at the beginning of World War II was the captain of a cruiser. In May 1942, he was promoted to rear admiral and was eventually placed in command of a task force of destroyers and heavy cruisers in the waters around Guadalcanal. On the evening of November 30/December 1, 1942, at the naval Battle of Tassafaronga, Admiral Wright led his task force out to intercept a Japanese squadron of destroyers attempting to bring supplies to their troops on Guadalcanal, and in the ensuing battle, Wright's ships sank one Japanese destroyer and managed to stop the resupply mission dead in its tracks. However, he lost one heavy cruiser and had three more heavily damaged. Although presented with a Navy Cross, the second-highest decoration by the navy after the Medal of Honor, Wright was subsequently assigned to shore duty in Washington, D.C. After a brief period on the water again in 1944, he returned to shore duty and was eventually assigned as the commander of the 12th Naval District in San Francisco.[2] A lifelong navy man, Wright had seen combat up close and fully realized the significance of the cessation of hostilities. He was glad to be able to grant his upcoming new recruits, who were being

## Chapter 8. Quiet

spared the possibility of death on a warship, the opportunity to enjoy themselves.

Following "the pattern of a routine Sunday," most downtown San Francisco stores remained closed on Wednesday, August 15, and would close again "during the undetermined holidays to come." While all taverns in the Bay area had shut down two hours after the 4:01 p.m. announcement by President Truman on August 14, and the Board of Equalization was hoping that they would remain closed until 10:00 a.m. Thursday morning, August 16, the bartenders' union and the Liquor Dealers Association once again indicated that they might open sooner. "[U]nless the damage toll of last night's goings-on looks too forbidding," they stated, they would open for regular business at 6:00 p.m. that evening—Wednesday. However, in Oakland and other adjoining communities, the bars and liquor stores would remain closed. Noted a San Mateo newspaper, "The hardest thing to find today was a place to get a drink or buy a bottle."[3]

During the daylight hours of Wednesday, August 15, 1945, downtown merchants tried to clean up the mess that had been left in the streets and on the sidewalks from the late night/early morning revelry. Many merchants began sweeping broken glass from the sidewalks in front of their stores and righting overturned shelves and furniture within. Some nailed plywood and boards over the broken windows while others simply taped signs that read "Broken Glass" over gaping holes of jagged glass. At the same time, emergency city workers, exempt from the city holiday, tried to resurrect "No Parking" signs that had been torn down or collect the numerous trolley car bumpers that had been left sitting in the streets after being pulled off the fronts and rears of numerous streetcars.

Naturally, some people, including many couples with children, came down to Market Street and the Civic Center during the daylight hours and continued to celebrate the end of the war, but not with the sense of destructiveness that had marred the revelry of the past two nights. "Chinatown was crowded during the day with visitors," wrote an Associated Press correspondent. "Firecrackers continued to crack and sputter." Among one of the more comical sights that the daylight partygoers noticed were some drunken pigeons wobbling around Union Square. "Someone has apparently been feeding them grain soaked in bourbon," summed a local reporter.[4] August 15 was a day to celebrate the end of World War II and a lot of people knew how to do it right.

While some people and families went downtown to rejoice or stayed home to celebrate in their own way, many others took time on this declared holiday to go to their place of worship to give thanks that the conflict that had cost the lives of over 418,000 Americans had finally come to a successful conclusion. On August 16, the *San Francisco Examiner* noted, "Thousands of civilians and service men and women offered prayers of thanksgiving for peace yesterday as Protestant, Catholic and Jewish churches conducted special services."[5]

Despite the closing of all state and city governmental buildings, and the voluntary closing of most retail shops, workers in the many San Francisco factories treated Wednesday, August 15, as a normal workday and went to their jobs. "Hundreds of workers reported at the various Bay area shipyards," noted one San Francisco correspondent. However, it was also reported, "Some yards sent them home at once, while others operated [only] until noon."[6] There was still a feeling of jubilation in the air.

Although many of the war-related industries remained open, workers could at least rejoice in the fact that the Washington, D.C., Office of Price Regulation (OPA) had finally ceased the rationing of gasoline. "[T]oday came the announcement from Washington that gasoline rationing has ended," crowed the *San Mateo Times*. "Gasoline stamps and A, B, C stickers will go into the discard, and once more will ring the familiar American cry of 'Fill 'er up!'" Wrote a United Press correspondent, "Rationing stop orders are effective immediately." In response, San Francisco and other Bay-area service stations were overrun with car owners. Reported the *San Francisco Examiner*, "Beginning at 10 a.m. when gas ration stamps became history, most of the handful of stations remaining open during the holiday reportedly had tripled their wartime sales."[7]

Beginning on December 1, 1942, the OPA was forced to issue ration cards for civilian personnel since the armed forces needed so much gasoline to fuel their vehicles, planes, and ships. Most people, generically termed "the general public," received an "A" card to put in the front windshield of their automobile, allowing a driver to get about four gallons of gasoline a week. People with jobs considered "essential," such as business owners or employees working at a job supporting the war effort, received a "B" card, which allowed them to purchase eight gallons a week. A "C" card was given to people deemed "critical professionals," such as doctors, nurses, members of the clergy, and even farmworkers. A "C" card meant the owner of the car could purchase "a relatively unrestricted amount of gasoline." At the same time, a nationwide "victory speed limit" of 35 miles per hour was instituted, mainly to restrict wear and tear on tires, since raw rubber was almost impossible to obtain after the Japanese captured and occupied most of the rubber-producing countries of Southeast Asia.[8]

## Chapter 8. Quiet

Over the next few hours, for as long as the supply of gasoline held out, the service stations averaged between 80 and 100 customers an hour. As one San Francisco newspaper reported, "An old American phrase, discarded for almost three years, staged a rousing comeback in San Francisco ... as thousands of motorists drove into service stations to command jubilantly, 'Fill 'er up!'" Some drivers who had not heard about the cancellation pulled up to the pump and asked for only eight or 10 gallons of gas, offering their ration coupons to the service station attendant. They soon discovered that the coupons were no longer needed and called out "Fill 'er up." "It certainly can't come too soon as far as we are concerned," declared Price Administrator Chester Bowles. At one service station, one customer who ordered a full tank was heard to say, "First time I've had 'er filled since I owned 'er." Reported one person, "We simply cruised around, joyfully burning up gas." Despite the jubilation, however, the California State Highway Patrol reminded motorists that the wartime speed limit of 35 miles per hour was still in effect and hoped that all motorists would be careful since replacement parts were hard to come by. "It may be months before new cars are available and tires are still on the scarce list," said the public safety department. "Those who are reckless in use of their automotive equipment with unlimited gasoline may find they have 'rationed' themselves back to little or no travel."[9]

With their tanks filled with gas, many drivers headed to downtown San Francisco. By midafternoon, Market Street was lined with cars, bumper to bumper, from the Embarcadero to the Civic Center, in both directions. Soon, the drivers were blowing their horns and their passengers were shouting and making all kinds of noise, turning the motorcade into a boisterous, noisy celebration. By early afternoon, thousands of people had once again crowded into downtown San Francisco.[10]

Although it was hoped that all the San Francisco taverns would remain closed until Thursday morning, many of the bar owners, seeing the large number of potential customers, decided to open early. Most of the celebrants were navy sailors who had been granted leave through the sweeping announcement of Admiral Wright and had headed into downtown San Francisco to party. Said Bruno Mannori, president of the bartenders' union, "[The bartenders are] under orders to put on their coats and hats and go home any time they believed the situation to be dangerous."[11] It seemed as though, as long as there was a buck to be made, the bars would remain open.

While cars jammed Market Street, thousands of people once again began to line the sidewalks along either side of the main thoroughfare.

## The San Francisco V-J Day Peace Riots

"Crowds jammed the sidewalks on Market Street almost solid," wrote United Press reporter Hennen Hackett. "But until many of the city's taverns reopened at 4:00 p.m. the throng had not spilled into the street." After many bars opened just 24 hours after President Truman's momentous announcement and liquor once again began to flow, the scene deteriorated quickly. Once again, the celebrants spilled off the sidewalks and into the street. "Three hours later," Hackett continued, "traffic was completely stalled for the third straight night. A noisy crowd of at least 10,000—chiefly sailors and teen-agers—began to turn what had been a disorderly celebration into a mob scene." As one San Francisco resident stated, "We had a holiday on Wednesday, but Wednesday night they did the wrong thing, opening up the bars and liquor stores. It was worse than Tuesday, RIOTS EVERY PLACE."[12]

Fortunately, many of the couples with children, and most of the older individuals, had seen the writing on the wall and had deserted the downtown area. They could readily see that trouble was about to begin.

CHAPTER 9

# Renewal

"San Francisco's downtown area had an orderly summer holiday appearance during yesterday's daylight hours," stated one Associated Press reporter on Thursday morning, "but crowds began to gather about 6 p.m. Vandalism and rowdyism quickly developed." Added one eyewitness, "Late in the afternoon, hundreds of servicemen, again mostly young sailors, milled around Market Street. It looked like the whole thing was going to begin all over again." With most liquor stores and bars reopening at 4:00 p.m., alcohol was once again readily available and the tavern owners were not too discreet as to whom they sold their liquor to. As one newspaper reporter said, "Bobby-soxers, teen-age youths and boys who didn't look as if they had reached their teens reeled on streets throughout the downtown area. Bottles passed from hand to hand. When they went dry, they were smashed on the sidewalk."[1]

Fueled by alcohol, the celebrants began their evening of uncontrolled merrymaking simple enough. For the first few hours, the crowd of civilians, most in their late teens and early twenties, and sailors seemed to revel in simply breaking empty bottles, kissing, dancing, and making as much noise as possible. Around 6:30 p.m., Wednesday, August 15, as the crowd began to get ugly, the Market Street trolleys, which had been so badly damaged the night/morning before, were immediately rerouted to a calmer avenue. Anticipating trouble, Superintendent Marshall of the Municipal Street Railway had told the trolley crews to avoid Market Street if trouble seemed imminent. It was not long before all the trolleys were gone from the main downtown thoroughfare.[2]

Disabled army veteran Sidney Georgeson was down on Market Street again on Wednesday evening and noticed the trouble rekindle. "And start all over again it did," he wrote. "Except that this night few women were involved, and those that were, wanted it. That night the mob lost its lust and turned mean instead. The rioters systematically smashed windows along Market and other streets and looted whatever they could get their

## The San Francisco V-J Day Peace Riots

hands on. They beat up civilians who tried to interfere with them, but left people alone who didn't hinder them."³

As darkness settled on San Francisco, the slightly rowdy, fun-loving crowd suddenly turned into a destructive mob. "The situation began to get out of control as early as 7:30 p.m. after an orderly day of victory celebration," stated one reporter. In trying to describe the composition of the mob, one Oakland reporter wrote, "Sailors were by far in the majority among servicemen, [but] the unruly, destructive crowd also included bobby-sox girls and teen-aged boys." It was later reported that most of the men in uniform were drunk, with an estimated one-quarter being "staggering drunk." Starting around 8:30 p.m., the Navy Shore Patrol officers "began making arrests at the rate of one a minute."⁴

Group of elated servicemen celebrating the news of Japan's surrender (San Francisco History Center, San Francisco Public Library).

Even in 1945, California had one of the most liberal liquor laws in the land. Still, people under the age of 21, or people already inebriated, were prohibited from being served or from purchasing alcohol. On the evening of Wednesday, August 15, 1945, many of the bartenders and liquor store owners seemed to have suddenly forgotten all the laws and restrictions. "Boys of 18 and 19, who could not be served at (some) bars, were able to purchase liquor by the

## Chapter 9. Renewal

bottle, and to drink it openly in the streets," editorialized the *San Francisco Examiner* a few days later. "The State law definitely prohibits the sale to intoxicated persons—that law was ignored by many of the bartenders. The State law prohibits any sale to minors—package liquor stores ignored that law."[5] With liquor so readily available to young people who were unaccustomed to drinking such hard brew, trouble was not far off.

While many of the Market Street merchants had spent the daylight hours boarding up their broken windows in response to the destruction of the night before, and perhaps in anticipation of what might follow, it did not seem to matter to the Wednesday night crowd. An automobile crashed through the boarded-up front windows of an already frequently looted liquor store. Stated an eye-witnessing reporter, "The crowd poured through the entrance and helped themselves from the shelves." As witnessed by many, "automobiles were being shoved bodily through the windows, mostly liquor stores, for purposes of looting." Although the chief object for the rioters were liquor stores, no store along Market Street was safe from the crowd of "window-breakers." Wrote an Associated Press reporter, "Jewelry and clothing stores were looted by a mixed crowd of servicemen and bobby-soxers." Another chronicler wrote, "One merchant [later] said $1,000 worth of luggage was taken from his display window."[6]

Although many young teenage girls, wearing their bobby-sox, had been escorted to the downtown area by young civilian men, their presence alongside the young beauties, in many cases, seemed to make no difference to the drunken sailors. Robert Frederickson, the young teenager working at the Fox Theater, felt that Market Street was "no place that night for a woman alone or even with a male escort." "Girls were kissed and manhandled and escorts of some were beaten when they tried to defend the girls," wrote a reporter with the *Oakland Tribune*. "Some girls were dragged into alleys, and a few instances of public assault were reported."[7] As Robert Frederickson had said, it appeared as if no female was safe in the downtown area on the night of August 15, whether she had an escort or not.

Perhaps hoping to return to civilian life as soon as possible, many sailors broke windows in department and clothing stores and began looting the merchandise from the shelves and hangers. Noted another reporter, "Both men's and women's civilian clothes seemed to be the chief target of the looters." Photographs taken on the night of August 15, 1945, show sailors wearing civilian neckties, fedora hats, and even a few suit jackets.[8] In addition to looting civilian clothing from the stores, many sailors also attacked revelers on the street, stripping clothing from anyone in the crowd. "Clothes were stripped from both men and women on the riot torn streets," wrote a correspondent from the *Oakland Tribune*. While the servicemen may have stripped the clothing from the civilian men to add the pieces of clothing to their own wardrobe to hasten their move back to civilian life, for the most part, the stripping of the women had more sinister intents.

A United Press reporter wrote, "Some of the demonstrators attempted to tear dresses from women in the crowd." Like the night before, this Wednesday night riot, as it was now being called, soon included the "public molestation and rape of women and teen-age girls." Stated an Associated Press chronicler, "[W]omen were seized and roughly handled." Wrote an *Oakland Tribune* correspondent, "Several cases of criminal assault on young women were reported." Young women, including "bobby-soxers," were reportedly "accosted and dragged into alleys and doorways and molested in public squares by both enlisted and officer personnel of the Navy at the height of Wednesday night's orgy." Although the San Francisco Police Department would later make the ridiculous claim that no women were raped during the three nights of rioting, as early as August 16, newspapers were reporting that "[the police had] received numerous official and semi-official reports that women had been publicly molested."[9] This was a celebration that had gotten out of control.

In additional to the sexual assaults, four more people died on Wednesday night. Sixty-three-year-old Gustave H. Scobie, a teamster, collapsed in Oakland from an apparent heart attack brought on by all the excitement.[10] In San Francisco, 19-year-old Seaman Second Class Raymond Joseph Ramirez was found unconscious with a fractured skull on Mason Street, between Sutter and Bush Streets, several blocks north of Market Street. Police were unable to determine if he had been the victim of a hit-and-run automobile or a bottle-wielding assailant. He was rushed to Treasure Island Hospital, where he died shortly after arrival.[11]

Another serviceman who lost his life from the wild celebration was Private First Class William E. Flaherty, with the 62nd Radio Intelligence Company at Two Rock Training Center near Petaluma, California. The 20-year-old native of Philadelphia, Pennsylvania, was found suffering from a fractured skull at Tenth Avenue and Geary Street in San Francisco, far west of the main area of celebration. Transported to Letterman Hospital, he managed to tell hospital assistants that his "assailant had been an unidentified Marine" before lapsing into unconsciousness. He died very early on Thursday, August 16.[12]

The fourth individual to die that night, a heartbreaking incident, occurred in front of the Hotel Stewart at 353 Geary Street, only a few blocks

## Chapter 9. Renewal

off Market Street. Eighty-year-old retired bank clerk John Sutherland Batchan was walking on the sidewalk in front of the hotel when he was suddenly struck in the head by a water-filled wastepaper basket dropped out of a seventh-floor window, the highest floor, of the hotel. "A small crowd collected," an eyewitness remembered. "The old man's head was caved in, spilling out blood and brains through a wide dark gash." A group of sailors lifted the old man and moved him to a doorway. Later a civilian police officer carried Batchan to a less crowded street for transport to a nearby hospital. Wrote the eyewitness, "An ambulance couldn't have gotten through [the crowd]." Eventually, Batchan was taken to San Francisco Hospital, where he soon died. Unbelievably, a coroner's jury would later determine that Batchan had died from an "accidental death."[13] Batchan was the 10th person to die because of the San Francisco celebrations.

Trying to come up with a reason why the crowd had suddenly turned so destructive, one reporter felt that it was the sudden availability of alcohol. "The violence that raged up and down Market Street was fed by drunkenness," he reasoned. "Many bars there opened at 4 p.m., at the end of the 24-hour period following President Truman's announcement of Japan's capitulation, and they were immediately stormed." One San Francisco reporter stated, "Barrooms and liquor stores, theoretically closed until 6 p.m., began opening at noon with a rush or patronage; night clubs were open from sundown on; soldiers, sailors, and Marines poured into the city in unprecedented numbers and high spirits." Once the bars and taverns were out of alcohol, the crowd turned to other outlets to feed their desire. "The surging celebrants smashed windows of [closed] liquor stores and looted the shelves," the reporter continued. "Bottles of liquor were consumed on the street."[14]

As the disturbances increased and spread, the military and civil authorities had to admit that this crowd was not the crowd of the night before. This was now an "ugly, destructive" crowd. It was noted that this Wednesday evening crowd "had little in common with the universal and spontaneous joy that Tuesday's victory announcement had set off." Explained one United Press reporter, "Fist fights and fights with jagged ends of liquor bottles were a common sight." Despite their drunken condition, however, many sailors and civilians alike still maintained an air of decency when it came to the Stars and Stripes. "During the orgy of window smashing and looting," noticed one correspondent, "there was only one instance where a window displaying an American flag was shattered. Even uncontrolled as they were, the people retained their respect for the Flag under which they had fought and worked for victory."[15]

## The San Francisco V-J Day Peace Riots

"The major disturbance was on the north side of Market from Montgomery to Sixth, where 41 store windows were broken. On the south side of Market, from the Palace Hotel to Sixth, 24 stores were damaged. There was other damage on side streets," reported the Associated Press. "Nearly every plate glass window on lower Market Street was shattered, [and] display shelves were cleaned out." Although Chief of Police Dullea later felt that the Wednesday night mob, estimated to be about 10,000 in number, was "only a fraction of the boisterous crowds of the past two nights," he admitted that this smaller crowd was more destructive, breaking "every window within three blocks." Stated one irate Market Street merchant who witnessed his store being destroyed, "Fun's fun, but this is pure vandalism."[16]

Not satisfied with simply breaking and looting stores, many of the rioters also battered anything and everything within sight. Both civilians and military personnel attacked cars parked along the curbs. "Crowds of people would climb aboard any automobile within reach," said one reporter, "stamp and jump on the roof, and scratch the fenders and hood." Stated one Associated Press reporter, "[T]he few parked automobiles parked at curbs were badly battered." An eyewitness to further mayhem wrote, "Barber poles were broken from their bases, stop-and-go traffic signals were smashed, glass marques were shattered and signs ripped off theaters." Even at City Hall, which was closed, a crowd of young civilian males smashed through the door of the Polk Street entrance and forced their way inside the building. When Watchman Claude Mansfield attempted to call for assistance, the rioters tore the phone off the wall and stole his timeclock. "I'm lucky that I'm alive," he commented.[17]

"Within a two-minute period shortly before 10 p.m.," wrote one San Francisco journalist, "the police received calls that twenty street windows had been smashed in." Between 6:00 p.m. and 10:00 p.m., though undoubtedly aware of the situation, the police received four riot calls from concerned citizens. During those same four hours, police also responded to 64 automobile accidents, which "resulted in thirty-one personal injuries cases." Around that same time, the San Francisco Fire Department received "thirty-seven false fire alarms" and 94 calls for an ambulance.[18]

At exactly 10:45 p.m., the riotous mob broke the glass on the base of the large freestanding Albert Samuel Clock in front of Albert Samuels Jewelry Store at 856 Market Street, which had managed to avoid the first two nights of destruction. The ornate clock had been built in 1915 and was described as "one of San Francisco's historic landmarks [which] has seldom recorded inaccuracy or failure." While the timepiece had four

## Chapter 9. Renewal

large clocks at the very top of the monument, the base had four smaller clocks and four large glass panels showing the mechanical workings on the insides. The mob shattered all four glass panels at the base, leaving the above clocks frozen in time. Fortunately, the historic timepiece was insured by Lloyd's of London and would eventually be rebuilt.[19]

Finally, near 11:00 p.m. on Wednesday evening, after about five hours of wanton destruction, Police Chief Dullea, who had apparently been in contact with Admiral Wright and acting upon his request, decided that enough was enough. Personally invoking the San Francisco Riot Act and utilizing a "riot squad" consisting of about 1,000 city police officers, 924 Shore Patrol officers, and about 1,000 members of the Army Military Police, Dullea set his force in motion to quell the riot. Lining Market Street from curb to curb with six patrol wagons interspersed with officers on foot, Dullea used a truck-mounted loudspeaker to proclaim: "All persons in this area are ordered to disperse in the name of the people of the state of California. Attention all naval, Marine and Coast Guard personnel: The commandant of the 12th Naval District personally appeals to me to request that you return to your ships or stations."[20]

Sidney Georgeson was an eyewitness to the event and wrote, "Late that evening, [August 15] police authorities finally worked out a system. They closed off the downtown streets in tight ranks. Then they marched forward, squeezing the mob from the streets. This joint action by civilian and military law-enforcement agencies ended the San Francisco riots." As the phalanx of vehicles and officers spread out across Market Street, starting at Sixth Street, officers hung to the sides of the patrol wagons to keep revelers off. The police wedge headed northeast up the street toward San Francisco Bay and the Embarcadero. Over a truck-mounted loudspeaker, Deputy Chief of Police Michael Riordan's "rich Irish brogue" could be heard intoning, "This is an illegal assembly.... I command you to disperse." Through another loudspeaker, Navy Shore Patrol officers ordered all sailors to report back to their ships and stations immediately. Noted United Press reporter Hennen Hackett, "Policemen, whose good nature had remained unmatched through two nights of celebrations, brusquely ordered civilians and sailors alike off downtown streets."[21]

As the phalanx of civilian and military officers moved "shoulder to shoulder" down Market Street toward San Francisco Bay, the voice of Chief of Police Dullea could be heard over a loudspeaker repeating, "All persons in this area are ordered to disperse in the name of the people of the state of California." The Riot Act had been invoked and any person resisting the order, either in civilian attire or in uniform, was now subject to arrest.[22]

With reporters watching, the police barricade moved up Market Street with the squad cars and patrol wagons leading the officers on foot. Wrote one United Press reporter, "A sound truck moved down Market St. from Sixth St. in the van of a dozen shore patrol wagons whose flashing red lights warned the celebrants to disperse." At the same time, mixed groups of both civilian and armed forces police officers moved along the sidewalks, using their batons freely to keep the rioters retreating and arresting any and all that resisted. Moving steadily forward, the police gave the crowd no time to react. The mixed group of both civilian and military officers kept moving forward, forcing the rioters back and into a tighter group.[23]

An Associated Press reporter wrote, "The 3,000 city and military policemen in patrol wagons and squad cars formed behind the first wedge at Sixth and Market. Red warning lights flashed as the cars moved into the throng, pressing them down Market Street." At each intersection, the massed police forced the revelers off Market Street and down the side street. After the wedge of patrol wagons and squad cars, and the great majority of foot officers, had passed, a few squad cars peeled off and turned down the side street behind the rioters, "to keep them on the go." At each intersection on Market Street, a select few patrolmen and a few squad cars halted to stand vigil. They wanted to prevent the rioters from spilling back onto Market and getting behind the wedge. As the main body of mixed officers continued down the main thoroughfare, the military officers ordered the rioting service personnel to return to their bases or face arrest while the city police threatened to arrest "hundreds of teenagers who [had taken] an active part in the looting."[24]

"At each side street a section of the mobile police pressed the crowd from Market Street and held the revelers there," noted an Associated Press writer. "This went on until all Market Street eventually was cleared and finally the crowds in the side streets disbanded and went home." As the accompanying group of reporters watched, they noticed that the police were showing no signs of favoritism. Any civilian and military personnel who resisted the order to move along, or showed any sign of disobedience, were quickly rounded up and thrown into the back of a patrol wagon.[25] After three nights of allowing the crowd to basically do whatever they wanted, the police were no longer fooling around.

In addition to every available regular San Francisco police officer whom he could call up, Chief Dullea had also called up all his auxiliary

## Chapter 9. Renewal

officers. It was reported, "Police Chief Charles Dullea ... [had] put in an emergency call for all civilian police, all naval patrolmen and all Army military police as well as his own." Along with the many Shore Patrol officers and the Army Military Police who responded to the request, there was also a small group of United States Marines and a handful of firemen. "Marines, carrying sheathed bayonets at their side, and firemen aided in dispersing the crowd," noted an Associated Press reporter. Near midnight, the wedge of city and armed forces police officers finally reached Montgomery Street, the city financial district. They were more than a half mile from where they had begun at Sixth Street. Almost the entire crowd had been broken apart and pushed off to the side streets.[26]

Shortly thereafter, even the side streets were cleared. As an Associated Press reporter later wrote, "Finally the crowds in the side streets disbanded and went home." Another reporter noted, "A half hour after the riot squad was called, [the] crowds appeared to be dispersing." Among naval personnel alone, the Navy Shore Patrol arrested 430 sailors and confiscated "some 400 open liquor bottles from naval personnel" during their sweep up Market Street.[27]

"Shortly after midnight," one reporter stated, "comparative peace reigned in the downtown district." At the intersection of Fifth Street and Market Street, one of the wildest spots in the city just a few hours ago, the only person in sight was "a lone MP swing[ing] his club in rhythmic circles."[28]

CHAPTER 10

# The Aftermath

"For the first time in three days," wrote United Press correspondent Hennen Hackett, "San Francisco's downtown area was quiet—even compared with wartime—after riot squads of 3,200 police and shore patrolmen quelled a mob of sailors and civilians who were turning [a] victory celebration into an orgy of 'pure vandalism.'" The same reporter had noted, "At 2 a.m. [Thursday, August 16] the only Navy men in sight were Marine military police, shore patrolmen and men who could prove they were on official business."[1]

Somehow, the San Francisco Chinatown area, and downtown Oakland, which had been scenes of wild merriment the night and early morning before, had both evaded the vandalism of Wednesday evening. Noted an Associated Press reporter, "[Chinatown] escaped the after dark outbreak of window smashing, brawling and looting." The city of Oakland had a bit of trouble when two city police officers tried to arrest a soldier for breaking a barber pole. During the attempted arrest, the officers were surrounded by a large mob of irate revelers, including several Navy Shore Patrol officer. The two city police officers quickly put in a call for assistance and "10 radio cars and a detachment of military police were rushed to the scene and broke up the mob." Beyond that one incident, Oakland had been quiet. Perhaps it was because their bars and liquor stores had remained closed all day and night.[2]

By the time the sun came up on downtown San Francisco on Thursday morning, August 16, 1945, city and military officials were already assessing the situation. Within a short time, Admiral Wright made the decision to cancel all leave for navy personnel, which included all sailors, Marines, and members of the Coast Guard. "Stations within 100 miles of San Francisco will grant no liberty until further orders," he stipulated. A little later he added, "The order means all naval personnel now on liberty within 100 miles of San Francisco will return immediately to their stations, except naval personnel subsisting at their homes, who will remain in their homes and off the streets." According to one-armed veteran Sidney

## Chapter 10. The Aftermath

Georgeson, "Rear Admiral Carlton Wright, commander of the 12th Naval District, had clamped down on liberty, and slowly the situation returned to normal. San Francisco licked its wounds." While Admiral Wright gave no reason for his sudden change in orders, a bright-eyed reporter with the *Oakland Tribune* wrote, "Although the Navy did not elaborate on the action, it was obvious the cause was the San Francisco riot."[3]

In writing to a friend the next day, one San Francisco resident spelled out the feelings of her fellow citizens toward the men in uniform. "Yesterday, they canceled all the liberty of servicemen to quiet the thing down," she wrote. "These demonstrations of vandalism and riots have aroused the indignation of all citizens. And while I celebrated ... I agree with the indignant populace regarding the wholesale destruction of property."[4] Most residents felt that partying was one thing, but wholesale destruction just for the sake of destroying something was beyond reason.

After the wild night of outright vandalism, the city began to clean up and assess the damage. "[W]ith daylight came street sweepers to pick up tons and tons of debris of all kinds," wrote one reporter. At the same time, the last of the revelers were also being swept up. Wrote Sergeant Georgeson, "[It was] not until Thursday afternoon that, augmented by additional shore patrol, they managed to clear the streets altogether." Although federal employees had been granted a two-day holiday by President Truman, the state and city authorities had opted for a single-day holiday. With businesses returning to their normal Thursday work schedule, San Francisco had to be ready.[5]

On Market Street, however, it would take quite some time to return to a normal operating schedule. After a quick police survey, it was estimated that at least 107 plate glass windows had been broken in 66 different businesses on Market Street, mostly along the five-block stretch between Montgomery (near Second Street) and Seventh Street. "It took days to clean up the glass and get over the hangovers," admitted Josette Dermody Wingo, who had been an early partier on August 14. Noted a United Press reporter, "Most window fronts on shops on the north side of Market St. between Powell and Mason Sts. were broken and jewelry and clothing stores were looted by a mixed crowd of servicemen and bobby soxers." Wrote one San Francisco resident, "Two five-ton trucks were busy carrying broken glass off Market Street." Noted Sergeant Georgeson, "I later found out that every single window in the long 900 block of Market Street, as well as many other windows elsewhere had been smashed." City Attorney John J. O'Toole announced that the merchants had 60 days to make a claim with the city for damages, which were estimated to be around

## The San Francisco V-J Day Peace Riots

the $25,000 range for Market Street alone. Throughout the city, however, insurance companies were reporting that more than 170 windows had been smashed. "Store owners and insurance companies still were trying to compute the swelling loss in terms of dollars," said one report. By January 1946, a total of 423 claims were filed in the city attorney's office because of "the depredations done during the celebration of VJ Day." As of that same date, "none of them have been tried."[6]

At the same time, the city of San Francisco was trying to assess the damage to city property. The Public Utilities Commission, which oversaw the running of the many downtown streetcars, reported that at least 300 windows had been broken on the trolley cars and that many were missing either their front or rear fenders, or both, and that many had damaged and bent trolley poles. Another city entity, the Board of Public Works, estimated that 135 parking signs had been uprooted and destroyed, which would cost the city $757 to replace. However, the board stipulated that it was still too early to know the full extent of the damage. The count of 135 was only a partial count. As one unknown resident of San Francisco wrote to a friend, "The news of peace and victory caused a celebration in San Francisco the like of which has never been witnessed before; however, the people's jubilation exceeded good judgement and caused a great amount of damage and vandalism." Even the federal government was trying to assess the damage to its property. The Post Office claimed that an unknown number of the big corner mailboxes had been tipped over and vandalized. It was still trying to assess whether any of the contents within the boxes had been damaged.[7]

While both city and federal departments were trying to come up with a number on the damaged items and an estimated cost to repair or replace each item, the district attorney for San Francisco, Edmund G. "Pat" Brown, and City Attorney O'Toole were trying to decide who would pay for the damage. Wrote one Associated Press correspondent, District Attorney Brown "said San Francisco taxpayers may have to pay for the broken windows, destroyed and stolen merchandise and ruined property left in the wake of the violent throng." Later in the day, City Attorney O'Toole announced that under the California political code, the taxpayers of San Francisco would have to foot the bill for the three nights of rampage.[8]

In addition to the property damage, five San Francisco hospital emergency rooms reported that in the 24-hour period between midnight Tuesday, August 14, and midnight Wednesday, August 15, they had treated 427 people, mostly for minor injuries. After midnight on Wednesday, another 41 people had been treated. Wrote a United Press reporter, "Most of them were

## Chapter 10. The Aftermath

sailors cut by glass, injured in fights or felled by drunkenness." At the Treasure Island military hospital, the medical officer-in-charge, Captain G.G. Herman, recalled years later that they treated 125 sailors on August 15. He wrote, "[O]ur busiest day of the hospital's history was V-J day when three complete surgical teams worked twenty-four hours around the clock doctoring casualties from the liberty celebration, including a whole ward of fractured jaws." Although it was originally reported that the San Francisco hospitals had treated a total of 624 people during the three days of rioting, that number would soon climb to over 1,000. Still, said one hospital official, "Doctors weren't sure because they were still too busy taking care of the injured to bother with bookkeeping."[9]

On that Thursday, August 16, Bruce Keith Tarkington, the 48-year-old railroad employee who had fallen on the sidewalk during Tuesday night's celebration, died of his fractured skull at Harbor Emergency Hospital. He left behind a widow and three young children, one only three years old. Tarkington was the 11th fatality from the wild three nights of celebration. Wrote navy Corpsman Greene, who was restricted to his barracks on Treasure Island, "As the military did penance by being restricted to their bases, we learned that 11 people had been killed and better than 1,000 had been injured in the war's end celebration, or riot in the city."[10] All of the deaths and injuries need not have happened. A fun celebration had somehow become a riotous situation, with people being injured left and right, for no apparent reason at all.

Although San Francisco now had 11 people dead and over 1,000 people injured, the city police proudly proclaimed that during the entire three-day upheaval, not a single woman had reported being raped. The police blotter was empty on the subject. Eyewitnesses to the rioting could not believe what they were reading. Numerous people, including several reporters, had seen women being assaulted by the mob. "Reporters said young women, including bobby-soxers, were accosted and dragged into alleys and doorways and molested in public squares by both enlisted and officer personnel of the Navy at the height of Wednesday night's orgy," wrote a United Press reporter. When Dr. Jacob Casson Geiger, the city health officer, heard the ridiculous claim, he vehemently commented on the six women whom he personally knew who had been treated at Central Emergency Hospital for rape. "What do they think we examined at the hospital that night—ghosts?" he exclaimed. And nobody was saying how many others had been treated at different hospitals. In response, the police department published the ridiculous statement that none of those sexual assaults "appeared to be direct outgrowths of the riots."[11]

## The San Francisco V-J Day Peace Riots

Within the week, because "police files failed to record such rapes as taking place during last week's peace riots," Dr. Geiger instituted a "new system for recording reports of asserted rape cases." As the city health officer explained, "Henceforth, reports of rapes will be kept in triplicate—one for the master file, one for the arresting or investigating officer and a third for the district attorney's office." Additionally, the investigating officer would be required to sign the report. Said Dr. Geiger, "[I am] of the opinion that a qualified medical examiner in criminal matters, under the district attorney's office, should be called in on all rape cases."[12] At least something positive was developed because of the San Francisco Peace Riots and the lack of reporting and response by the police department.

On Thursday morning, Mayor Lapham held a press conference to assess what had transpired in San Francisco over the past few nights. "It was evident that last night and night before last there was much bottle drinking by military personnel and civilians," he began. "I understand the Army and Navy will take disciplinary action against any member of the military hereafter found drinking in public out of a bottle." Speaking about the cooperation between the civilian and armed forces police that had finally put an end to the rioting, the mayor said, "As you know the city has worked hand in glove with the Army and Navy for the last four years. We have tried to work out our joint problems and have been successful. And we are going to continue to work together. Chief Dullea and Army and Navy officers have conferred to prevent a recurrence of this kind." Knowing that San Francisco was planning on holding a grand celebration once the official surrender documents were signed by Japan, Mayor Lapham predicted, "We have V-J Day coming in the future and we know that other shiploads of military personnel will reach this port. If they can celebrate without rioting and looting, God bless them, but we feel we can't have a celebration such as last night when real looting took place, property damaged and goods stolen." Although Mayor Lapham walked the narrow tightrope and refused to place the blame on the predominantly young servicemen who had destroyed much of his city, the many reporters present could certainly read between the lines. When a reporter finally asked the mayor where he placed the responsibility, Mayor Lapham gingerly said, "No comment. Dullea and the Navy did a good job when they finally took over."[13] The use of the word *finally* seemed to indicate that Mayor Lapham believed that things could have been taken care of much earlier than they eventually were.

As people throughout San Francisco tried to clean up the mess and evaluate the casualties and cost, city officials and military authorities

## Chapter 10. The Aftermath

were trying to figure out what had gone wrong on Wednesday night, the worst of the three nights of celebration. While it may have been a combination of many factors that had created the riot, most people were pointing to the early opening of the liquor establishments. Reported the United Press, "Officials blamed the riot partly to confusion over hours permitted for liquor sales." Although many bars and liquor stores had opened early, Admiral Wright's sweeping order granting liberty to all the sailors in the San Francisco area had sent thousands of servicemen into the Bay City to start their celebrating as soon as they arrived. It had not taken long for things to get out of control.[14]

While many people blamed the bar and liquor store owners for opening early, the United Press reported, "Civic authorities ... sharply criticized the Navy for failing to curb rioting last night, before Adm. Wright issued his order [canceling liberty]." The most vocal critic of the navy was Police Chief Dullea, who felt that the riot was due to the "unbridled and unrestrained action on the part of a lot of uniformed men." In his eyes, the wild celebrations were "the culmination of unrestrained liberty granted by the Navy to its men." He added, "The damage to civilian property is to be deplored, but this was a celebration not by San Franciscans but by men in uniform." Commenting on why the sailors did not fear the consequences of their riotous activities, Dullea alluded to past examples where military personnel had been arrested by city police officers only to discover that courts simply gave the offenders a slap on the wrist because they were in uniform. Dullea concluded, "They wrapped the flag about their shoulders when they were arrested previously and juries dismissed them after acts of violence. Other sailors heard of this, felt they wouldn't be punished and so let themselves go."[15]

When questioned why it had taken so long for him to invoke the State Riot Act, Dullea said that initially, the city police had stayed in the background because he felt that "the policing of naval personnel is a naval shore patrol job." However, when the celebration got completely out of hand on Wednesday night and the crowd turned to destruction, "city police moved in and took over." Dullea promised that there would be no further recurrence of mob action and promised to put additional city police officers on the streets in the days to come.[16]

Although San Francisco had been declared off-limits to naval personnel by Admiral Wright's early morning cancellation order, some sailors remained in the downtown area throughout the day. Near 4:00 p.m., however, Navy Shore Patrol officers, assisted by the additional police officers mobilized by Chief Dullea, began arresting any sailor they ran across, throwing them into the brig. Commented Sidney Georgeson, "By 4 p.m.

of the next day [August 16], additional hundreds of shore patrol men augmented the 2,300-man local police force and regular military and shore patrol cops. All servicemen were ordered off the streets, even those that lived in San Francisco."[17]

At 7:00 p.m., the army issued an order similar to that issued by Admiral Wright, prohibiting soldiers stationed within a 100-mile radius of San Francisco from getting liberty. Two hours later, however, the order was rescinded when it was shown that "the city [had] remained without new disorders" throughout the day on Thursday, even though hundreds of uniformed soldiers had been within the city since morning.[18] It appeared as though men in the army knew how to behave themselves.

That Thursday evening, Mayor Lapham had a three-hour meeting with Chief Dullea; District Attorney Brown; Don Marshall, the chief liquor enforcement officer in San Francisco for the State Board of Equalization; members of the Chamber of Commerce; and members of the Police Commission. Also in attendance was Admiral Wright; Major General Henry Conger Patt, commander of the Western Defense Command, responsible for coordinating the defense of the Pacific Coast; and Major General Homer M. Groninger, in command of the San Francisco Port of Embarkation. To prevent any repeat of the past three nights, Don Marshall, perhaps feeling the wrath of city officials and others, said that he would ask liquor store owners to open for only two hours each day, from 10:00 a.m. until noon, until the official observance of V-J Day, which was expected to take place shortly after the Japanese signed the official surrender documents. On that official observation date, hopefully sometime soon, the stores would remain closed for 24 hours. Afterward, they would open as usual. Although Marshall, like George R. Reilly, the local representative of the San Francisco district of the California Board of Equalization, had no real authority over the liquor store owners, as Mayor Lapham termed it, the request was "a straight business proposition."[19] Unfortunately, the request did not apply to bars and taverns or places that sold liquor by the glass or single bottle, such as restaurants or cafés.

During the same meeting, in the presence of Admiral Wright and the other military officials, Mayor Lapham and the other city officials "deplored [the] public molestation and rape of women and teenage girls," especially by members of the military. Although Mayor Lapham stipulated that servicemen were "not entirely to blame" and that access to available liquor "aggravated if it did not cause" the riot, he got Admiral Wright to agree that most of Wednesday night's damage had been caused by "young

*Chapter 10. The Aftermath*

kids who never served overseas" and "young boots—sailors who have not yet completed their training."[20]

Surprisingly, the admiral then took the opportunity to announce that he was going to rescind his early morning order making San Francisco "off-limits" to all naval personnel. Instead, the order would be enforced only until noon the next day, Friday, August 17. After the noon hour, sailors would be allowed to return to the City by the Bay. However, Admiral Wright assured Mayor Lapham and the others that he was planning to put more Shore Patrol officers on the streets to patrol alongside the supplemented city officers.[21] By working together, both civil and military authorities hoped that they had finally put a stop to the wild, unbridled celebrations. One unanswered question remained, however: Who was to blame?

## Chapter 11

# The Blame Game

On Friday morning, August 17, the *San Francisco Examiner* reported on the special "star chamber" meeting held by Mayor Lapham on Thursday evening. "With V-J Day yet to be proclaimed and celebrated officially," the paper stated, "local authorities, the Army and the Navy yesterday and last night took steps to prevent [a] recurrence of the riotous victory revelry which in seventy-two hours took a toll of eleven lives, caused hundreds of personal injuries and thousands of dollars in property damage in San Francisco." For the first time in three nights, the San Francisco streets, especially Market Street, had been quiet. "Hundreds of vigilant city police and shore patrolmen patrolled San Francisco to prevent further victory 'celebrations' when a temporary 'off limits' order affecting 100,000 naval personnel is lifted at noon today," wrote a United Press reporter. "They kept a weather eye on Market Street, where [the night before] thousands of drinking, looting and boisterous sailors surpassed even the most raucous binges of the city's gold-poke bonanza days."[1]

That same morning, District Attorney Brown announced that he had spoken to "several grand jurors" the day before and was going to continue polling additional members to see if he should start an investigation to "fix responsibility for the disorders." Then, as now, San Francisco had a standing civil grand jury and a criminal grand jury. California state law requires that each of the 58 counties in the state impanel a civil grand jury. The San Francisco Civil Grand Jury comprised 19 members who served a one-year term. Their "primary function is to investigate the operations of the City & County of San Francisco's officers, departments, and agencies, and to make recommendations." Unfortunately, the Civil Grand Jury had "no authority to compel compliance" with any of the recommendations that it might suggest.[2] Although District Attorney Brown knew that the Civil Grand Jury had no power to punish any person or agency that it determined was responsible for the three nights of rioting, he felt that a fact-finding investigation was needed. Where it went from there, only time would tell.

## Chapter 11. The Blame Game

Edmund G. "Pat" Brown had been born in San Francisco in 1905 and had been given the nickname of "Pat" as a youngster, when during World War I he had sold Liberty Bonds on the streets of San Francisco shouting the immortal words of Patrick Henry, "Give me liberty or give me death!" Graduating first in his class from the San Francisco College of Law in 1927, he went into private practice until entering public service as the district attorney for the city and county of San Francisco in 1943. He was a no-nonsense litigator, and most San Franciscans were glad to see that District Attorney Brown was looking into whether he should convene the grand jury to get to the bottom of who was responsible for the San Francisco "Peace Riots."[3]

While he was working on the decision of whether or not to sit the jury, Brown began gathering statements from several eyewitnesses who had seen "specific acts of violation and misconduct." He also conferred with Superior Court Judge Robert McWilliams to "determine the legal limits of the jury's actions." Perhaps to sway the grand jurors to pursue the question of responsibility for Wednesday night's riot, the *San Francisco Examiner* published an editorial on August 17 titled "Where Responsibility Lies." Driving right to the point, the article began by attacking the bars and liquor store owners for opening early and supplying the revelers with easy access to alcohol. "Instead of keeping properly and decently closed on the second day of the peace celebration," read the editorial, "almost all saloons and package stores opened, and thus contributed to the disorder on the street." After explaining that other places of business had stayed closed on Wednesday, the editorial stated, "But many liquor dealers, both in bars and stores selling by the bottle, opened greedily to grab a few extra dollars—and to jeopardize their future business life.... The result was a disgrace—a disgrace to the greedy, unscrupulous, impatient liquor dealers."[4] According to the *Examiner*, the almighty dollar had won out over common sense and decency.

Only 12 years removed from prohibition, the *San Francisco Examiner* pointed out that "California ranks among the States with liberal liquor laws," while some states, such as Oregon, still had very restrictive laws and other states, namely Kansas, Oklahoma, and Mississippi, still enforced prohibition. "If saloonmen abuse the relative freedom of trade they enjoy in California," the article scolded, "they will be thrown out of business and a restrictive law [will be] imposed here." *Oakland Post-Enquirer* columnist A.E. Anderson said, "[Let's] see what such as demonstration as last week's around the bay does to the liquor question. It plays right into the hands of those who insist that the only

## The San Francisco V-J Day Peace Riots

way of dealing with the problem of strong drink is to prohibit its use." Because the bars and liquor establishments had deemed it necessary to open early to cash in on the victory celebration, the editorial ended with the admonition, "As a consequence much damage was done to property by misguided celebrants, citizens were assaulted and women were insulted—and the liquor business in San Francisco bred a lot of trouble and disrepute for itself." Added writer Anderson, "It's ironic that several liquor stores were smashed and looted in last week's celebrations. They were the victims of their own wares, getting a sample dose of what they, too, irresponsibly inflict on the community."[5]

Also on August 17, in a letter to the editor of *The Sacramento Bee* titled "Disgraceful Orgy," the letter writer added his voice to the growing number of people who felt the whole three nights of rioting in San Francisco had given a big black eye to the City by the Bay. "It was a healthy thing for a war tense nation to blow off steam in the form of celebrations when the Japanese surrendered," the writer began, "but there is a line at which a celebration leaves off and an orgy begins." Commenting on the guilty parties, the writer continued, "This line seems to have been crossed in San Francisco, where sailors, bobby sock girls and civilian hoodlums staged a shockingly disgraceful demonstration. The city counted 12 [sic] dead and at least 648 injured in the three day celebration and riot. It would seem the metropolis which prides herself as 'the city that knows how' did not seem to know how to celebrate sanely the end of the war."[6] Others were watching San Francisco and they were not happy. What would city authorities do to quell this mounting dishonor?

At nine that Friday morning, Mayor Lapham held a meeting with the liquor enforcement officers and representatives of the city liquor businesses, trying to get an assurance that the city liquor stores would abide by the request to open for only two hours a day until the official celebration of V-J Day. Before the meeting convened, however, Samuel J. Jones, the attorney for 380 local retail liquor stores, protested that the request was discriminatory since it did not pertain to bars, restaurants, and every other establishment holding a liquor license. "We are not going to conform to any such request," Jones flatly asserted against the two-hour limit. Digging in his heels, he stipulated that the liquor store owners would not abide by the request unless the California State Board of Equalization so ordered it. When asked what liquor store owners would do if the military posted liquor stores "out of bounds," Jones concluded that this too would be discriminatory but, he conceded, "We would be helpless. Of course, we would accede to any such military order."[7]

## Chapter 11. The Blame Game

Prior to the meeting, Mayor Lapham made a statement in which he once again gingerly avoided placing blame on anybody or anything. He said:

> It was unfortunate that many individuals, not familiar with what goes to make up a typical San Francisco celebration, saw fit to be excessive in their jubilance and created conditions which do not redound to the city's credit.
> 
> I am sure that if these individuals—most of them, at least—were familiar with San Francisco, what the city is and what it stands for, they would have exercised better judgment in their enthusiasm and would have confined their celebration to a different plane.
> 
> Certainly, I have no desire to scoff at anybody who wishes to unlimber after forty-four months of war which have been a great strain on all of us, but I do most respectfully request all persons in this city, be they residents or visitors, to realize that some forms of enthusiasm cannot be allowed.
> 
> The war was fought to protect the rights of individuals, their lives and their property. All of us should bear this in mind in any future celebration.[8]

No single group had been insulted or put to blame. Mayor Lapham had managed to walk a neat political tightrope.

Present with Mayor Lapham when the 9:00 a.m. meeting took place were representatives of organized liquor dealers, cabarets, restaurants, hotels, bars, and the bartenders' union. Unlike the closed-door meeting of Thursday evening, when he met with both civil and military leaders, this meeting was open to the press. During the meeting, Mayor Lapham again requested that liquor stores agree that "packaged liquor, beer and wine would be sold only between 10 a.m. and 12 noon until official Victory day is declared." On the officially celebrated V-J Day, all establishments selling liquor would be closed, and remain so for another day and night. This time, however, the mayor admitted that the request had been made by the army and navy.[9]

As Mayor Lapham explained, the two-hour selling time until V-J Day would not apply to taverns, restaurants, cabarets, and hotel bars. They would be able to remain open as usual. Only on V-J Day and the day immediately following would they close. In agreement, Bruno Mannori, the president of the local bartenders' union, said his members would abide by the request to "refrain" from working on those two days, while Harry Troup, the secretary of the San Francisco Hotel Association, indicated that the hotel bars would do the same.[10] Only the liquor store owners seemed bothered by the proposal.

Knowing that the liquor stores would lose considerable money by being open for only two hours every day over the days between then and the officially recognized V-J Day, whenever that would be, and only in the late morning, when most people would be at work, R.G. Mannheimer, a member of the Liquor Dealers Association, felt that although the mayor's request was "sensible and logical," he admitted, "I don't think everybody will fall in line with it."[11] There seemed to be too much money to lose now that liberty was about to be restored to navy personnel and San Francisco would again be an "open city."

At noon on Friday, August 17, liberty was once again granted to navy, Marine Corps, and Coast Guard personnel. While the newspapers reported, "Soldiers, sailors and Marines again 'invaded San Francisco,'" they also reported that "there was no repetition of 'peace riots' which broke out three consecutive nights earlier in the week." One of the major differences this time was, although the army had lifted all its restrictions, there were still conditional restrictions on navy personnel, something being called "limited liberties." This time, "the Navy would permit only 50 per cent of its petty officers and 25 per cent of its nonrated men to be given liberty." Additionally, Admiral Wright had warned that any sailor in possession of an open bottle in a public place would be subject to arrest and punishment. All police officers, both city and military, would be keeping their eyes open for any sailor walking around on the streets with an open bottle.[12] Cut down by a considerable number, there would be only a few hundred sailors on the streets of San Francisco at any given time.

Before the day was over, District Attorney Brown finally announced that he would convene the Civil Grand Jury on Tuesday night, August 21, and "present a full report on the rioting." Having weighed all his options and sought advice from several individuals, Pat Brown was now bound and determined to get to the bottom of the mess and was hoping for full cooperation from both civil and military authorities. As Brown told reporters, "We will have two or three witnesses there, and after hearing their testimony, the Grand Jury, if it likes, may invite Admiral Wright and Chief of Police Dullea to attend a session on Wednesday and Thursday night."[13]

That Friday evening, with the addition of a limited number of naval personnel receiving liberty, both the civilian and armed forces police worked together this time from the start. Joint police groups, made up of one city officer, one Shore Patrol officer, and one Military Police officer, set up at several different spots along Market Street. It was hoped that this new "triple patrol system" would terminate the long-standing agreement that each agency would be responsible for policing and arresting only its

## Chapter 11. The Blame Game

own people. Under this new system, any officer of any agency, either military or civilian, either army or navy, could arrest anyone committing a violation of the law.[14]

Since Chief of Police Dullea had promised that no new "peace riot" would ever happen again, he issued General Order No. 80. The sweeping order canceled all days off for his officers, had all officers not on the current shift standing by, and had an additional 50 uniformed officers patrolling the side streets. As reported, "The plan will be continued until it is certain trouble will not recur." Fortunately, Friday night in San Francisco was quiet. The city police reported only the usual number of automobile accidents and incidental arrests. Although the Navy Shore Patrol reported that the evening was "comparatively quiet," it was later reported that officers were using their nightsticks "for the first time ... to quiet unruly sailors." The only real trouble among the visiting sailors occurred after midnight when the bars closed and "sporadic fistfights involving naval personnel broke out."[15]

In reaction to what had transpired in San Francisco over the three-night period of August 13, 14, and 15, many residents decided to sound off in with letters to the editor. Mr. B.A. Reedy wrote to the editor of the *San Francisco Examiner*, "I am a native of San Francisco in the third generation, and now living in Los Angeles," he began. "I am quite content to remain here, after reading about the hilarity in San Francisco on V-J Day." He continued, "Such doings ... will relegate San Francisco to second place in Pacific coast cities, and perhaps further down the list. I still love San Francisco ... but no more living in your city for me."[16]

Although things seemed to have quieted down by Saturday August 18, news of the three-day riots had reached some of the warships in the Pacific. On board Admiral John S. McCain, Sr.'s, flagship, the *Essex*-class aircraft carrier USS *Shangri-La* (CV-38), stationed off the coast of Japan, a group of chief petty officers met in conference and issued a statement to the press. Describing the rioting in San Francisco by navy personnel as a "disgrace to the Navy," they went on to say, "The activities of those Market Street commandoes does not represent the true Navy. They very likely waged little war outside port. Radio reports say they were accompanied by bobby socked girls but we think that the sailors wore bobby socks, too. All we want is a chance to go home and take up life where we left off when the war began and we deeply resent such a nonrepresentative group jeopardizing our stand with the people at home. Those peace riots in San Francisco were a disgrace to the Navy."[17] It was an angry statement fired off by angry warriors. They did not appreciate the "Market Street commandoes" giving the "real navy" a black eye.

## The San Francisco V-J Day Peace Riots

The people of San Francisco also heard from a group of 134 veteran sailors, about half the ship's crew, aboard the battle-damage repair ship USS *Nestor* (ARB-6). "It was a great shock to us serving in the Pacific to hear of the demonstration put on by sailors in San Francisco," they started. "We want you to know how much we disapprove of such a thing. Certainly, we felt exultant out here with the surrender of Japan, but it was an emotion which was deep inside of us. We realized at long last our chances of being once again with our loved ones was not too far off." As might be expected from the veteran sailors, the thoughts of the men had turned to home. They continued, "What happened to those girls in San Francisco could have and maybe did happen to the wife or sweetheart of a man out here. Regardless of that, we want you to know that the men out here most certainly do not uphold the sailors back there in the way they acted." Their thoughts then turned toward their future. "All we ask," they said, "is to come home and start over again in a nice, peaceful home life which so many of us have been deprived of." They finished with some thoughts regarding the future of the sailors who had riotously taken to the streets of San Francisco on the nights of August 13, 14, and 15. "We earnestly hope the sailors involved in that sordid demonstration are dealt with severely—namely, eighteen months out here. We licked the enemy and his atrocities. Let's not have them at home."[18]

Another active sailor, though already back in the Bay area, sent a letter to the editor of the *Oakland Post-Enquirer*. He wrote, "I would like to take this opportunity to apologize for the outlandish conduct of certain so-called 'sailors' during the recent celebration of V-J day." Believing that the rioting sailors had never faced combat or been in a combat area, the writer continued, "I should like to estimate that the majority of the enlisted men involved in wholesale destruction of property were men (or should I call them youngsters wearing naval uniforms?) who have never been to sea and seen [the] destruction that the Japs were able to dole out." Although the author of the letter had been on shore at the time of President Truman's momentous announcement, he and his friends had elected to stay out of the city. "Quite a number of us were so happy over V-J day that, even though we rated liberty, we stayed in off liberty and just enjoyed ourselves." In an attempt to smooth over the ruffled feathers caused by the rioting sailors, the author ended, "I hope the people of San Francisco, Oakland, and all of the bay area will accept this apology from the majority of the sailors who feel as though it is our duty to apologize for the minority, some of whom are just too inconsiderate of other people's rights to care."[19] It was a heartfelt letter from a

## Chapter 11. The Blame Game

young man who had worn the navy blue for a number of years and was proud of it.

Equally as heartfelt, though a bit more caustic toward the young navy recruits who had rioted along Market Street, a chief pharmacist mate with "20 years service" wrote to the editor of the *Oakland Post-Enquirer* "regarding the clowning of Market street commandoes." He started by praising the citizens of San Francisco: "Have been coming into the bay area for 20 years with the fleet and have always been treated royally and Frisco-Oakland cops have always treated navy men one hundred percent." The chief pharmacist mate then went after the navy rioters. "I'm certainly glad war is at an end so all the ice cream sailors can go back to the farm. Some of these plough jockeys who are such great clowns in uniform haven't seen a lighthouse much less any combat duty."[20] Veteran sailors had taken the gloves off and were not about to pull their punches.

Perhaps in response to the angry and apologetic letters from so many navy veterans, one new sailor, simply identifying himself as "Coastie," sent a rebuttal letter to the *San Francisco Examiner*. "I hear and read what a black eye the Navy is getting for damage done to stores in San Francisco," he began. "I want the readers to know I wasn't one of the rioting servicemen, and I do not approve of such destruction, but it was something that has been brewing in sailors for some time, and they just let loose when the opportunity came." Although he stated that he had not taken part in the breaking of windows and the rape of several young women, "Coastie" was trying to rationalize the destruction caused by his overexuberant comrades. "This town has been for sometime what is commonly called a gyp town to sailors. Too many merchants have been overcharging, and some places just plain highway robbery for merchandise and service to servicemen." After admonishing the San Francisco merchants for overcharging service personnel, Coastie then went after the people of San Francisco. "It's up to the public to put a stop to this outrage, as your town is built around its port and the men who enter it. Don't kick … the Navy—get on your police department to do their jobs."[21]

Another new sailor who wrote to the editor of the *San Francisco Examiner* to defend the actions of his fellow sailors was responding to the letter published a few days earlier by B.A. Reedy, whose family had lived in San Francisco for three generations. "I imagine you members of the third generation were a little shocked by the antics of the 'strangers' in your lovely 'burg,'" the recruit, calling himself "A Sailor," started. His first line had set a disparaging tone to his reply. "I am not a stranger in this town,"

## The San Francisco V-J Day Peace Riots

he continued, "I'm a 'captive' as are the rest of the servicemen who can't possibly realize why this place was chosen as a main point of embarkation except for the natural resources. If you think I or we like the treatment your mismanaged city hands us, you may reconstruct your thoughts." "A Sailor" then got on his soapbox and attacked the good citizens of San Francisco.

> Servicemen and their families have been "last" in line for a decent place in which to live ever since war began. We're sick of "dollar" haircuts, "75 cents" shaves, "50 cents" sandwiches that used to go for a dime, entertainment at bootleg prices, your lousy transportation systems and then finally to be blamed for the V-J blowup which was caused by one thing—your greedy whisky peddlers selling it by the quart to teenagers who had never even had a legal drink yet.
>
> Don't call me a stranger. Call me an ex-resident as soon as I get out of here.[22]

While "Coastie" was correct in attacking the police for not doing enough during the riots, especially on the second and third nights, and "A Sailor" was correct in attacking the liquor dealers for selling alcohol to underaged revelers, both "Coastie" and "A Sailor" were wrong to go after the merchants and people of San Francisco. Throughout the war, prices on civilian goods were high and quantities were limited on many items. They were also regulated by the Office of Price Administration (OPA), which set price ceilings on most goods and started the system of rationing certain items to help combat the hoarding of scare or hard-to-come-by materials. If "Coastie" and "A Sailor" were unhappy with the prices that San Francisco merchants were charging, they should have complained to the OPA, not the newspapers. Likewise, while most San Franciscans accepted the fact that their city had become a main point of embarkation toward the Pacific theater, they also wanted the recruits and draftees who came through San Francisco on a temporary basis to behave themselves. They knew that San Francisco would always be a "navy town" but they hoped that once the war was over, the number of sailors in the city would go back to prewar levels, which would be much more manageable for the city and armed forces police to handle. While "Coastie" made it a point to stress that he had not been one of the rioting servicemen who had broken store windows and looted the wares, "A Sailor" made no such proclamation. By simply reading between the lines of his complaining letter, one could get the impression that he had certainly been among the rioters getting retribution for the "treatment your mismanaged city" had given him in the short time he was a "resident."

On Saturday morning, August 18, street sweepers continued cleaning

## Chapter 11. The Blame Game

up the streets, and repair crews continued boarding up the broken windows. Simultaneously, the politicians and civic leaders began sweeping up and repairing the political damage done to the city. Everybody in San Francisco, and across the nation, was aware of what had been happening in the City by the Bay, and everybody was watching and waiting to see what, if anything, would be done to punish those responsible.

CHAPTER 12

# Liquor Wars

On Saturday afternoon, August 18, 1945, District Attorney Brown announced that he had finished his preliminary investigation into the three nights of rioting. To get "the fullest opportunity to obtain a complete picture" of the circumstances, he had interviewed several eyewitnesses and had studied dozens of photographs snapped by newspaper cameramen and camerawomen. In commenting on the rioting himself, Brown stated, "There's something fundamentally wrong some place when a situation can develop such as that which permitted three nights of 'demonstrations' in San Francisco." With the knowledge of what he had already learned, Brown later added that the responsibility for the riots might be placed on "the Navy or the police—or both."[1]

Next, he would take his finding before the Civil Grand Jury on Tuesday evening. In stipulating the job of the grand jury, Brown emphasized that the jury would only be a "fact-finding body." It would simply hear the testimony and view the evidence but there would be "no criminal action to be taken." The Civil Grand Jury did not have the power to refer criminal charges but Pat Brown did. If necessary, the grand jury could, and was certainly expected to, recommend that the district attorney's office take criminal action.[2]

In hoping to convene the grand jury by the end of the next week, Brown was already lining up people to be interviewed. Among them was Admiral Wright. "If the Grand Jury wants to talk to Admiral Wright about [the rioting]," Brown stated, "I'll certainly see that he be requested to attend."[3] District Attorney Brown's use of the word "request" was intentional. When Chief of Police Dullea and his phalanx of both civilian and armed forces police officers, including several hundred Shore Patrol officers, had moved up Market Street on Wednesday evening to break up the riotous crowd, predominantly young sailors, the chief had shouted into the police loudspeaker, "The commandant of the 12th Naval District personally appeals to me to request that you return to your ships or stations." Although windows were being broken on a regular basis, and San

## Chapter 12. Liquor Wars

Francisco was being torn apart on Wednesday night, Admiral Wright did not "order" his sailors to cease and desist and return immediately to their ships or barracks buildings. Instead, he had merely made a "request" that they stop what they were doing and retire for the night. In that same vein, District Attorney Brown was now simply stating that he would make a "request" for Admiral Wright to appear before the Civil Grand Jury.

When Admiral Wright was told that District Attorney Brown might ask him to sit before the grand jury, the admiral "expressed surprise." Not knowing what he might possibly contribute to the investigation, or what Pat Brown might ask of him, Admiral Wright said that he would "seek more information before taking the witness stand." Although Brown admitted that he did not know what power civil officials had over high-ranking military officers, he was hopeful that Admiral Wright would fully cooperate. "I am sure," Brown said, "the Admiral will be only too anxious to help us get to the bottom of this thing—why San Francisco can have such rioting and lawlessness."[4]

As the weekend progressed, irate citizens were finally sounding off about the rioting, sending letters to the editors of local newspapers. Paul White, a resident of San Francisco, wrote to the *San Francisco Examiner*. He began by admonishing the "dry land sailors and home guard soldiers and other home folks." He wrote, "Did you ever see a man die? Did you ever see a man suffer the tortures of hell and live? Have you watched those boys come back? Sailors? Soldiers? Marines? Have you seen them on Market Street, or elsewhere? One foot off at the ankle. An empty sleeve. Maybe that leg came off at the hip. I'll bet those boys were not down blowing the horns that are in my ears right now. No, no, no, no, no. I'll bet they are just saying: 'Thank God, thank God, it's over.'" The Reverend Clement Berberick of Saint Boniface Catholic Church also commented on the rioters. He felt that the people in the streets had acted more like barbarians than civilized individuals. He wrote that the riot was a "savage, barbarous, riotous and uncontrolled mob passion."[5]

Another angry resident of the Bay area, Melanie L. Matignon, wrote, "As a mother of a sailor giving his services to our country, I am very much incensed to have all the blame for the rioting put on the servicemen. In the first place where did the liquor come from? Why were not the places to buy liquor closed?" Mrs. Matignon went on to criticize the parents of young men and women who felt that the only way to celebrate was with alcohol. "Because a man has on a uniform," she reasoned, "it will not make much difference, he will still reflect the home he was brought up in."[6]

In defense of the parents of the young sailors who had wreaked such havoc upon San Francisco, columnist A.E. Anderson summarized, "The mothers of boys we saw lurching through the streets with dazed eyes and unsteady legs would be horrified to tears if they could have seen their sons." Anderson wondered if it was the U.S. Navy that had broken the morals of many of the young recruits. "He was a good boy, clean and high-minded," Anderson imagined the parents saying. "Was it necessary that in the task of serving his country he should learn to be a hoodlum and a drunken sot?" Anderson then went on to admonish the city officials who let the celebration get so out of hand. "[T]here was no parade, no organized festival, nothing to do but mill around in the streets and … [take] another nip of strong liquor." The columnist ended by reflecting on the young sailors themselves, "Most of them, you can be sure, are cleaner, more decent boys than they seemed during those days.… I'll bet a very big proportion of the fellows were disgusted with themselves after it was all over."[7]

In another letter to the editor, a San Franciscan calling him or herself "Long Time Resident" went after the chief of police for his attacks on the military. "Police Chief Dullea has criticized the naval shore patrol because of what he terms THEIR 'inefficient handling' of the riot of Wednesday, August 15," Long Time Resident wrote. "First, the primary function of the shore patrol is to assist the civil authorities. A man in uniform is NOT immune from civil law and restraint. For drunkenness, destruction of private property, molesting women, etc., he is subject to civil law as well as military law."

Long Time Resident went on to complain that the city police made only the average number of arrests on Wednesday night. "A riot of sufficient proportions to attract national attention occurred in our city," the complainant explained, "and the civilian police arrested only the 'average' number. How come?" The author then pointed to the statement Chief Dullea made on Thursday, that "the policing of naval personnel is a naval shore patrol job." According to Long Time Resident, this was "buck passing at its peak." The resident asked, "Since when are the taxpayers who pay police salaries dependent on naval shore patrol for the protection of their property? Who relieved Chief Dullea of his delegated authority? No amount of whitewash will cover the eyes of sober citizens who witnessed the disgraceful lack of initiative displayed by the civilian police on the night of August 15."[8] Long Time Resident clearly placed the slow response by both the city police and armed forces police squarely on the shoulders of Chief Dullea.

Another individual who blamed Chief Dullea for shirking his duties signed her name "A Sailor's Wife." She wrote in the *Oakland Tribune*,

## Chapter 12. Liquor Wars

"After reading a news story on the San Francisco riot, I must say that I am disgusted with the opinion that Chief of Police Dullea voices. He blames the riot wholly on the sailors. I will say that there were sailors in the riot but the greater percentage of the ones taking part were civilians." Unfortunately, what "A Sailor's Wife" was saying was not true. Photographs taken at the time of the riot clearly show that upward of three-quarters of the people on the streets, or on the top of streetcars, or draped all over city monuments, were sailors. Still, she ended, "I suggest that the chief of police quit worrying about the sailors and start taking care of the juvenile delinquents that are infecting his fair city."[9]

As seen in the numerous letters to the editor, the citizens of the Bay area had varied opinions as to who was responsible for the riots. It would be up to the grand jury to sort through everything and come up with the responsible party or parties.

With the weekend upon them, a war of words erupted between Sam J. Jones, the attorney for the city Liquor Dealers Association, and George R. Reilly, the local representative of the California Board of Equalization. Attorney Jones still felt that it was "discriminatory" for liquor stores to be requested to open for only two hours each day while bars and cabarets and other places selling alcohol by the glass could be open all day and evening. Likewise, he was angry at the fact that cigar stores, drugstores, and other retail stores could still sell bottled goods as usual. He was threatening to end the practice of having his liquor dealers being open for only two hours per day. At the same time, representative Reilly was telling the liquor association members to ignore the lawyer.

Attorney Jones said he had received "a flood of complaints" from the liquor store owners saying that bars and nightclubs were selling bottled goods to customers to be consumed outside of their premises, "whether or not they had off sales licenses." Bars, taverns, and most other "by the glass" establishments had only "on sales" licenses, meaning that the liquor had to be consumed on-site. Now, according to the complaints that Jones was receiving, many of these establishments were selling beer and liquor to go.[10]

"Unless we get a modification of the request that we restrict off sales business by tomorrow," Jones said, "I will ask off sales liquor stores to resume their regular hours. We do not intend to be made the goat. We are in a legitimate business and there is no reason to penalize us and not bars, tavern and night clubs." He was quick to add that to the best of his knowledge, most city liquor stores had been abiding by the two-hour restriction, except for perhaps "some little chiselers in the outlying areas."[11]

## The San Francisco V-J Day Peace Riots

Fighting back, Reilly hoped that the store owners would ignore Jones, admitting that he was not concerned with the desires of a Liquor Dealers Association lawyer. Reilly felt that the liquor stores would continue to close early. While admitting that the Board of Equalization could "do nothing to enforce the restricted [two] hours," Reilly was hoping that the liquor stores would continue to sell alcohol for only two hours each day. He said, "Off sales establishments will retain far better public relations by listening to the chief of police, the military and the board of equalization than they will by listening to Jones." Added Reilly, "I ask all off-sale licensees to ignore the advice of Attorney Jones, and take the advice of the Board of Equalization. I think they will take Reilly's advice and ignore Jones' because, in this case anyway, Jones doesn't know what he's talking about." As a show of good faith, however, Reilly stated that he expected to meet with both military and city officials later in the day to discuss the "necessity of continuing the restricted hours." He praised the many liquor store owners who "gave full co-operation" so far and promised to do what he could to ease the restrictions. However, he also said that his men would note any license numbers of liquor store owners that violated the two-hour rule.[12]

At the meeting that evening with army, navy and city officials, including Mayor Lapham, it was decided that the San Francisco retail liquor stores would return to their normal schedules on Tuesday, August 21, after it was agreed that "the business curtailment to two hours a day is no longer necessary." As Mayor Lapham stated, "The military suggests, and I concur, that the two-hour restriction on sale of bottled goods be off as of tomorrow. We are going back to normal." However, it was still understood that on the official V-J Day, whenever that would be, all the liquor stores, taverns, and any other establishment selling alcohol—both on sales and off sales—would shut down for two full days. Attorney Jones, feeling that his pressure campaign had worked, was reveling in the triumph. He proclaimed, "Had the State Board of Equalization not rescinded its request order, as it did, we would have resumed regular selling hours [anyways]. We were obeying the request, but these other establishments were benefiting by it."[13]

Wanting to have the last word on the matter and show that he had not been pushed into anything by Mr. Jones, Reilly simply said, "[N]ow that [the navy and army] are ready to rescind it, so are we." He added, "Anything which the military wants is O.K. with us."[14] In Reilly's mind, the change had nothing to do with pressure by Jones and the liquor stores, it was what the military authorities preferred.

CHAPTER 13

# The Grand Jury

Each weekend evening, and on Monday night, August 20, the streets of San Francisco remained quiet as the triple patrol of city police officer, shore patrolman, and Military Police officer walked the beats together. Although there were still the usual arrests for public intoxication and occasional fisticuffs, there was no repeat of the week before. However, many wondered if trouble would rear its ugly head again on Tuesday evening, when the liquor stores once again remained open until midnight.

During the day on August 20, District Attorney Brown spoke to the press regarding the Civil Grand Jury meeting scheduled for the following evening. In outlining the case he would present to the jury, he mentioned that he would be reading several newspaper accounts of the rioting and also introduce "photographs, records of hospital treatments of those injured[,] and arrest reports." Brown also explained that his evidence would include the "testimony of four or five citizens who saw [the] window smashing." In addition to the citizens who had been present during the destruction, Pat Brown's list of witnesses included Chief of Police Dullea, Navy Shore Patrol heads, and a few merchants whose stores had been damaged and looted. Admiral Wright was also included on the list. "Admiral Wright attended the Mayor's meeting [on Thursday evening, August 16] to discuss the rioting," Brown pointed out. "He had several ideas, and I think it would be a good idea if these were given [to] the jury."[1]

After listing all his witnesses, District Attorney Brown reiterated what he was attempting to accomplish by bringing the details of the riot before the jury. "I won't merely present the evidence—I shall recommend that the grand jury investigate fully, with a view to making specific findings and recommendations," Brown said. "With the Navy and the police both blaming each other for the riots, we'll attempt to fix responsibility," he said. "If there is any indication that something is wrong with the way these two forces operate, or a lack of co-operation, I think we should find it out."

## The San Francisco V-J Day Peace Riots

Realizing that thousands of young men and women would soon be returning from the Pacific war, the district attorney ended his statements by expressing his desire that the current investigation might also investigate ways to help with the "peacetime conversion of servicemen back into civilian life." Hoping to wrap everything up within a couple of days, Brown stated, "There is every indication this investigation will be carried to a completion with dispatch."[2]

That next day, August 21, Radioman Third Class Sonny Thompson died at Treasure Island Hospital from the skull fracture that he had received after being thrown out of a second-story window on August 14 on Market Street. He was the 12th person to die because of the celebrations/riots. He was only 20 years old.[3]

That evening, the Civil Grand Jury met and listened to District Attorney Brown lay out the evidence that he had gathered on the San Francisco "peace riots" of the nights of August 13, 14, and 15, 1945. Eyewitness testimony began with Larry Marshall, division superintendent of the Municipal Street Railway, who told the grand jury that 30 streetcars had been "wrecked on Market Street" during the first two days of rioting. Marshall next pointed out that "25 of 52 streetcars operating the night of August 14 on Market Street were taken out of service because of bent trolley poles and other damage." After that, anticipating another night of rioting on Wednesday, August 15, Marshall had ordered his trolley crews to divert their cars from Market Street to Mission Street upon the first signs of trouble. He reported that the first trouble arose at 6:30 p.m. and that the cars were immediately removed from Market.[4]

Following Superintendent Marshall were V.M. Zlokovich and A.D. Jacobson, co-owners of a Market Street cigar store. Both men stated that they had been at their homes on Wednesday night when they got phone calls from the police telling them that the window on their store had been broken out and their establishment had been looted. They both stated that when they rushed down to Market Street, they found their store abandoned and the police nowhere in sight. Terrifyingly, the men also said that at the height of the riot on Wednesday night, they had witnessed five drunken sailors assaulting a young woman who was continually screaming for help.[5] No police officers were around and no help was forthcoming.

That same lack of concern by the police departments, both city and military, was voiced to the Civil Grand Jury members by Lloyd Taylor, the executive secretary of the Market Street Association. After describing some of the damage done to many of the association member stores, he went on to complain that on the first two evenings, and during the first

## Chapter 13. The Grand Jury

few hours of Wednesday night, he had seen very little cooperation between the city police and the Shore Patrol officers. However, as soon as the two law enforcement agencies began working together on Wednesday evening, "the situation was controlled in less than an hour." He then wondered why, when "signs of trouble were apparent by 5 p.m. Wednesday ... city and military police did not take determined action until nearly midnight when the crowds had gotten out of hand." Taylor estimated that the damage done along Market Street alone would amount to more than $25,000 (almost $450,000 in 2025).[6]

District Attorney Brown then presented hospital and health department records showing that 1,059 people had been treated in local emergency rooms over the three evenings of rioting and that many had been treated for "stab wounds and others for injuries caused by flying glass." However, the biggest bombshell of the evening came when Dr. Geiger, the San Francisco health officer, presented the grand jury with hospital records showing that six women had indeed been raped during the "Market Street demonstrations." The production of the records took those in attendance by surprise, since "no reports of such violence had been filed by police." Perhaps in an attempt to cover their butts, police later admitted "that rapes had been reported but that none appeared to be direct outgrowths of the riots."[7]

After the sitting, which lasted until the early morning hours of Wednesday, August 22, the grand jury extended an "invitation" for public officials to appear before that body and present their own views on the riot. District Attorney Brown announced that the grand jury was "inviting" the public officials to appear before the jury on Wednesday evening, stressing the fact that they were not being summoned but were being asked to appear voluntarily. Among those officials whom he wanted to meet with the jury were Mayor Lapham; Chief of Police Dullea; Jerd Sullivan, president of the San Francisco Police Commission; and George Reilly of the State Board of Equalization. Additionally, it was hoped that Admiral Wright would appear in response to the "invitation" or at least send a navy representative to act in his stead. Also called would be reporters who had covered the riots on all three nights. And again, Brown reiterated, "The purpose will be to fix responsibility for the disorders."[8]

Although it was expected that the Civil Grand Jury would continue its investigations at 7:00 p.m. on Wednesday, August 22, the jury members made the surprise announcement that morning that they would postpone the hearings and hold their final meeting on Tuesday, August 28. The postponement was being made to allow Police Chief Dullea, who was in

## The San Francisco V-J Day Peace Riots

Los Angeles, and George Reilly, who was in Sacramento, to be present to testify. Almost all the other officials on Pat Brown's witness list agreed to appear before the jury next Tuesday. Admiral Wright, however, was still questionable. When the jury eventually reconvened, District Attorney Brown said that he would "ask the body to affix blame for failure to control the demonstration" and would "request a constructive report containing recommendations for the future handling of rioting mobs."[9]

Then, in an even more shocking move, early on Wednesday morning, the San Francisco Junior Chamber of Commerce, concerned with leadership training in business development, management skills, community service, and international connections, among other attributes, appealed to District Attorney Brown to stop the Civil Grand Jury investigation altogether. The Junior Chamber of Commerce was worried that continued investigation and press coverage of the rioting, especially with an emphasis on responsibility leaning toward the navy, might prompt the Navy Department to remove its permanent installations from the Bay area, thereby costing San Francisco millions in lost revenue. "The San Francisco Junior Chamber of Commerce is conscious of the regrettable incident which occurred last week on the down town streets of San Francisco," they wrote to Brown in a telegram. "We, too, are aware of the past excellent record of the United States Naval Forces in our community. In view of all the facts, it is therefore recommended by this organization that no further public action be taken of this incident and that we welcome the permanent assignment of the Navy here in the area."[10]

Perhaps somewhat taken aback by this request to end the investigation just to ensure a continued influx of government money into the San Francisco area, District Attorney Brown responded with the following telegram:

> I am well aware of the extreme importance to San Francisco of the permanent assignment of our great and splendid Navy. I do feel, however, that there is a moral issue involved that transcends money values. I intend to continue my investigation until the Grand Jury knows all of the facts.[11]

District Attorney Brown and the Civil Grand Jury were determined to get to the bottom of the matter and pin the blame on those responsible, no matter where the finger of guilt pointed.

## Chapter 14

# Support and Planning

Many of the citizens of San Francisco were glad that District Attorney Brown had not caved to the wishes of the Junior Chamber of Commerce. Perhaps the greatest proponent for DA Brown and the Civil Grand Jury continuing with the investigation, and continued coverage by the media, was the Reverend John Compton Leffler, rector of Saint Luke's Episcopal Church of San Francisco and president of the San Francisco Council of Churches. In a formal statement authorized by the council, he wrote, "We commend the local press for their excellent work in reporting the facts and regret any criticism leveled against the newspapers for doing so. We believe that what happened in public should be faced by the public from the highest officials to the common citizen, nor do we have any sympathy with those who for any reason want to hush up the sorry mess." After stating that the riot was "too reminiscent of some of the actions of our recent enemies," Rev. Leffler went on:

> It is not within our province to attempt to fix blame, but we do believe the grand jury, as requested to do so by the District Attorney, should seek an honest and frank answer to the following questions:
> Why were the bars reopened on Wednesday afternoon when they were not so reopened in any other county in the State? Why were not the city authorities prepared for such an occurrence in view of what transpired on Monday and Tuesday nights? Why was there not a coordinated plan worked out in advance between the Civil, Naval and military police for controlling what any amateur knew would be an acute situation?
> The limitation of authority as between the police, Shore Patrol and Military Police may have worked well in normal wartime situations, but it seems strange that anyone could have expected anything but the completest coordination to work during a Victory celebration in a city like San Francisco.

As Rev. Leffler said, "The serious blot on our city's reputation should not be ignored or hushed up."[1] Being scolded by an irate public in letters to the editor was one thing. Being scolded by the president of San Francisco's Council of Churches was another. As far as District Attorney Brown and

## The San Francisco V-J Day Peace Riots

the Civil Grand Jury were concerned, Rev. Leffler and the citizens of San Francisco would get their full investigation.

While many people were pointing fingers at the sailors for taking a large part in the riots, some, as seen earlier, felt that the sailors had been made scapegoats. Both a mother of a sailor and a wife of a sailor had rushed to their defense through letters to the editor. Another resident of San Francisco, Mrs. H.E. Maus, also wrote to defend the sailors. "I feel a dire necessity of expressing deep regret at the condemnation of our sailor boys and the horrible destruction which occurred during the past few days," she began her letter to the editor of the *San Francisco Examiner*. She felt embarrassed that the "fine boys who served us nobly and honorably, willing to sacrifice their all for the honor and safety of their home and country" were now being "condemned by the very people they were protecting."[2] Unfortunately, Mrs. Maus was incorrect. Most of the sailors who had participated in the riots had been new recruits, fresh from their training base on Treasure Island. They had never been asked to "sacrifice their all for the honor and safety of their home and country."

Mrs. Maus continued,

> Why not be honest—place the blame justly where it should be? Why were these liquor purchasing places permitted to function with no restraint. Had they been closed for three days, this disgusting and expensive loss would have been eliminated, our fine young men and women would have found a clean and wholesome fun, their celebration a pleasant memory, bringing sorrow to none. Don't blame the sailor—blame we the people.[3]

Again, Mrs. Maus was arguing a flawed premise. Many of the liquor stores had indeed shuttered their doors on Tuesday and Wednesday evening. It made no difference. The sailors, aided by many civilians, had simply shattered the front windows and helped themselves to the stock on the shelves. They had even shoved automobiles through some of the storefronts. If the stores had "been closed for three days," as Mrs. Maus suggested, the rioters would simply have gotten their liquor by shattering the plate glass windows the way they did. It would have taken more than just closing all the liquor stores for three days to have prevented the rioting.

On Friday, August 24, at the navy base on Treasure Island, Seaman Second Class Hans Herbert Pfister, not yet 20 years old, passed away at the base hospital after suffering for 11 days with a fractured skull sustained when he was shoved through a plate glass window on Market Street on Tuesday evening, August 14. His body was prepared and shipped home to his family in Newark, New Jersey. On the application for a government headstone, his discharge date had the notation "Died in

## Chapter 14. Support and Planning

Service, August 24, 1945."[4] Seaman Pfister was the 13th, and last, fatality of the San Francisco peace riots.

On Saturday, August 25, a sister of a sailor wrote in response to the comments made by the mother of a sailor and the wife of a sailor. "In answer to two letters ... I who am a sister of a sailor, wish to say that they are not in possession of the facts," she started. In referencing the statement made by Chief Dullea that most of the rioters were unruly young sailors, she wrote, "Chief of Police Dullea is not expressing an opinion, but is voicing facts as reported by injured parties to the police department. Surely those who made such reports must know whether or not it was a sailor or a civilian who made the attack."

The sailor's sister explained that "about twenty sailors ambushed me" on Tuesday evening in downtown Oakland. "[T]he smell of liquor was strong and I for one wish the stuff could all be thrown in the bay." Although her brother was a sailor, the author did not sugarcoat the activities of the unruly servicemen during the rioting. "The sailor had greater cause for celebration than the civilian," she concluded. "Mob fever and liquor did the rest. I sing my praises to the sailors and their great part in America's victory, but those who are offenders to all that they fought for, should be punished accordingly. Many sailors take advantage of their uniform. Let us face facts."[5] Unlike the mother and wife of sailors, and Mrs. Maus, the "sailor's sister" had taken the blinders off and was willing to call a spade a spade.

While numerous letters were sent to the editors of newspapers of cities that lined San Francisco Bay, one resident of faraway San Diego felt the need to write to the editor of his hometown newspaper regarding the San Francisco Peace Riots. "San Diego can look back upon its recent victory-day celebration, compare its record with that of other cities, notably San Francisco, and say 'Well done; we're proud of ourselves.'" In describing the activities in San Diego, the author said, "[T]his city took the event in stride. Its people, including thousands of servicemen and women, whooped, threw paper, tossed a few uniformed men into the Plaza fountain, kissed a few girls and did themselves no harm. Some of the more exuberant got into slight legal entanglements; some automobile horns blew themselves hoarse. Then folks went home and to bed."

Going further, the San Diego letter writer asked, "And who can say that we were less joyous than in San Francisco where people on the streets, including servicemen, went wild and killed a half dozen [sic] persons? Who is to chide us for failing to break windows and loot shops? One of the tenets of patriotism is orderliness. We had that."[6] Unfortunately, cities throughout California, and even in other parts of the country, had taken

## The San Francisco V-J Day Peace Riots

note of what had been transpiring in San Francisco immediately after President Truman's announcement of the Japanese surrender.

In finalizing his comments on the way San Diego residents had performed after the surrender announcement had been made, the author speculated, "San Diego's celebration may have been tamed considerably by advance preparations made by Chief of Police C.E. Peterson and his men. It may have been guided into calm channels by the presence of shore patrolmen. But it is probable that it did not get out of hand simply because there was a spirit of law and order on its streets. It is entirely in order for [San Diego] to pat itself roundly upon its back and repeat, 'Well done.'"[7] A spirit of law and order. That was something that was sorely missing in San Francisco on the nights of August 13, 14, and 15, 1945.

That Saturday morning, Mayor Lapham appointed a citizens committee to begin formalizing an official "V-J Day" celebration. On September 9, San Francisco would be holding its annual Admission Day celebration, recognizing the date in 1850 when California became the 31st state in the Union. Fixing on that date, the committee decided to combine the two celebrations into one giant festival. While Mayor Lapham was already planning for the official V-J Day celebrations, Police Chief Dullea was busy gathering information for his appearance on Tuesday before District Attorney Brown and the Civil Grand Jury. In gathering material, Chief Dullea reached out to the police captains of the Central, Southern, and Northern stations, looking for data on the three nights of rioting, especially regarding the number of officers on duty at different points throughout the city and how many arrests at each station.[8] Questions had arisen as to the activities, or lack thereof, by the San Francisco police during the three nights of rioting. Police Chief Dullea knew that he had to go in armed and ready if he was going to defend his actions, and those of his officers, on the three nights in question.

Also on Saturday, the San Francisco Police Board of Supervisors began looking into the need for hiring more officers. Prior to the Japanese surprise attack on Pearl Harbor, San Francisco had a population of 650,000 and a police force of 1,302 officers. During the war years, the population of San Francisco had shot up to approximately 750,000 while the number of police officers had fallen to only 1,116 because of enlistments and the draft. Addressing the problem, Chief Dullea declared that "at a minimum, an additional 384 police officers are needed—but that's the minimum. We could use 500." Over the next few days, the board of supervisors would meet with members of the civil service commission and several city officials to address the budget provisions, civil service requirements, "and

## Chapter 14. Support and Planning

everything connected with quick action to relieve the police situation."[9] Although it was not stated, everyone seemed to understand that the rioting of the week before had drawn attention to the low number of police on duty throughout the city at any given time.

With Mayor Lapham and Police Chief Dullea busy with their committees and homework, District Attorney Brown continued to line up witnesses and gather evidence to present before the Civil Grand Jury, which was scheduled to meet for the final time on Tuesday evening, August 28. The four witnesses who had been "invited" to meet with the grand jury—Mayor Lapham, Chief Dullea, George Riley of the State Board of Equalization, and Jerd Sullivan, the police commission president—had all indicated that they would show up. "The grand jury has been fully informed of what took place and now the city's leaders will be asked to explain why," District Attorney Brown reported. "If the jury finds the riots resulted from inefficiency, I shall ask that they fix responsibility where it belongs." He finished by saying, "On conclusion of the testimony, I will ask the grand jury to make specific findings and recommendations. In their findings, the jurors will be asked to determine just who was to blame for the riots, whether it was the police, the Navy or the mayor. In their recommendations, the jurors will be asked to outline a means by which such riots can be prevented in the future."[10] Noticeably missing from the witness list was Admiral Wright.

Instead of appearing in person before Pat Brown and the Civil Grand Jury, Admiral Wright agreed to "answer questions submitted in writing in advance." His answers would then be read aloud to the jury on Tuesday evening.[11] In this way, Admiral Wright could go over each question with a group of navy attorneys and come up with the best, and least discriminatory, answer to each question. Admiral Wright undoubtedly wanted to cast himself and the navy in the best light possible. By avoiding spontaneous answers before the Civil Grand Jury, Admiral Wright was playing it safe and taking the coward's way out.

On Tuesday evening, August 28, 1945, the grand jury assembled for its final meeting. Newspaper reporters from around the nation were gathered to hear Mayor Lapham, Chief Dullea, and the other officials explain what had gone wrong during the three tumultuous nights of the riots. While the San Francisco Junior Chamber of Commerce had been the only organization to officially condemn the investigation and call for its early termination, many individuals had criticized the inquiry while many others were eagerly awaited its findings. What would the final conclusion be?

CHAPTER 15

# Passing the Buck

The grand jury met as planned on Tuesday evening, August 28. The first one to sit in the witness chair was Mayor Lapham. He began by explaining the conditions leading up to the victory riots but, always the consummate politician, deflected all the questions regarding who he felt bore the most responsibility for the rioting and refused to answer any of the questions put to him about responsibility. Reported the *Oakland Tribune*, "Mayor Lapham refused to tell of the topics under discussion during his appearance before the jury."[1] It was a nice way of avoiding pointing the finger toward any of his constituents and making enemies of someone he might need in his corner in the future.

Next to testify was Police Chief Dullea. Almost immediately he went on the offensive, completely exonerating his police department and laying the blame squarely on the shoulders of the navy. Chief Dullea told the jurors that "90 per cent of those involved in the riot were sailors." He then stated that the responsibility for policing the sailors rested with the Navy Shore Patrol and not with his police officers.[2]

Although Admiral Wright "declined an invitation" to appear in person and "refused to send a member of his staff" to meet with the jury, he did answer 16 written questions provided by District Attorney Brown. To one question, Admiral Wright wrote that only "normal liberty" was granted to sailors on ships in the Bay area or at adjacent naval bases. In another answer, the public was told for the first time that 540 Shore Patrol officers were on duty the first night, 813 the second, and 924 the last. In answer to one of the questions, the admiral wrote that he had no way of knowing how many of the men on liberty headed to San Francisco during the three days in question.[3]

In defending his sailors, the admiral wrote, "While the foregoing answers pertain to the participation of Navy personnel in the celebration, no implication is intended that the disorders were confined to Naval personnel. The announcement of termination of years of hostilities stimulated civilians to pack the streets and intermingle with military personnel and

## Chapter 15. Passing the Buck

give vent to pent-up emotions."[4] Although newspaper photographs taken at the time show that perhaps between 50 and 75 percent of the rioters were dressed in the dark blue navy uniforms and white "Dixie cup" caps, Admiral Wight refused to accept the truth.

Next, he went on the offensive, attacking Chief Dullea and the San Francisco Police Department. "Crowds made up solely of Naval personnel could have been controlled by the Shore Patrol," he reasoned correctly, "but the Patrol has no authority to curtail liquor sales or to compel crowds to move on. On the other hand, the civil authorities have jurisdiction over Naval personnel in the streets and the Shore Patrol is required to assist the police in enforcing the law with respect to Naval personnel." In this regard, Admiral Wright was correct. The city police should have taken a more active role in curbing the destruction by both civilians and military personnel. The admiral explained, "No formal arrangement existed between the San Francisco Police Department and the Navy for joint operation on the three days in question, but, as usual, the shore patrol expected to assist the police in controlling naval personnel as required."[5] On Wednesday night, when the two forces finally worked together, the rioting was brought under control in less than an hour.

Knowing that more than 100 store windows had been broken during the riots, mostly by sailors, District Attorney Brown had asked the question, "Did any apparent vindictiveness exist on the part of naval personnel against San Francisco shopkeepers during the riot?" In response, Admiral Wright simply wrote, "None reported or overheard."[6] Some of the rioting sailors may have held a grudge or animosity toward the city shop owners, but more than likely, Admiral Wright would have been the last to know. It was almost impossible to believe that a low-rank sailor would have sounded off about a beef he had with a San Francisco store owner within hearing distance of Admiral Wright or one of his staff. It was a ridiculous question answered the only way possible.

Then, perhaps offering an olive branch, Admiral Wright concluded his written statements with, "The Commandant feels that measures now in effect, as set forth by the San Francisco Police Department General Order No. 80, appear sufficient to prevent future disorders from reaching the serious proportions of those experienced on August 15."[7] From now on, with the Shore Patrol and the San Francisco Police Department working together, Admiral Wright believed that the upcoming official V-J Day celebrations would be safe for all.

The next person called to testify, Jerd Sullivan, the police commissioner, came to the defense of the police department and tried to explain why it had taken until Wednesday night before the city police and armed forces police had gone into action. "After all we couldn't anticipate what was going to happen," he explained. "Japan never surrendered before. We were surprised and overwhelmed. But you have our assurance it won't happen again."[8] But the city authorities had been aware of what had happened in Halifax, Nova Scotia, after VE Day in May. They had been given three months to get ready. They should have been better prepared.

George Reilly, the area representative of the State Board of Equalization, was questioned for 25 minutes and told the jurors that the board had issued an appeal for both liquor stores and taverns to close for 24 hours upon the announcement by President Truman that the Japanese had surrendered. "We got fine cooperation for the first twenty-four hours," he explained, "but, we didn't have time to request an additional twenty-four hours closing. Nevertheless, many liquor dealers remained closed. Unfortunately, those who closed had their windows broken and stocks stolen while the stores which remained open sold out."[9] According to representative Reilly, the rioting celebrants would have gotten the alcohol one way or the other.

After listening to the last witness, the jury went into consultation and within a short time came forward with a startling conclusion: Nobody would be held responsible for the three nights of rioting. They absolved "all parties concerned." In justifying their verdict, Civil Grand Jury foreman J. Leslie Vogel stated that the rioting had been caused by "a large number of young men who didn't want to be in the service and who suddenly realized by the surrender announcement [that] they might not have to be in service long." This was a veiled reference to the navy personnel who had caused much of the destruction. According to the Civil Grand Jury, the young men in navy uniforms, prowling the streets, breaking windows, damaging streetcars, destroying other items, stealing liquor bottles and anything else they could get their hands on, and molesting women, had simply gotten overly excited that they would not have to be in uniform much longer. In the eyes of Vogel and the 18 other jurors, the "young men" had simply gone out and celebrated.

While hinting that the navy personnel might have gotten a little out of control in their excitement over the end of the war, the Civil Grand Jury admonished, but did not place any responsibility, on the young civilian participants. Foreman Vogel said that the jury felt the rioting had been caused by too much "enthusiasm" among the younger people, both civilian and military personnel. In the eyes of the jurors, the young participants had gone a little wild and had gotten a bit out of hand. Kids will

## Chapter 15. Passing the Buck

be kids. One has to expect them to let their hair down occasionally. One could not hold them responsible for that.[10]

In exonerating the San Francisco Police Department and the Navy Shore Patrol officers, Vogel suggested that the officers had shown great restraint in not using tear gas to break up the rioters. In the opinion of the grand jury, tear gas would have escalated the problem. In other words, any anti-riot maneuvers by either civil or military law enforcement would have exacerbated the situation, not subdued it. In the eyes of the Civil Grand Jury, the two law enforcement agencies had done the right thing by letting the crowd celebrate until they burned themselves out. There was no need to step in with undue force. That would have only made things "worse."

Going beyond their unbelievable conclusion that nobody was to blame for the three nights of rioting, the grand jury went on to praise Chief of Police Dullea for the exemplary way he had handled his officers during the entire situation. In their year-end Report of the Grand Jury for the year 1945, the Civil Grand Jury wrote, "[T]here is one individual who we must name, a man who in spite of deficient manpower and in the face of traffic problems not exceeded, perhaps, anywhere else in the United States, managed, somehow, to accomplish this outstanding job of law enforcement. He provided the leadership and the executive capacities which made possible the smooth functioning of this intricate organization. That man, of course, is our Chief of Police, Charles W. Dullea." The Civil Grand Jury did send a slight jab at Chief Dullea regarding the traffic jam during the V-J Day celebrations but not the riot itself. "Chief of Police Charles Dullea did a splendid job in handling traffic [during the United Nations conference and the VJ Day celebration] until the fatal disturbance of mob violence during VJ Day."[11] Although the "mob violence" was mentioned, it was never addressed. In the eyes of the jurors, Chief Dullea had done an "outstanding job" during the V-J Day riots. It was as if all the witness testimony of police officers standing by while windows were being shattered, while items were being stolen, and while women were being molested had fallen on deaf ears.

Perhaps the only redeeming part of the grand jury conclusion was their praise of State Board of Equalization representative George Reilly. They praised Reilly for requesting that liquor stores and saloons remain closed for more than 24 hours after President Truman's announcement of the Japanese surrender. Unfortunately, with no power to enforce the continued closings, Reilly could only "request" that the liquor establishments stay closed. He had done everything in his power to get the liquor store owners to abide by his request, but in the end, many of the owners had put the want of money over the need for safety.[12]

In finishing their report, the grand jury recommended that California Governor Earl Warren, who had already called for a special session of the state legislature, include the proposal to amend state liquor laws and allow the presiding chief of police of any community the power to close "any and all distributors of liquor in his jurisdiction in [the] event of a riot or near-riot."[13] That was the only recommendation that the Civil Grand Jury delivered to prevent future riots throughout California.

As should have been expected, there was an immediate backlash to the Civil Grand Jury's final report. Dozens of irate letters were sent to the editors of the leading San Francisco and Oakland newspapers, berating the conclusion of the grand jury and the people involved. At the same time, numerous newspaper editors published scathing editorials in their publications. From Redwood City, along the southwestern edge of San Francisco Bay, the editor of the *Redwood City Tribune* chipped in on the controversy on the first day of September in an editorial titled "Extraordinary Conclusion."

> San Francisco's grand jury, after investigating the city's recent "peace riots" came to an extraordinary conclusion. It will be recalled that there had been considerable buck-passing as to the responsibility for the disorders—the mayor's office, the police department, the shore patrol, the saloons and others sharing in both the blame and the blaming.
>
> The grand jury took no chances on hurting anyone's feelings. It absolved "all parties concerned" of any blame.
>
> The disorders resulted in 13 deaths, 1059 cases of injury to persons, six cases of rape, and a vast amount of property damage. Yet, nobody was to blame.[14]

That same date, the editor of *The Bakersfield Californian*, from Bakersfield, California, not far from Los Angeles, also chimed in on the lack of courage showed by the San Francisco Civil Grand Jury in refusing to place the responsibility on the guilty parties. Wrote the editor, "The investigations by a grand jury in San Francisco as to the responsibility for the recent rioting on V-J Day and other days, rioting which destroyed 11 [sic] human lives and a vast deal of property, has been about as productive as to what really happened at Pearl Harbor." The editor was referring to a series of investigations performed by the U.S. Army, U.S. Navy, and even a committee from the U.S. Congress that had all looked into the surprise Japanese attack on Pearl Harbor on December 7, 1941, to see who was responsible for the lack of awareness on the part of the United States military on that fateful day. After gathering reams of evidence and hearing

## Chapter 15. Passing the Buck

from dozens of eyewitnesses, each investigative body had come to the same conclusion: They could not fix the responsibility on any one individual or group of individuals. The editor of *The Bakersfield Californian* went on about the San Francisco grand jury decision. "One metropolitan official says that it was all due to the 'exuberance of enthusiasm' and really nobody was to blame. Certainly not the Chief of Police, nor the Navy, nor any organized authority," he wrote. "Circumstances, as stated by one publication, 'were too unusual to permit anything to be done about it.' So this is probably the end of the chapter."[15] Like seemingly everyone else, the editors of both the *Redwood City Tribune* and *The Bakersfield Californian* could not comprehend the milquetoast outcome of the San Francisco Civil Grand Jury.

The grand jury had listened to dozens of people connected to the riots, from Mayor Lapham and Admiral Wright to some of the shop owners whose windows had been shattered and whose stores had been looted. District Attorney Brown had promised to "fix responsibility for the disorders" and had said, "There's something fundamentally wrong some place when a situation can develop such as that which permitted three nights of 'demonstrations' in San Francisco."[16] In the end, no one was held responsible and there appeared to be "something fundamentally wrong" with the conclusion of the Civil Grand Jury.

## Chapter 16

# The Quiet Holiday Weekend

One thing that all parties in authority had stressed when being interviewed by the Civil Grand Jury was that when the Japanese finally signed the surrender documents, and the "official" V-J Day proclamation finally happened, both the city and military would be ready. George Reilly, the State Board of Equalization representative, had gotten assurances that "both on and off sale liquor establishments ... [will] close immediately after the V-J Day announcement is made and [will] remain closed for the entire next day." The request, according to Reilly, had been made by Police Chief Dullea with full backing by the navy and army. It was reported, "The Bartenders Union has ordered all members to comply with the request, and all off-sale liquor firms are expected to comply."[1] Without the flow of alcohol throughout the city, San Francisco officials were hoping to curb any inclination toward destruction and violence.

To add a little strength to George Rielly's request, Robert W. Kenny, the attorney general of California in Sacramento, weighed in on what had transpired in San Francisco and ruled that anybody drinking alcohol past the midnight hour inside an establishment that had closed its doors at midnight would be "a clear violation of state law." As Kenny declared, "The present law which controls liquor selling hours would be defeated if it were legally possible to procure a sufficient supply to enable patrons to continue consumption within the licensed premises beyond the permitted hour of sale."[2] This ruling would prohibit people from buying several bottles of beer or hard liquor in advance of the closing of the bar or restaurant and then continuing to consume the contents even after the establishment had shuttered its doors.

Hoping to build off the ruling by Attorney General Kenny, Mayor Lapham waded in and called for "all who dispense liquor either by the drink or by the bottle, to abide by the agreement reached in my office on August 17, whereby no liquor will be sold in San Francisco on official VJ Day and the following day." He then added that he had been "advised that members of the bartenders' union will not work on VJ Day or the following

## Chapter 16. The Quiet Holiday Weekend

day, and I hope those employees who dispense packaged liquor also will take a holiday." In a veiled threat to any service personnel, he finished by stating, "I reiterate that this entire program has the strong indorsement of the Army and Navy."[3] This time, San Francisco, and indeed all of California, would be ready for the official V-J Day celebrations.

During the last days of August, news had filtered out that the Japanese would sign the formal surrender documents aboard the battleship USS *Missouri* in Tokyo Bay near 9:00 a.m. on September 2, 1945. Being 16 hours ahead of San Francisco, the date and time in the Bay City would be near 5:00 p.m. on September 1. President Truman would make the formal announcement of the signing shortly thereafter. Therefore, beginning at 4:00 p.m. on Saturday, September 1, Chief Dullea put all 1,116 San Francisco police officers on alert and canceled all days off.[4]

To facilitate better coverage of the entire city, San Francisco was divided into several sections. As noted, "Special attention will be directed to downtown districts." Motor traffic would be barred from Market Street along the six blocks from Second Street to Eighth Street, where most of the rioting had taken place on the nights of August 13, 14, and 15, but the streetcars would still be allowed to travel along the tracks "unless the crowds make it impossible to operate them." Extra patrols would be assigned to the "downtown section south of Market, along Third, Fourth, Fifth and Sixth streets and Market and Mission [one block south of Market]," the area where "most of the damage occurred previously." This time the patrols would consist of a city police officer, a naval shore patrolman, and an Army Military Police officer. All three law enforcement agencies were given the authority to arrest any person breaking the law, whether they be civilians or in uniform. Although the papers reported "no formal arrangement existed for co-operation between the shore patrol and the local police during the trouble period" of August 13, 14, and 15, the Shore Patrol officers were now "instructed to support Police General Order No. 80" and "assist police in controlling naval personnel."[5]

At that same time, 4:00 p.m., Police Chief Dullea augmented his General Order No. 80, which had been issued on August 17 and had called all regular and auxiliary police officers to duty with limited time off until after V-J Day. According to Chief Dullea, this time the army, navy, and city police would "co-operate" and "co-ordinate" their activities and patrols "to forestall further victory riots." As the addition read, "These units are to work in the closest co-operation … but the police officer is to remember that a crime committed in violation of any ordinance of this city or any statute of this State is punishable, whether committed by a civilian or by a member of the armed forces." To further stipulate the cooperation required between the three law enforcement officers, the order also stated, "If any resistance is made to the order of the shore patrol officer, he shall be immediately supported in carrying out his order by the police officer of the unit. The same procedure shall be followed in supporting the orders of the military police against their personnel." According to Chief Dullea, "special orders had been issued by the service regarding conduct of their personnel."[6]

Putting out a strong presence, police patrol wagons were being brought in from outlying districts to help patrol the downtown area, and Captain George M. Healy, in charge of the San Francisco Police Department Juvenile Bureau, would have members of his special unit patrolling the streets looking for "unattended juvenile celebrants." Additionally, plain clothes police would be stationed in all the hotel lobbies and up and down the streets keeping an eye on anyone showing the first signs of public intoxication or starting trouble.[7] This time, both civil and military authorities would not be fooling around.

At 10:00 p.m. in Washington, D.C., 7:00 p.m. in San Francisco, on Saturday, September 1, 1945, President Truman got on the radio airwaves and informed the American public that the surrender documents had been signed. World War II was officially over. "My fellow Americans, and the Supreme Allied Commander, General MacArthur, in Tokyo Bay," he began. "The thoughts and hopes of all Americans—indeed of the civilized world—are centered tonight on the battleship *Missouri*. There on that small piece of American soil anchored in Tokyo Harbor the Japanese have just officially laid down their arms. They have signed terms of unconditional surrender." Near the end of his speech, Truman said, "As President of the United States, I proclaim Sunday, September the second, 1945, to be V-J Day—the day of formal surrender by Japan."[8]

While some San Franciscans immediately rushed out to celebrate the announcement, most decided to wait until the morning and the "official" start of V-J Day. "Bars and liquor stores throughout San Francisco closed almost immediately tonight after the announcement that the Japanese had signed the surrender terms and President Truman's proclamation that tomorrow would be official V-J Day," noted a United Press correspondent. Earlier that day, as planned, the civilian and armed forces police patrols took their stations and began walking their beats.[9] However, as the newspapers later reported, the "mobilized police, shore patrol and military police found themselves with nothing to do." As an Associated Press reported noted, "Special police precautions against renewed rioting were unneeded."[10]

## Chapter 16. The Quiet Holiday Weekend

"S.F. Is Quiet" read the title of an article written by an Associated Press reporter that appeared in *The Fresno Bee*. "The ebullient city of San Francisco, which exploded in a three day demonstration at the capitulation of Japan, celebrated today's formal surrender ceremonies soberly, for the most part, tonight. All bars closed." Shortly after Truman's speech, Chief Dullea reminded the tavern owners of their promise to close, and Bruno Mannori, president of the bartenders' union, ordered his members to "put on their coats and go home." Because of these acts, only a few non-union establishments remained open after 7:00 p.m. However, they were soon being closed by the civilian and military patrols. "There was a lot of grumbling from soldiers and sailors," noted one newspaper, "but they gave little trouble." Only two men, both ensigns in the U.S. Navy, were arrested on Saturday night and taken into custody by the Shore Patrol.[11]

In contrast to the riotous nights of mid–August, most people spent the Sunday morning of V-J Day in church, giving "thanks for the end to nearly four years of total war." As the *San Francisco Examiner* reported, "V-J morning dawned on few hangovers, with on-sale and off-sale liquor establishments [having been] closed since President Truman's announcement of the surrender signing." In commenting on the calm, the paper said, "Officials attributed some of the surrender-day quiet to its anticlimax after the first impact of peace last month."[12]

Calling the rest of the Sunday celebration an "orderly anticlimax to the 'victory riots' of three weeks ago," the newspapers revealed that Sunday was quieter than an "ordinary Saturday." As the police noted, typically, a Saturday "brings an average of 120 drunk arrests, thirty-five to forty misdemeanors, [and] sixty accidents." Throughout the entire V-J Day Sunday, the roving law enforcement patrols reported "but 104 arrested drunks, twenty-four misdemeanor arrests, forty-eight accidents with fifteen minor injuries and but one drunk driver arrest." And, since that first weekend in September was officially the Labor Day weekend, it was thought that the "first gas-rationless holiday weekend since the war … [had] lured thousands out of town."[13] The small celebration in San Francisco was beyond orderly.

Across the bay, in Oakland, the scene was the same. "Prepared for the official announcement [of the signing of the surrender documents]," reported *The Oakland Post Enquirer*, "police patrolled the streets with shore patrol and auxiliary policemen, but in no case was a disturbance reported." As the officers told the reporters, the day was actually "more quiet than a normal Sunday."[14]

On Labor Day, Monday, September 3, San Francisco celebrated with

## The San Francisco V-J Day Peace Riots

a sanctioned, peaceful parade down Market Street. The following morning, the *San Francisco Examiner* explained, "On Sunday, San Francisco paid homage to the front line heroes who had won V-J Day—and yesterday, Labor Day, it was the home front production workers who were honored." The paper went on, "For four years … wartime production had kept workers on their jobs on Labor Day. But yesterday, the first peacetime Labor Day observance since 1941, silence had settled on the waterfront, the shipyards, the factories, the production lines."[15] Instead of working on Labor Day, the San Francisco laborers had marched in a parade and had celebrated their accomplishments.

"The San Francisco parade was staged by 30,000 CIO [Congress of Industrial Organizations] members, and featured a tribute to the 200,000 American workers who died in the war," stated one newspaper article. Interspersed throughout the marchers were 16 bands playing patriotic tunes. Noted the *Oakland Tribune*, "Thousands of workers marched in the parade from the Ferry Building to the Civic Center." Afterward, a rally was held at the Civic Center. Continued the *Oakland Tribune*, "Veterans from Army and Navy hospitals were introduced at the start of the rally and taps were sounded while the huge crowd stood in silence in tribute to the men and women who lost their lives in the war."[16]

Although the highways surrounding San Francisco Bay were heavily crowded on this "first work-free Labor Day week-end in four years," the area police stated that there was "an exceptionally low record of automobile accidents and fatalities." Only four deaths were recorded in the entire Bay area. As indicated, the police attributed the low record to two reasons—many drivers had driven more cautiously, being aware of the "faulty conditions of their cars," and most of the state taverns and liquor stores had been closed over the long V-J Day/Labor Day weekend.[17] Unlike those tumultuous days and nights of mid–August, the official V-J Day/Labor Day weekend had been a joy for most San Franciscans.

CHAPTER 17

# Celebration Done Right

Although most people in San Francisco probably missed the article, the *Alameda Times-Star* of Alameda, California, across the Bay from the big city, ran a small blurb on the front page of its September 3, 1945, issue. As reported by the United Press, Adele Wainwright, wife of Lieutenant General Jonathan M. "Skinny" Wainwright, was reporting from her hometown in Skaneateles, New York, that "she hoped to meet General Wainwright in San Francisco some time this week." That meant that the exalted general would be arriving in the Bay City sometime soon. Within a day of the *Alameda Times-Star* blurb, San Francisco authorities were making plans to welcome the returning hero with a Victory Parade.[1]

In March 1942, when General Douglas MacArthur left the Philippines by order of President Franklin Delano Roosevelt, he gave command of the forces still holding out in the Philippines to General Wainwright. On April 9, giving in to starvation and overwhelming odds, 70,000 American and Filipino troops on the Bataan Peninsula had been forced to surrender. A month later, on May 5, General Wainwright and another 11,500 men who had been holding out on the island fortress of Corregidor at the mouth of Manila Bay had surrendered. The combined Bataan/Corregidor surrender was the largest capitulation of troops in U.S. history. Already tall and slim, which had earned him the prewar nickname of "Skinny," Wainwright lost even more weight as he languished for over three long years in Japanese prison camps. All the while, Wainwright was haunted by the fear that he would be court-martialed after the conclusion of the war for his surrender of the Philippines forces. By contrast, he became a symbol of American fortitude and resilience. Instead of a court-martial, Wainwright received the adulation of an adoring public. Liberated from his Japanese captors at the cessation of hostilities, he had the honor of being present on the deck of the battleship *Missouri* when the Japanese signed the official surrender documents. He was even presented with one of the pens used in the signings. Two days later, on September 4, 1945, Wainwright, and British General Arthur Percival, who had been forced to surrender Singapore and 85,000 British and Commonwealth troops to the Japanese in February 1942, stood over Japanese Lieutenant General Tomoyuki Yamashita as that officer was forced to surrender the Philippine Islands back to the Allies.[2]

Wainwright, now being called the "hero of Corregidor," was due to arrive back in the United States, at Hamilton Field at Novato, California, a few miles north of San Francisco, within the next few days. Coming with Wainwright would be "eight generals, two other officers and two enlisted men who [had been] imprisoned with Wainwright." Two of the returning generals were residents of San Francisco. According to the War Department, although Mrs. Wainwright had changed plans and had decided to reunite with her husband in Wahington, D.C., instead of the Bay City, the wives and families of all the other men were "being provided air transportation to San Francisco" to be on hand when their men arrived home.[3]

Teaming with Major W.C. Powers, an army liaison officer, Supervisor John J. Sullivan of the San Francisco citizens' committee, parade chairman Paul Verdier, and parade director Edward Sharkey began working diligently to honor the liberated individuals with an official Victory Parade. "Lt. Gen. Jonathan Wainwright, hero of Corregidor, will lead a victory parade here Sunday [September 9], army officials informed Mayor Roger Lapham today," the United Press reported on September 6. As envisioned by Major Powers and the three directing citizens, "Wainwright will ride at the head of a parade of 20,000 service men and war workers." The parade would be "San Francisco's official celebration of victory, and a salute to the armed forces that made victory possible. All units of the military service will be represented, as well as the homefront [sic] activities that backed up the men and women in uniform."[4]

It was planned that the parade would kick off at 12:30 p.m. from in front of the Ferry Building at the foot of Market Street and the waterfront and then proceed up Market for two miles, to Grove Street and then to a reviewing stand in front of the Civic Center. Reporting on the occupants of the first car, the position of honor, the *Oakland Tribune* wrote, "General Wainwright will ride with Gov. Earl Warren, his own son, Lieut. [Cmdr.] Jonathan M. Wainwright V of the U.S. Merchant Marine, Mayor Lapham and Chief of Police Charles Dullea." Once at the reviewing stand, Wainwright was scheduled to stand beside other "high ranking Army and Navy officers" for a short time before being whisked away for a flight home to the East.[5]

In addition to the distinguished dignitaries, Major Powers promised that 300 army planes of the Fourth Air Force from March Air Reserve Base near Los Angeles would appear overhead, "as a symbol of the air power

*Chapter 17. Celebration Done Right*

Lieutenant General Jonathan M. "Skinny" Wainwright (center), the hero of the Philippines, at the reviewing stand during the September 9, 1945, San Francisco Victory Day Parade (Karl R. Youst, West Virginia & Regional History Center).

that played such a decisive part in the war." Likewise, "Armored units will symbolize their part of the battle might that led to victory." Behind 7,000 marching army personnel would be several thousand navy marchers,

## The San Francisco V-J Day Peace Riots

while up above, "Navy torpedo planes and dive bombers [will] take over the skies." Next would come 700 marching WAVES, floats from Mare Island Navy Yard, U.S. Marines, WACs, SPARS (Coast Guard Women's Reserve), Veterans of Foreign Wars, and "800 marchers from the Chinese colony." The civic leaders arranged for 17 marching bands to be spread throughout the marchers and an estimated 2,000 mounted police officers from northern California. Helping to represent the work of the home front throughout the war would be members of the American Women's Volunteer Services, the Red Cross, labor organizations, and similar groups.[6]

On Sunday, September 9, 1945, the San Francisco Victory Parade went off without a hitch. A successful, fun, exuberant parade without any trouble was exactly what San Francisco needed. Roger Johnson, a United Press staff correspondent, wrote, "People crowded ten-deep on the sidewalks to catch a glimpse of Wainwright. Sailors and soldiers scaled the sides of office buildings and theaters. Orange crates sold at inflationary prices to standees." Richard V. Hyer, with the *San Francisco Examiner*, noted, "People from all over northern California had been pouring into the city all morning. By the time the parade started at 12:30 p.m., they were packed solid from building fronts to the curbs where they strained against police lines." The police, however, did not mind. A patrolman at Powell and Market Streets was heard to say, "This is a good day to be a cop. We can get right out front and watch."[7]

In comparing the successful and peaceful Victory Parade with the riotous three nights in August, correspondent Johnson stated, "San Francisco already had experienced a three-day peace 'celebration' that developed into a semi-riotous outburst of looting and drunkenness. Today, the celebration was wildly enthusiastic but almost self-consciously orderly." Noting the heavy police presence, Johnson added, "Hundreds of city and military policemen enforced the peace."[8] As noted before, however, the police had no trouble with the joyous, orderly crowd.

Riding in a flag-decorated limousine behind a mounted color guard of the San Francisco Police Department, General Wainwright acknowledged the accolades of the crowd. "All the way up Market from the Ferry Building to the review stand at the Civic Center," wrote Richard Hyer, "General Wainwright, erect, shoulders squared, his army cap firmly set on his graying head, grinned and waved in the traditional salutes of a champion, with hands clasped and held aloft. And the crowds loved that." As the general's car passed and the rest of the parade marched up Market Street, "the roar of acclaim rose and swelled and rolled up the broad thoroughfare in a deafening torrent of sound." Added Roger Johnson, "This was America's official welcome to Wainwright, the symbol of triumphant U.S.

## Chapter 17. Celebration Done Right

Lieutenant General Jonathan M. "Skinny" Wainwright's flag-draped limousine travels along Market Street past well-behaved cheering crowds during the September 9, 1945, San Francisco Victory Day Parade (Prelinger Archives).

military might, and the throngs that jammed the center of the city roared a jubilant greeting to the skinny man who is only three weeks out of a Manchurian prison camp."9

As the different marching groups followed behind General Wainwright's car, loud cheers went up as the people in the crowd read the banners being carried in front of some of the groups. The Marine Superintendent's Branch, which had been responsible for the coordination of the operation and maintenance of all vessels in the various shipyards, marched behind a banner proudly stating, "The impossible we do immediately. The miraculous takes a little longer." Immediately behind was a float in the shape of a merchant marine Victory ship carrying the name "Wainwright Victory." In front of a group of workers from an army ordnance factory, a few young ladies carried a banner reading, "We packed the equipment that packed the wallop that whipped the Japs." But cheers that "came close to rivaling those given Wainwright were reserved for one very special section of the parade," noted reporter Hyer. "A long line of olive green buses rolled by, each loaded with disabled men from Letterman General Hospital."10

## The San Francisco V-J Day Peace Riots

**Servicemen and servicewomen, along with civilian defense workers, march up Market Street during the September 9, 1945, San Francisco Victory Parade (Prelinger Archives).**

It was estimated that a "half million men, women and kids ... lined Market Street and festooned themselves from windows, roofs, signboards, fire escapes and every other conceivable point" to witness the "pageant of military and civilian might" that was the United States of America. All along the route, people in the upper floors and on the rooftops of office buildings showered the marching men and women with confetti. "Clouds of ticker tape, blotters and [pages from] telephone books fluttered down" from the buildings on either side of Market Street, recalled reporter Johnson. Hundreds of American flags were draped from those same buildings and dozens of light poles. The marquee of the Newsreel Theater at 978 Market Street proclaimed, "Welcome Gen Wainwright." Ships in San Francisco Bay sounded their horns and sirens in jubilation. Just before General Wainwright's car turned off Market Street toward the reviewing stand, "A huge formation of P-38's thundered overhead." Added reporter Hyer, "The general looked up and saw more air power than was ever at his disposal in the Philippines."[11]

Upon reaching the reviewing stand, General Wainwright, Governor Warren, and the others exited their vehicle and joined Major General Julian C. Smith, the Marine Corps commander of the Department of

## Chapter 17. Celebration Done Right

**The marquee of the Newsreel Theater at 978 Market Street proudly proclaims a welcome to Lieutenant General Jonathan M. Wainwright on Sunday, September 9, 1945, during the San Francisco Victory Parade (Prelinger Archives).**

the Pacific, and Rear Admiral William K. Scammell, Coast Guard commandant, on the review stand. "The crowd saved its greatest welcome for the climactic moment when Wainwright stepped out of his limousine and mounted the reviewing stand in front of city hall," wrote Johnson. The crowd immediately in front of and around the reviewing stand was estimated to be between 50,000 and 75,000 people.[12]

Although the parade was expected to last three hours, it took nearly four. After about 30 minutes at the reviewing stand, however, General Wainwright's aides, "fearful less the strain be too much, whisked him into City Hall, to the mayor's office." Wrote United Press correspondent Johnson, "Wainwright stood without his cane at the reviewing stand, but he was plainly weary from the strain of his trans–Pacific flight and the strenuous round of welcomes." In addition, Johnson reported that the general "was troubled by an abscessed tooth. His jaw was swollen, and the smiles came with effort." Once inside the mayor's office, Wainwright reportedly said, "It was a wonderful parade. I was deeply impressed by the reception given me by the city of San Francisco. I only wish my wife could have been here to experience it with me." Within an hour or so, the slim general was on his way to the airport for the flight to Washington, D.C., and his long-awaited meeting with his beloved Adele.[13]

## The San Francisco V-J Day Peace Riots

Rightly proud of his city, Mayor Lapham was heard to say, "It's one of the greatest crowds I've ever witnessed." Comparing the crowd size to the amount of people who had cheered on President Truman when he had visited San Francisco for the closing of the first meeting of the United Nations in April 1945, Lapham added, "It is as large as the crowd that welcomed President Truman. That was estimated at half a million."[14]

In contrast to the raucous celebrations that had taken place within San Francisco over three nights in mid–August, the General Wainwright Victory Parade saw San Franciscans and the military personnel stationed around the Bay area at their best. Only 15 people were treated at city hospitals. One Shore Patrol officer was treated for cuts on his scalp after being hit by a large pane of glass that had accidentally been loosened by viewers in a third-floor window. Another individual had sustained minor injuries when he accidentally fell into an open City Hall lightwell and had to be rescued by an ambulance crew. The other 13 casualties were all victims of fainting, "apparently as the result of excitement."[15]

For three days and nights in mid–August 1945, San Francisco had been a disgrace. For three days in September—the official V-J Day, Labor Day, and during the Victory Parade—San Francisco had redeemed herself. On September 14, the huge aircraft carrier USS *Saratoga* (CV-3) steamed under the Golden Gate Bridge and into San Francisco Bay. Only one month removed from the disastrous riots of August 13–15, many of the arriving sailors wondered what kind of a reception they would receive from the people of a city that had been torn apart by their fellow men in navy blue. "We're still sore about the black eye those boots gave the Navy and San Francisco in the V-J riots," stated Aviation Storekeeper (AK) William Scanlon. He questioned, "Did those Market Street commandos leave anything liquid for us after those victory nights?" Fortunately, Scanlon and the others had nothing to worry about. San Francisco welcomed the returning heroes with open arms and plenty of liquid refreshments. Willing to forgive and forget, the people of San Francisco even welcomed the recruits from Treasure Island back into their midst, if they behaved themselves. "San Francisco took it graciously," commented Navy Corpsman David S. Greene, who had been in the city during the riots, "and when we were again permitted liberty we were received warmly. That's one reason, I think, why the bay city is the one city everybody loves."[16]

As time went on, the people of San Francisco tended to forget what had happened on the nights of August 13, 14, and 15, 1945. The San

## Chapter 17. Celebration Done Right

Francisco Board of Supervisors paid the store owners for the damage done to their stores and for lost merchandise. The final price tag eventually came to $200,000—in 1945 dollars. The broken glass windows were replaced and the damaged streetcars were repaired. The scars of those horrible days and nights eventually faded away. As more and more ships returned to San Francisco Bay, bringing home the thousands of warriors who had battled their way across the Pacific to victory, the City by the Bay greeted them warmly. There were no more raucous celebrations, no more riots. Eventually the citizens forgot the ugliness of mid–August 1945. Sixty years later, in 2005, Charles Fracchia, founder of the San Francisco Museum and Historical Society, simply said, "You know, it's something which has been understandably buried historically. People don't want to go back and remember this."[17]

While Rev. Clement Berberick admitted that "the city has received a black eye throughout the nation," Chief Dullea, who bore much of the responsibility for letting the rioters get so out of hand, hinted that he wished that the whole matter would simply just go away, believing that the past was the past. Even Mayor Lapham, who also bore much of the responsibility, said that he was sorry that the rioting had been reported throughout the nation the way that it had been and simply wanted San Francisco to start anew. Noted San Francisco historian Charles Fracchia, who was a young boy at the time of the riots, "There were fears that San Francisco would get a bad name from the riot, but it was quickly swept under the rug and forgotten."[18] It happened. It was over. Forget about it.

But some people could never forget and did not want others to forget either. In 1958, one-armed veteran Sergeant Sidney Georgeson wrote a magazine article about his experiences on the evenings of August 13, 14, and 15 in San Francisco. He stated:

> Newspapers printed little about it, then or since. It would have been bad "publicity" all around.... But now, at last, the truth finally can be told about those frantic hours when rowdy, reeling mobs of drunken, boot camp sailors, led by criminal elements within their ranks, ran wild with lust and vandalism.
> I was there. I saw it happen. I was an Army combat veteran who—like the out-numbered police and shore patrol—was forced to watch helplessly one of the most disgraceful episodes in our national history.
> Perhaps it was resentment that the war was over before they could get in their own licks, perhaps it was a compulsion to prove that they were as tough as their combat-hardened older brothers, that made young servicemen go off the deep end. Most were teenage sailors from nearby training bases. There were a few Marines and soldiers. It was a good bet that not one in a hundred had ever heard a shot fired in earnest.[19]

## The San Francisco V-J Day Peace Riots

Thirteen years after the rioting, Georgeson was still angered at the city police for letting the rioters get away with the destruction of Market Street. "Police," he complained, "…shrugged their shoulders about the mess. They said the liquor control was up to the State, and they had never even been officially notified to enforce it. Also, they said they felt control of servicemen was up to the services." Georgeson wanted everybody to remember, "A grand jury investigation some weeks later quietly whitewashed both the civilian and military authorities, gently placed the blame on liquor, and then discreetly dropped the whole thing." The army veteran was shocked that so few people remembered what had happened in San Francisco in mid–August 1945. "The 100,000 or so young, punk sailors and other rookies," he reminded everyone, "…sure left the town and its women in a helluva mess for the fighting men to come home to from a hard-won war."[20]

As Georgeson reminded everyone, the rioting in San Francisco after the announcement of peace by President Truman had occurred. Citizens of San Francisco, along with thousands of young servicemen, mostly sailors, had caused considerable damage to the beautiful bayside city. Despite his rhetoric, District Attorney Brown had not prosecuted those responsible for the rioting and the Civil Grand Jury had not determined the responsible parties. The whole affair had been nicely whitewashed and then forgotten.

But it had happened. And people should be aware of the past, and hope that it never happens again.

## Chapter 18

# Compare and Contrast

San Francisco historian Charles Fracchia has written, "The only city in the United States that celebrated the end of the war with a riot was San Francisco." This is correct. Undoubtedly every village, every town, and every city in America celebrated the end of World War II. While most of the celebrations were boisterous but fun, something went wrong in San Francisco.[1]

Why? What had gone wrong in San Francisco, or more correctly, what had gone right in so many other towns? Only two other towns suffered anything near a riot. In Monroe, Wisconsin, after the chief of police arrested two high school youths for their activities during the Peace Celebration, about 2,000 angry citizens surrounded the police station and then "broke aerials off the police car, broke car windows, and let air out of the tires while hurling eggs and oranges at the chief." The chief asked the governor to call out the Wisconsin National Guard but the governor refused. Eventually the chief left town, the two youths were set free, and the "rioters" went back to a peaceful celebration. Of course, the population of Monroe was only about 6,500 people in August 1945, so it was nowhere near the riotous crowd that flooded San Francisco.[2]

The second near-riot occurred in New Bedford, Massachusetts. There, fisticuffs broke out when a Shore Patrol officer asked a young man to "get off the fender of a stalled car because he was obscuring the light from the headlight." "After an hour and a half of street fighting," city police, Navy Shore Patrol officers, and a 53-man company of the state National Guard arrested four adults and two juveniles and managed to quell the disturbance. Police later admitted that "there was no injuries and … no serious damage" to property.[3] With a 1945 population of approximately 105,000 people, the number came closer to that of San Francisco but was still too far away from the City by the Bay to be a fair comparison.

While it might be improbable to compare what happened in San Francisco, a city of about 750,000 inhabitants in August 1945, with the smaller villages and towns in the United States, it would be well within reason to compare the celebrations and responses with cities of a similar size, or larger.

In the 1940 census, the town of New Orleans, Louisiana, with 494,537 people ranked 15 out of the most populous cities in America. (San Francisco was number 12 with 634,536.) When the people of New Orleans heard President Truman's announcement, they spontaneously rushed into the streets in "celebrations, bearing the earmarks of a Mardi Gras." "Soldiers, Sailors and civilians joined in the bedlam," wrote an Associated Press reporter, "...and early reports indicated that the celebrations, although noisy, were orderly." The reporter said, "Liquor and beer dispensing establishments were closed down over most of the area but the celebrants appeared to be in no need for artificial spirits." Unlike in San Francisco, as soon as word of Japan's surrender hit the airwaves, "The police chief promptly ordered all bars and liquor establishments closed and cancelled all police leaves. One hundred additional officers were distributed about Canal and the French quarter." Knowing full well where the revelers would generally congregate, the New Orleans chief of police had immediately dispatched extra officers to those areas.[4] The same could not be said regarding Chief Dullea in San Francisco.

The 14th most populous city in the United States was Buffalo, New York, with a 1940 population of 575,901. An estimated 100,000 flooded the downtown area after the surrender announcement. "At 7:04 p.m.," while President Truman was still addressing the American people, the "assistant chief desk sergeant, sent out a prearranged order mobilizing the police department." Like San Francisco, the Buffalo police had prepared for the announcement ahead of time and had mobilized immediately. Unlike San Francisco, however, each officer had been assigned a specific job to do and a specific place to be. "Cyclemen patrolled Main St., keeping the crowd on the sidewalk," wrote a reporter with the *Buffalo Courier Express*, "[and there] were two patrolmen at every important intersection to keep traffic moving and prevent jams."

Although Buffalo was soon drenched with rain, it did not curb the enthusiasm of the celebrants. Near 9:00 p.m., just two hours into the celebration, the police cordoned off the entire downtown area, shutting it off from automobile traffic "from all directions." The San Francisco police never shut down traffic on Market Street, although the mass of people made it almost impossible to move a car along the thoroughfare. And although Buffalo taverns and bars in the downtown area remained open with people "lined five deep in front of the bar," the top Buffalo police inspector indicated that the police "would remain mobilized at full

## Chapter 18. Compare and Contrast

strength" to "prevent any trouble that might occur during the late hours in downtown drinkeries." Despite the huge, "spontaneous celebrations" in downtown Buffalo, there were no reports of broken windows and only a few reported injuries.[5]

Milwaukee, Wisconsin, with almost 600,000 people in 1945, ranked 13th among the most populous places in the United States. According to the Associated Press, about half of the population, or about 300,000 ecstatic people, "jammed the barricaded 'playground' area set aside for celebrants in the heart of the city's business district." Despite the size of the crowd, the police reported "just a few calls, nothing important." It was a large beer-drinking community, but there seemed to be no undo unruliness in the crowd. Instead of breaking windows, as the crowd had done in San Francisco, an Associated Press reporter noted, "Everything tearable was ripped up for confetti and the streets and celebrants were covered with the paper that cascaded down from offices and stores."[6] Instead of sweeping up broken glass the next morning, the Milwaukee sanitation crews were busy cleaning up bits and pieces of torn paper.

Just slightly larger than San Francisco in population was Washington, D.C., which registered 663,091 people in 1940. Home to the White House and President Truman, the wartime capital's population surged considerably more by 1945, and an estimated 500,000 people from the city and nearby suburbs joined the V-J Day celebration. "Half a million delirious people celebrated victory and peace in Washington last night," wrote an *Evening Star* reporter, "loosing a maelstrom of noise and merrymaking that swept through the downtown streets from the announcement of peace until dawn, leaving in its wake on nearly empty streets this morning a clutter of paper and debris that looked as if the city literally had been torn to shreds."

Almost immediately after President Truman's announcement of peace, the "police radio advised all policemen off duty to report to their precincts," said the *Evening Star* reporter. "Two emergency operators were called in to help handle the calls which flooded the switchboard at headquarters. Extra policemen mingled with the celebrants downtown, but they rarely interfered with the exuberance of the merrymakers, overlooking such technical violations of the law as tilting up liquor bottles on the street." While the San Francisco police had been seen among the crowd, most of them had been spotted standing transfixed on street corners, almost reluctant to "mingle with the celebrants." Had the San Francisco and armed forces police been more visible and more involved, perhaps less vandalism and violence might have occurred.

## The San Francisco V-J Day Peace Riots

Although it was reported that a "dense crowd" near the White House had gotten "out of hand for a time," both civilian and armed forces police worked together from the start to quiet things down. Before getting control of the crowd, however, it was reported, "Several soldiers climbed on top of a street car. Others clambered on the roofs of stranded automobiles." Still, the military and civilian police soon had the matter well in hand and there were no reports of excessive damage.

While the Washington nightclubs and bars were never given an order to shut down, most decided to close early for fear "that late crowds might prove too rough." Late in the evening, when 10 fire engines responded to a false alarm in the downtown area, "a score of celebrants clambered aboard a truck and refused to get off," similar to what had taken place in San Francisco. However, while the young rioters in San Francisco were reportedly seen attempting to steal the personal equipment of the firemen, playing tug-of-war with fire hoses and hijacking and damaging a few fire trucks, the citizens in Washington, D.C., only seemed playful. "They stayed on the perch for 20 minutes," explained the *Star* reporter, "before consenting to allow the vehicle to return to its station."[7] Albeit the crowd was extremely large, the Washington, D.C., celebrants were more joyful than destructive.

Pittsburgh, Pennsylvania (population 671,659 in 1940), heard the news of the surrender at 7:02 p.m. Eastern War Time and was soon inundated with civilian and service personnel alike. "Men who fought on every front and on every sea mingled with untold thousands as they shrieked, screamed, yelled, laughed, kissed, cheered, paraded and snake danced through the golden triangle [i.e., downtown Pittsburgh]," stated reporter Chester Potter of *The Pittsburgh Press*. "Paradoxically, the roaring throng was orderly. It was too happy to be otherwise. There weren't any serious fights or arguments. There was plenty of shoving, but everyone took it good naturedly."[8]

Unlike in California, the governor of Pennsylvania, Edward Martin, immediately ordered all licensed liquor establishments to lock their doors. "Few [celebrants] were seen under the influence of liquor," reporter Potter wrote. Stated the *Pittsburgh Post-Gazette*, "Governor Martin issued the proclamation at 7:30 o'clock last night, half an hour after President Truman's announcement of surrender terms." The *Post-Gazette* continued, "The proclamation was put on the Pennsylvania State Police teletype system along with orders to enforce it and five minutes later Pittsburgh police squads were making the rounds of all liquor establishments in the districts." About the same time, all trolley traffic was being detoured around the downtown business district.[9] Had the San Francisco bars and liquor

## Chapter 18. Compare and Contrast

stores closed immediately instead of remaining open for two hours and had the numerous trolley cars been almost instantly redirected from Market Street, the drunkenness and the destruction of the numerous streetcars may have been avoided. The governor of Pennsylvania was not afraid to wield his power to close all the bars and liquor stores throughout the state. The same could not be said of Governor Warren or Lieutenant-Governor Houser of California.

Writing about the Pittsburgh police, Chester Potter said, "The police did a swell job with a maximum of good humor. They entered into the spirit ... and did all they could to make sure no one was hurt or unduly disturbed. Aiding them after being on most of the day was the Auxiliary Police. They had trained for their jobs to meet emergencies should war ever come to Pittsburgh." Added a reporter with the *Pittsburgh Post-Gazette*, "Every available member of the police force was on duty, plus military and auxiliary police and downtown stores, in many cases, boarded up their windows to avoid breakage." In San Francisco, several eyewitnesses reported that many of the civilian and armed forces police had remained in one location, almost refusing to get involved with the rioters. In Pittsburgh, where there were no windows broken and only minor incidents of misbehavior, the police and the auxiliaries had actively made sure that "no one was hurt or unduly disturbed."[10] What a difference between the two cities.

Boston was the ninth largest city in population in the United States in 1940, with 770,816 residents. "Pent-up tension, which had been mounting since the first surrender hint five days ago," wrote a journalist with *The Boston Daily Globe*, "exploded like a giant firecracker with President Truman's announcement at 7 p.m. and sent deliriously happy crowds pouring into the downtown area." The reporter described the crowd as "spontaneous but orderly." By 10:30 p.m., the police commissioner estimated there were 750,000 people, many from the outlying areas, jamming "downtown Boston's narrow streets."

It was subsequently reported, "The entire personnel of the Police Department, 2000 men, augmented by auxiliaries, naval and military police, were on duty to keep the celebration within reasonable bounds. Police, though, were tolerant, and only a few arrests were made." Even with a little over three-quarters of a million people, the crowd was said to be "orderly and always good natured." No serious injuries or accidents were reported, and although additional doctors and nurses had been called in, only about 200 people were treated for "minor hurts."

While alcohol was prevalent, the drinking never seemed to get out of hand. "Bars and package stores did a rushing business through the evening,

## The San Francisco V-J Day Peace Riots

but the liquid consumption seemed only to increase the generally friendly spirits," said the *Globe*. "On the streets it seemed that everybody had a bottle containing his favorite beverage. And these bottles were freely handed around among persons who were total strangers a moment before." The *Globe* went on to inform the public, "Beer parties around bonfires were going on all over the Common and the Public Garden. Later, after package stores and bars closed, these spots became the favorite rendezvous for the remaining celebrants. They were jammed until the early hours today."

At one point during the celebration, fire trucks responded to what turned out to be a false alarm in the famed Boston Commons. "There six fire engines, hopelessly stalled in the swarming crowds, were quickly covered with joyriders," a reporter wrote. "One ladder truck must have had 100 persons, mostly sailors, aboard as it tried to make its way down the street." Although similar to what was happening in San Francisco, with sailors leading the charge, the big difference was that the Boston firefighters were not attacked or molested and their equipment was not taken from them.[11] The Boston merrymakers appeared more disciplined.

With 816,048 people listed in the 1940 census, St. Louis, Missouri, ranked eighth among the most-populous cities in the U.S. Within minutes of the surrender announcement, downtown St. Louis was filled with "throngs" of jubilant revelers. Just like in San Francisco, the *St. Louis Post-Dispatch* noted, "Central figures in every group were men in uniform, returned veterans and recent recruits alike. WACs, WAVEs and SPARs were cheered, and were robustly reminded that they had 'won the war.'" Shortly after the president's announcement, "a stream of motor traffic," with the cars running "bumper to bumper," filled the downtown streets. "Soon the plan for suspending streetcar and bus service ... had to be put into effect," stated the *Post-Dispatch*. Such a plan was implemented in San Francisco only after a few trolley cars had already been damaged.

Many St. Lous tavern owners closed their establishments as soon as a request was sounded over the radio. They would remain closed for two full days. However, as the *Post-Dispatch* reporter wrote, "Some celebrators had prepared for such a contingency, and bottles were displayed in hotel lobbies and in street gatherings." Despite the consumption of alcohol, even among the thousands of servicemen and servicewomen in attendance, there were no egregious episodes of violence or destruction. No windows were reported broken and only minor injuries occurred among the celebrants.

About 30 miles east of St. Louis, near Shiloh, Illinois, was Scott Field, a training base for thousands of military radio operators and mechanics. "News

## Chapter 18. Compare and Contrast

of the end of hostilities was met with mixed feelings by the thousands of men stationed at Scott Field," stated the *St. Louis Post-Dispatch*. While saying that "most of the soldiers stationed there had not been overseas," they reacted calmly to the announcement that would keep them out of war. "Many of the Scott Field men spent the evening listening to the radio for additional news, and scanning newspapers," said the *Post-Dispatch*. "One group marched around the post singing victory songs played for them by several impromptu bands." Admitted the *Post-Dispatch* correspondent, "Scott Field soldiers were under orders to confine their festivities to the Field."[12] What a difference from the San Francisco Naval Base on Treasure Island.

An estimated 50,000 people flooded into downtown San Francisco on August 15, 1945. In seventh-ranked Baltimore, Maryland (population 859,100 by the 1940 census), "more than 200,000 persons and pranksters" flooded the downtown area, "cheering, singing, shouting, [and] dancing." Despite a crowd that was four times larger than that in San Francisco, the celebrants were generally orderly. "In the seven hours from 5 p.m. to 1 a.m., [a police inspector] said only 21 arrests for minor law infractions took place throughout the city," reported the *Baltimore Sun*. "During that period there was not a single call for a crash investigation car. [The inspector] attributed a record of good behavior by last night's celebration in part to the fact that all alcoholic beverage establishments closed immediately after the victory announcement." Again, unlike in San Francisco, the liquor distributors had closed immediately. Also unlike San Francisco, the police immediately shut down all traffic lanes into the downtown area. "As soon as possible after the announcement, police began blocking motor traffic from the [downtown area]," explained an Associated Press reporter. It was told that "the crowd was so dense that the Baltimore Transit Company detoured all street cars from [the downtown area.]"[13] The result of no alcohol, no traffic, and no streetcars meant almost no destruction.

Regarding the response by the Baltimore police and authorities, the *Sun* wrote, "State Guardsmen with rifles appeared to assist city and auxiliary police, shore patrols and military police. Four battalions of the State Guard were mobilized by a prearranged plan as a precautionary measure." After the first or second night in San Francisco, why had Mayor Lapham not asked the governor, or lieutenant governor, to mobilize the California National Guard or the California Highway Patrol (i.e., state police)? A previous arrangement had been made between Baltimore authorities and the Maryland National Guard to mobilize and be ready for a call immediately after the surrender announcement. Why had the same not been done in California?

## The San Francisco V-J Day Peace Riots

Several military bases were either in or around Baltimore. At the Aberdeen Proving Ground, a military installation northeast of Baltimore, soldiers having some harmless fun reportedly "tied down the whistle of a railroad locomotive and ran it madly up and down the four miles of track inside the post." At the Camp Holabird Signal Depot, inside the southeast corner of the city, and at Fort George G. Meade, southwest of Baltimore, soldiers at baseball games between rival companies paused only briefly as the participants and spectators erupted into spontaneous cheers. "On the whole, the soldiers took the news quietly after the first outbreak of the blowing of whistles and the tolling of bells," said the *Baltimore Sun*. And at the Coast Guard Training Station at Curtis Bay, the trainees rang the bells of ships tied at anchor.[14] Both soldiers and sailors alike around Baltimore celebrated the news in a fun but nondestructive way, and the commanders of the different bases elected to keep their men on base rather than let them flood into the city. Again, how different from San Francisco.

Despite a heavy rainstorm that struck at 9:25 p.m., 2½ hours after President Truman's announcement, the people of Cleveland, Ohio (number six in population with 878,366), continued to celebrate. As a reporter with *The Plain Dealer* explained, "The city which had taken V-E Day in almost complete silence blew its top. Whistles blew, until downtown Cleveland resembled a madhouse." As in so many other cities, the people immediately crowded the downtown area and the streets were soon jammed with automobiles. "Bars were closed as soon as victory came," noted a reporter. "Police furloughs and days off were canceled at once, and the entire force went into action…. From Hotel Statler a sign appeared in a matter of seconds advising that the sale of alcoholic beverages has been discontinued in keeping with the pre-arranged plan. Liquor stores already had been closed by Gov. Frank J. Lausche." The Cleveland police and the Ohio governor had acted quickly to shut off the sale of alcohol, something Mayor Lapham and Police Chief Dullea, and Governor Warren or Lieutenant Governor Houser, failed to do in California. Without alcohol to fuel the fire, the Cleveland crowd was well behaved. "In spite of the noise and the crowds and the commotion," reporter Loveland said, "there was remarkably little to trouble the rather lenient police."[15]

Although in the same state as San Francisco, Los Angeles, at number five in population with 1,504,277 residents, reported no unruly behavior by its residents. "Despite a thunderous, paper-strewn reception of President Truman's announcement of the Jap surrender," wrote a United Press reporter, "sheriff's offices reported no damage to property, no looting and no trouble save for 20 drunks who were stored away." Only 157 people were

## Chapter 18. Compare and Contrast

treated in Los Angeles hospitals.[16] Unlike in San Francisco, squads of Los Angeles police had been standing by and rushed into trouble spots when needed.

Although showers throughout the day dampened the streets of the fourth largest city in the United States, Detroit, Michigan, with 1,623,452 people, celebrated the end of the war with great enthusiasm but little damage. "The people sprang up in the streets like mushrooms after the rain," said the *Detroit Free Press*. The police commissioner "came rushing down to headquarters to take charge of the full muster of police who had been put on twelve-hour duty during the first frolic [on Sunday evening]. He alerted 1,200 State troops." Although the Detroit police reported that "impromptu celebrations have sprung up" in almost every neighborhood, there was no window breaking and very few injuries. "Most of the injuries," said the *Free Press*, "resulted from persons falling off autos, street fights and minor mishaps."[17] There were no injuries from broken windows.

Philadelphia (the number three city with 1,931,334 residents in the 1940 census), which had "the wildest celebration in its history," suffered "one dead and more than 100 injured," according to *The Philadelphia Inquirer*. A 69-year-old man accidentally shot and killed himself while examining an army officer's rifle during an impromptu parade and 108 people were brought to area hospitals "for causes ranging from cuts and bruises suffered in fist fights, minor automobile accidents, falls and window-smashings." Like San Francisco, it was reported, "[A] rioting crowd of celebrants smashed store windows in South Philadelphia." Still, the police had responded immediately and the destruction came nowhere near what had happened in San Francisco, just a dozen or so windows in a city with a population of almost three times that of San Francisco.[18]

Of all the major cities in the United States, besides San Francisco, only Philadelphia suffered anything close to a riot, but it was quickly subdued by city police and firemen. Shortly after the surrender announcement aired on the radio, summer-school students from the University of Pennsylvania rushed into Woodlawn Avenue in front of the school and built a barricade out of garbage cans, trash, and a few wooden crates, halting the flow of all automobile and trolley traffic. The young celebrants soon started bonfires on the trolley tracks and swarmed over automobiles that were halted by the fires and barricades. "The rioters stalled scores of passing trolley cars by pulling the trolley poles from the wires, and engaged in a number of fist fights with police reserves and firemen sent to the scene," said *The Philadelphia Inquirer*. Soon, regular police arrived and quickly had the demonstration under control, with the firemen "spraying the crowds with water in an effort to break up the riot." Only two people were arrested.[19] While the civil and armed forces police in San Francisco had thought it unwise to use tear gas to break up the rioting mass of people on Market Street, why had they not instructed the firefighters to use water to quell the destruction? It had worked in Philadelphia. Might it have worked in San Francisco? One will never know.

The number two city in size of population in the United States was Chicago with 3,396,808 residents in 1940. In Chicago, an estimated half a million people jammed into the downtown area known as "the Loop." The *Chicago Daily Tribune* reported, "Thousands of sailors, soldiers, and marines were there. Young girls kissed them until their faces were smeared with lipstick." The bars, taverns, and nightclubs closed immediately after the announcement, thereby cutting down on drunkenness. Chicago police reported that "only two windows were broken in the loop and both of these were caused by pressing crowds." There seemed to be no wanton destructiveness among the revelers. Out of 500,000 people, only 61 were arrested, mostly "for drunkenness or fighting," and although the police had been put on an emergency footing immediately after Japan's surrender was announced, the *Tribune* proudly proclaimed, "The police department went back on its normal schedule at midnight." The next day, an estimated 250,000 revelers returned to the downtown area. Again, the celebration was orderly. Proclaimed the Chicago police commissioner regarding the two celebrations, "The people of Chicago are to be congratulated on their high spirited but orderly victory celebration. I don't think any city in the nation can match us in the real joy of Chicago's celebration and have a similar display of orderliness."[20] Certainly San Francisco could not.

Perhaps the only city that could possibly match Chicago for orderliness and joy was New York City, the largest U.S. city, with a population of 7,454,995 people in 1940. An estimated two million people flooded Times Square after President Truman's announcement and yet it was reported that only four people died during the celebrations—"two celebrants were killed by automobiles, one by stabbing and one in a fall from a window." Knowing that Times Square was the "traditional center of New York mass demonstrations," the police had made previous arrangements to protect the many windows. "Only the precaution of [wooden police] barricades kept store windows intact, especially in the theatrical district," wrote one newspaper reporter. The police barricades had kept the revelers from pressing up against, or getting close to, the many store windows. Immediately after the president's announcement, "restaurants and bars began closing." As noted, "The proprietors considered this a wise move to keep their establishments

## Chapter 18. Compare and Contrast

from being taken apart by the merrymakers." The next day, the merrymakers returned, numbering about 1,200,000 people. Although "soldiers, sailors, and Marines" were everywhere, and "the night clubs and saloons were jammed," the windows remained intact.[21] The New Yorkers were out to celebrate, not to destroy, and the New York police had been prepared. Common wooden barricades had saved the windows of America's largest city.

Above everything else, the V-J Day celebration in New York became famous for one event: a spontaneous kiss. In an iconic photograph taken in Times Square by Alfred Eisenstaedt from *Life* magazine, a sailor in his dark blue uniform and wearing his Dixie-cup cap is seen bending a beautiful young lady in a white nurse's uniform over at the waist and giving her a victory kiss. At the time, the man and woman were strangers to each other and unknown to Eisenstaedt. Subsequently, the two were identified as George Mendonsa and Greta Zimmer Friedman.[22] In contrast to what had happened in San Francisco, James O. Clifford of the Associated Press wrote, "Allied victory produced [a famous photo]: a sailor kissing a nurse in New York's crowded Times Square…. San Francisco had historic pictures too. But they show drunken men and women, some naked or barely dressed, shinnying up street lamps or frolicking in fountains."[23] The contrast could not have been more pronounced between the two cities.

In most every city near a military base or port, the streets were soon filled with joyous soldiers, sailors, Marines, and Coast Guard personnel kissing every girl in sight. It was reported happening in Washington, D.C., in Pittsburgh, in New Orleans, in Baltimore, New York City, Chicago, and thousands of other cities, both large and small. In Boston, reporter Seymour R. Linscott noticed, "When the excitement really got under way, servicemen—and again sailors seemed to dominate the picture—began the interesting game of trying to kiss every pretty girl they saw."[24] While such silliness had occurred in San Francisco on August 13, the first night of the celebration, the situation had soon gotten out of hand, with the servicemen, again mostly sailors, often manhandling the girls for unwanted kisses. On the second and third nights of rioting, the women had been attacked. One wonders what might have happened, or might not have happened, had the celebration been restricted to only one night, as it was in most every other city. Still, in cities such as Chicago and New York, the celebrants returned for a second night but no rapes or molestations had occurred. San Francisco had definitely acquired an unwanted black eye.

# Conclusion

So, what had gone wrong in San Francisco that had given it that black eye? Despite the whitewashing of the Civil Grand Jury, the responsibility was manifest, with multiple parties involved. At the top, Governor Warren, and in his absence, Lieutenant Governor Houser, failed to properly prepare for the situation. They both knew full well that San Francisco was a major port and training base, home to thousands of sailors and army personnel. They should have mobilized the California Highway Patrol prior to President Truman's announcement and sent them into the Bay City to help the deflated number of San Francisco trained police officers. And, if necessary, they could have mobilized the California National Guard and sent them to San Francisco, especially after the first night of celebration and the unruliness of the crowd. They did neither.

Likewise, Governor Warren or Lieutenant Governor Houser should have closed all the bars and liquor establishments throughout California immediately after the president's announcement, much as governors had done in several other states. They had the authority. They had the responsibility to protect the public. This lack of initiative had undoubtedly cost San Francisco over a hundred broken windows, untold looted items, and much damage throughout the city, as well as 13 deaths, at least six women sexually assaulted, and over 1,000 injuries. It was irresponsibility at its height.

Second down the line was Mayor Lapham. He should have insisted that the bars and liquor establishments, including restaurants and cafés, close immediately after the surrender announcement, instead of waiting two hours. He also should have requested additional help from Sacramento. At the start, he could have shut down traffic going into Market Street and prohibited trolley cars from using the thoroughfare. He did none of those things. Having promised to hold office for only one term, he should not have been afraid to step on a few toes or anger some of his constituents by making hard, though necessary, decisions. He should have made better preparations to protect downtown San Francisco, such as the

## Conclusion

erection of wooden police barricades along the sidewalks or designating a specific area for celebration, such as in front of the Civil Center or in Golden Gate Park and Kezar Stadium. Mayor Lapham undoubtedly knew what had happened in Halifax, Nova Scotia, another city with large numbers of servicemen present at all times, after the surrender of Nazi Germany. He should have foreseen the possibility of the crowd getting out of hand, especially with an expected large influx of sailors from Treasure Island and the various ships in the Bay. He should have worked hand in hand with Admiral Wright prior to the surrender announcement to make sure that there were plenty of Shore Patrol officers present in downtown San Francisco, and he should have made certain that the military officers worked side by side with the civilian police from the very start. The mayor should have instructed the police, both civil and military, to make arrests of anybody causing a disturbance or destruction, whether in uniform or not, and he should have instructed the fire department to use water from their fire hoses to quell the rioting. His lack of initiative and lack of wielding his authority did much to foment the lawlessness.

Next in line is Chief Dullea. The chief knew full well that his force was understaffed. Even with the auxiliary police, which were not trained to handle rioters but instead trained mainly for traffic control, he did not have enough people on hand to stop what was happening on Market Street. Chief Dullea should have worked together with his counterparts in the Military Police and Shore Patrol and made previous arrangements to have the different branches of law enforcement work together. And he should have instructed his officers to keep moving, to show their presence, to work in pairs or groups. Single officers had been intimidated by the large, rebellious crowd. Numbers might have helped. Special squads of riot police would have been able to rush to a hot spot to overwhelm the rioters with numbers. None of this happened, so San Francisco suffered.

On Sunday, August 12, when the false news flash was broadcast, both Chief Dullea and Mayor Lapham had been shown what might happen during the actual V-J Day celebration. Hundreds, if not thousands, of people had flooded into the downtown area, especially Market Street, after the false flash. The sailors and other servicemen had begun kissing any girl in sight and the street had quickly filled with automobiles. This happened almost 24 hours before President Truman's actual announcement of peace, giving the mayor and police chief plenty of time to change what plans they already had and come up with a good response to deal with a huge, boisterous, and perhaps rowdy crowd. They should have put in a call to Sacramento for the National Guard or state police, just in case. They should

# Conclusion

have planned for the worst but hoped for the best. A golden opportunity had slipped through their fingers.

Another responsible party was Admiral Wright. Perhaps insulated by his staff, he may not have been aware of the unruliness his young recruits could attain. Shame on him. He should never have granted full liberty to the entire base at Treasure Island. A combat veteran and ships' captain, he was well-aware of the practice of captains to grant only partial liberty to a crew in port, typically only one-half of the crew. To grant full liberty to 100,000 young recruits was asking for trouble. He also should have had a curfew in place from the very start. A midnight curfew would have given the sailors almost eight hours to enjoy themselves prior to returning to their base to be counted. And, from the start, he should have flooded downtown San Francisco with Shore Patrol officers and coordinated with either Mayor Lapham or Chief Dullea to have his patrolmen walk beside the city police. On the third night of rioting, 924 Shore Patrol officers were present to assist in finally stopping the riot. Where were those officers on the previous two nights? There was no good answer to that question.

Responsibility for the destruction of downtown San Francisco also rested on the shoulders of the many liquor store and tavern owners. Most of them stayed open for two hours after peace was declared. Much alcohol can be consumed in two hours—and was. Later, after experiencing one night of small rioting, most of the bars and liquor dealers decided to reopen after only 24 hours of being closed. They opened late in the afternoon of the second day, when the streets were once again teeming with unruly celebrants. They should have expected the consequences, yet the almighty dollar seemed to be their only passion. Had their establishments remained closed, with civilian and armed forces police standing by to retard the breakage and looting of the closed establishments, much of the drunkenness and destructive behavior may have been avoided. One will never know.

Others shared some of the responsibility, from the managers of the various streetcar lines who continued to send their trollies into the mob even though the streets were already packed, to the thousands of sailors, soldiers, Marines, Coast Guard personnel, and citizens of San Francisco who felt it was well within their right to destroy and steal things in the name of good fun. For the Civil Grand Jury to exonerate everybody and proclaim that it was simply a bunch of "boys being boys" was a travesty unto itself. The Civil Grand Jury shirked its responsibility to call out the responsible parties and hold them to the fire.

## *Conclusion*

Many things had gone wrong in San Francisco on the nights of August 13, 14, and 15, 1945, and many people were responsible. Fortunately, the city learned from its mistakes and made a fine showing with the V-J Day parade, the Labor Day parade, and the welcoming tribute to General Wainwright. Yet, the three nights of Peace Riots should never be forgotten. It happened. Learn from it.

# Chapter Notes

## Introduction

1. Lockwood, *VJ Day: The End of WWII in the Pacific*, np.

## Chapter 1

1. McManus, *To the End of the Earth*, 298; Hopkins, *The Pacific War*, 333–339.
2. Bay Area Census, San Francisco County, 1940, http://www.bayareacensus.ca.gov/counties/SanFranciscoCounty40.htm.
3. National Park Service, "Travel World War II Sites in the San Francisco Bay Area: Places of World War II in the San Francisco Bay Area," https://www.nps.gov/articles/000/places-of-world-war-ii-in-the-san-francisco-bay-area.htm; Martini, "Seacoast Defense: Fortress San Francisco," https://www.nps.gov/articles/000/seacoast-defense-fortress-san-francisco.htm.
4. Wardlow, *United States Army in World War II: The Technical Services—The Transportation Corps: Responsibilities, Organization, and Operations*, 99, 106; National Park Service, "Fort Mason Historic District," https://www.nps.gov/places/fort-mason-historic-district.htm.
5. McDevitt, *The Naval History of Treasure Island*, 5, 29.
6. Bonnett, *Build Ships! San Francisco Bay Wartime Shipbuilding Photographs*, excerpted in National Park Service, "World War II Shipbuilding in the San Francisco Bay Area," https://www.nps.gov/articles/000/world-war-ii-shipbuilding-in-the-san-francisco-bay-area.htm.
7. National Park Service, "Travel World War II Sites in the San Francisco Bay Area," https://www.nps.gov/subjects/travelbayareawwii/stories.htm#:~:text=The%20San%20Francisco%20Bay%20Area's,world's%20largest%20combined%20shipbuilding%20complex.
8. Simmons statement, *Keep the Spirit of '45 Alive*, http://spiritof45.org/storiess0.aspx; "That Old Gang of Mine," *Bangor* [ME] *Daily News*, October 14, 1942, 10; "With the Colors," *The Tensas Gazette*, St. Joseph, LA, October 16, 1943, 2.
9. "News of Our Men and Women in Uniform," *The Sioux Center* [IA] *News*, November 18, 1943, 2; "As One Goes Around," *Ukiah* [CA] *Republican Press*, August 22, 1945, 1; Simmons statement, *Keep the Spirit of '45 Alive*, http://spiritof45.org/storiess0.aspx.
10. Greene, "War Was Ended in Fun, Tragedy," *Greensboro* [NC] *Daily News*, August 14, 1965, 9.
11. Garvey, *Images of America: San Francisco in World War II*, 7.
12. "S.S. Victory Fete Awaits Jap Defeat," *San Francisco* [CA] *Examiner*, May 8, 1945, 1.
13. "Solemnity Marks Observance of V-E Day in San Francisco," *San Francisco* [CA] *Examiner*, May 9, 1945, 6.
14. "Solemnity Marks Observance of V-E Day in San Francisco," *San Francisco* [CA] *Examiner*, May 9, 1945, 1, 4.
15. "Solemnity Marks Observance of V-E Day in San Francisco," *San Francisco* [CA] *Examiner*, May 9, 1945, 6; "California Went Ahead with Work," *Santa Cruz* [CA] *Sentinel-News*, May 8, 1945, 9.
16. Ibid. [AU: Which source is repeated from note 15?]
17. "V-E Day a Sober Occasion in S.F.," *San Francisco* [CA] *Examiner*, May 10, 1945, 26.

## Chapter Notes

18. "$1,000,000 Damage in Victory Riots," *Oakland* [CA] *Tribune*, May 9, 1945, 1; "Nova Scotia Towns Guard Against Further V-E Day Celebration Riots," *Oakland* [CA] *Tribune*, May 10, 1945, 3.

19. Canadian War Museum, "Canada and the War: The Halifax VE Day Riots, 7–8 May 1945," https://www.warmuseum.ca/cwm/exhibitions/newspapers/canadawar/halifax_e.html.

20. Online Archive of California, "A guide to the Roger D. Lapham photograph collection, 1892–1956," https://oac.cdlib.org/findaid/ark:/13030/c8jm2c1f/admin/; Found SF, "Mayor Roger Lapham," https://www.foundsf.org/index.php?title=Mayor_Roger_Lapham.

21. Museum of the City of San Francisco, "San Francisco Police Dept. World War II Years," https://sfmuseum.org/sfpd/sfpd6.html.

22. Hartsell, "One big enthusiastic block party," *San Francisco* [CA] *Examiner*, August 11, 1995, 18.

23. "Police Readied for V-J Day," *San Francisco* [CA] *Examiner*, August 10, 1945, 9; "Grand Jury to Sift S.F. Peace Riots," *Oakland* [CA] *Tribune*, August 20, 1945, 13.

24. Georgeson, "The Rape of San Francisco," *Real War*, 36.

25. "Bars Asked to Close at War's End," *The Vallejo* [CA] *News-Chronicle*, August 10, 1945, 6.

26. "Police Readied for V-J Day," *San Francisco* [CA] *Examiner*, August 10, 1945, 9.

## Chapter 2

1. "Allies Reported Split on Acceptance of Jap Offer," *San Francisco* [CA] *Examiner*, August 11, 1945, 1.

2. "Peace Offer Touches Off Celebrations," *Wilmington* [CA] *Press-Journal*, August 11, 1945, 1.

3. "Peace Rites to Be Dry," *San Francisco* [CA] *Examiner*, August 11, 1945, 1.

4. "Radio Programs Announced for Sunday," *Oakland* [CA] *Tribune*, August 12, 1945, 36; "Coast League Box Scores," *Oakland* [CA] *Tribune*, August 13, 1945, 11; Anderson, "The Human Side of It: Suspenseful Waiting," *Oakland* [CA] *Post-Enquirer*, August 17, 1945, 22.

5. "Premature Victory Celebrations Follow False Peace Report," *The Vallejo* [CA] *News-Chronicle*, August 13, 1945, 6.

6. "Premature Victory Celebrations Follow False Peace Report," *The Vallejo* [CA] *News-Chronicle*, August 13, 1945, 6; "False Flash Brings Short Celebration," *San Mateo* [CA] *Times*, August 13, 1945, 1; San Mateo Theater Advertisement, *San Mateo* [CA] *Times*, August 11, 1945, 2.

7. "False Flash Brings Short Celebration," *San Mateo* [CA] *Times*, August 13, 1945, 1.

8. "False Flash Brings Short Celebration," *San Mateo* [CA] *Times*, August 13, 1945, 1; "Premature Victory Celebrations Follow False Peace Report," *The Vallejo* [CA] *News-Chronicle*, August 13, 1945, 6.

9. "False Report of War's End Starts Noise," *Norfolk* [VA] *Ledger-Dispatch*, August 13, 1945, 2; "Radio Broadcast of Erroneous Surrender Report Touches Off Premature Peace Celebrations," *Rushville* [IN] *Republican*, August 13, 1945, 4; "Fake Flash Starts Many Celebrations," *The Chico* [CA] *Enterprise*, August 13, 1945, 1.

10. "False Report of War's End Starts Noise," *Norfolk* [VA] *Ledger-Dispatch*, August 13, 1945, 2.

11. "False Flash Brings Short Celebration," *San Mateo* [CA] *Times*, August 13, 1945, 3.

12. "S.F. Whoopee Marks Time," *San Francisco* [CA] *Examiner*, August 14, 1945, 6.

13. "'Peace' Reports Start Short-Lived Celebration Here," *Oakland* [CA] *Tribune*, August 13, 1945, 2; Greene, "War Was Ended in Fun, Tragedy," *Greensboro* [NC] *Daily News*, August 14, 1965, 9; Georgeson, "The Rape of San Francisco," *Real War*, 36.

14. Greene, "War Was Ended in Fun, Tragedy," *Greensboro* [NC] *Daily News*, August 14, 1965, 9.

15. "S.F. Whoopee Marks Time," *San Francisco* [CA] *Examiner*, August 14, 1945, 6.

## Chapter 3

1. "Japs Send Surrender Note," *Anaheim* [CA] *Bulletin*, August 14, 1945, 1.

2. "Japs Send Surrender Note," *Anaheim* [CA] *Bulletin*, August 14, 1945, 1; "Wild S.F. Crowds Set Fires in Street,"

## Chapter Notes

*San Mateo* [CA] *Times*, August 14, 1945, 1; "S.F. Blows Its Top as Japs Surrender," *The Hayward* [CA] *Review*, August 14, 1945, 2; McManus, *To the End of the Earth*, 299–300.

3. "Early Reports Touch Off 'Peace' Festivities from Coast to Coast and in Pacific Isles," *Oakland* [CA] *Tribune*, August 14, 1945, 2; "Celebrating Crowds Jam Streets Here," *Oakland* [CA] *Tribune*, August 14, 1945, 1; Morgan, "Joyous Nation Is Premature," *Anaheim* [CA] *Bulletin*, August 14, 1945, 1.

4. "Celebrating Crowds Jam Streets Here," *Oakland* [CA] *Tribune*, August 14, 1945, 1; "Mad Crowds in S.F. Set Fires on Market St.," *San Mateo* [CA] *Times*, August 14, 1945, 2; "S.F. Blows Its Top as Japs Surrender," *The Hayward* [CA] *Review*, August 14, 1945, 2; "Riotous Celebrants in S.F. Wreck Property," *The Modesto* [CA] *Bee and News-Herald*, August 14, 1945, 2.

5. "Riotous Celebrants in S.F. Wreck Property," *The Modesto* [CA] *Bee and News-Herald*, August 14, 1945, 2; Greene, "War Was Ended in Fun, Tragedy," *Greensboro* [NC] *Daily News*, August 14, 1965, 9; "Market Street...," *Imperial Valley Press*, El Centro, CA, August 16, 1945, 8; Anderson statement, *Keep the Spirit of '45 Alive*, http://spiritof45.org/storiesa0.aspx; Morgan, "Joyous Nation Is Premature," *Anaheim* [CA] *Bulletin*, August 14, 1945, 1.

6. "Riotous Celebrants in S.F. Wreck Property," *The Modesto* [CA] *Bee and News-Herald*, August 14, 1945, 2; "Celebrating Crowds Jam Streets Here," *Oakland* [CA] *Tribune*, August 14, 1945, 1; "Frisco Wild Over News of Jap Acceptance," *Mandan* [ND] *Daily Pioneer*, August 14, 1945, 2; Bodenweck, "City Went Crazy When WWII Ended," *San Francisco* [CA] *Examiner*, August 13, 1985, 9; Burns, "Gleeful, Wild S.F. Uproar Recalls Pearl Harbor Horror," *The Fresno* [CA] *Bee*, August 14, 1945, 1.

7. "Wild S.F. Crowds Set Fires in Street," *San Mateo* [CA] *Times*, August 14, 1945, 1; Dailey, "SF Blows Its Top as Japs Surrender," *The Hayward* (CA) *Review*, August, 14, 1945, 2; "San Francisco Celebrants Run Up Big Damage Toll," *Oregon Daily Journal*, Portland, OR, August 14, 1945, 4; "Riotous Celebrants in S.F. Wreck Property," *The Modesto* [CA] *Bee and News-Herald*, August 14, 1945, 2; "Celebrating Crowds Jam Streets Here," *Oakland* [CA] *Tribune*, August 14, 1945, 1; Burns, "Gleeful, Wild S.F. Uproar Recalls Pearl Harbor Horror," *The Fresno* [CA] *Bee*, August 14, 1945, 1.

8. "Mad Crowds in S.F. Set Fires on Market St.," *San Mateo* [CA] *Times*, August 14, 1945, 2; Greene, "War Was Ended in Fun, Tragedy," *Greensboro* [NC] *Daily News*, August 14, 1965, 9; "A Letter to Buddy," *San Francisco* [CA] *Examiner*, August 11, 1995, 18.

9. "Riotous Celebrants in S.F. Wreck Property," *The Modesto* [CA] *Bee and News-Herald*, August 14, 1945, 2; Bodenweck, "City Went Crazy When WWII Ended," *San Francisco* [CA] *Examiner*, August 13, 1985, 9; Dailey, "SF Blows Its Top as Japs Surrender," *The Hayward* [CA] *Review*, August 14, 1945, 2; "Oakland Throngs Smash Windows in Victory Fete," *Oakland* [CA] *Tribune*, August 14, 1945, 1.

10. "Chican Describes Celebration in San Francisco," *The Chico* [CA] *Enterprise*, August 15, 1945, 3.

11. Dailey, "SF Blows Its Top as Japs Surrender," *The Hayward* (CA) *Review*, August, 14, 1945, 2; "Riotous Celebrants in S.F. Wreck Property," *The Modesto* [CA] *Bee and News-Herald*, August 14, 1945, 2; "Oakland Throngs Smash Windows in Victory Fete," *Oakland* [CA] *Tribune*, August 14, 1945, 1; "Wild S.F. Crowds Set Fires in Streets," *San Mateo* [CA] *Times*, August 14, 1945, 1; "Chican Describes Celebration in San Francisco," *The Chico* [CA] *Enterprise*, August 15, 1945, 3.

12. "Wild Celebration in 'Frisco," *Grand Forks* [ND] *Herald*, August 15, 1945, 2.

13. "Riotous Celebrants in S.F. Wreck Property," *The Modesto* [CA] *Bee and News-Herald*, August 14, 1945, 2; "Mad Crowds in S.F. Set Fires on Market Street," *San Mateo* [CA] *Times*, August 14, 1945, 2; Dailey, "SF Blows Its Top as Japs Surrender," *The Hayward* [CA] *Review*, August, 14, 1945, 2; "Oakland Throngs Smash Windows in Victory Fete," *Oakland* [CA] *Tribune*, August 14, 1945, 1.

14. Dailey, "SF Blows Its Top as Japs Surrender," *The Hayward* [CA] *Review*,

## Chapter Notes

August, 14, 1945, 2; "Oakland Throngs Smash Windows in Victory Fete," *Oakland [CA] Tribune*, August 14, 1945, 1; "Riotous Celebrants in S.F. Wreck Property," *The Modesto [CA] Bee and News-Herald*, August 14, 1945, 2.

15. Morgan, "Joyous Nation Is Premature," *Anaheim [CA] Bulletin*, August 14, 1945, 1.

16. Dailey, "SF Blows Its Top as Japs Surrender," *The Hayward [CA] Review*, August, 14, 1945, 2; "Riotous Celebrants in S.F. Wreck Property," *The Modesto [CA] Bee and News-Herald*, August 14, 1945, 2; "Oakland Throngs Smash Windows in Victory Fete," *Oakland [CA] Tribune*, August 14, 1945, 1.

17. "Oakland Throngs Smash Windows in Victory Fete," *Oakland [CA] Tribune*, August 14, 1945, 1; "Wild S.F. Crowds Set Fires in Streets," *San Mateo [CA] Times*, August 14, 1945, 1; "Riotous Celebrants in S.F. Wreck Property," *The Modesto [CA] Bee and News-Herald*, August 14, 1945, 2; "Celebrating Crowds Jam Streets Here," *Oakland [CA] Tribune*, August 14, 1945, 1; "Grand Jury Riot Probe Commends Authorities," *San Francisco [CA] Examiner*, August 30, 1945, 28.

18. "Wild S.F. Crowds Set Fires in Streets," *San Mateo [CA] Times*, August 14, 1945, 1; "Oakland Throngs Smash Windows in Victory Fete," *Oakland [CA] Tribune*, August 14, 1945, 1; "Riotous Celebrants in S.F. Wreck Property," *The Modesto [CA] Bee and News-Herald*, August 14, 1945, 2.

19. "Mad Crowds in S.F. Set Fires on Market St.," *San Mateo [CA] Times*, August 14, 1945, 2; "Radio Tokyo Says Imperial Note Accepting Potsdam Ultimatum Is Ready for Transmission to U.S.," *The Hayward [CA] Review*, August 14, 1945, 1.

20. "Celebrations Are Held Over Nation," *Anderson [IN] Daily Bulletin*, August 14, 1945, 9; "St. Louis Celebrates with Noise and Prayer," *St. Louis Star-Times*, August 14, 1945, 1.

21. "Celebrations," *New Orleans [LA] States*, August 14, 1945, 2.

22. "L.A. Calm at News on War," *Oakland [CA] Post-Enquirer*, August 14, 1945, 3.

23. "Early Reports Touch Off 'Peace' Festivities from Coast to Coast and in Pacific Isles," *Oakland [CA] Tribune*, August 14, 1945, 2.

24. "Celebrating Crowds Jam Streets Here," *Oakland [CA] Tribune*, August 14, 1945, 1.

## Chapter 4

1. Snyder, "Canteens, Centers Celebrate as Downtown S.F. Explodes in Jubilee," *San Francisco [CA] Examiner*, August 15, 1945, 18.

2. "Truman Statement and Capitulation Notes," *Evening Star*, Washington, DC, August 15, 1945, A-2; Harry S Truman Library and Museum, "The President's News Conference," https://www.trumanlibrary.gov/library/public-papers/100/presidents-news-conference.

3. "Coast to Coast Whoopee Meets A. M. Peace News," *The Fresno [CA] Bee*, August 14, 1945, 1; Siegel, "All Things Considered: Recalling an American Riot of V.J. Day," https://www.npr.org/2005/08/15/4800963/recalling-an-american-riot-on-v-j-day.

4. "Coast to Coast Whoopee Meets A. M. Peace News," *The Fresno [CA] Bee*, August 14, 1945, 1; Market Street Railway Museum, "Jubilation—and riots—on Market Street 75 years ago," https://www.streetcar.org/jubilation-and-riots-on-market-street-75-years-ago/.

5. Heagerty statement, *Keep the Spirit of '45 Alive*, http://spiritof45.org/storiesc0.aspx; "A Letter to Buddy," *San Francisco [CA] Examiner*, August 11, 1995, 18; "Chican Describes Celebration in San Francisco," *The Chico [CA] Enterprise*, August 15, 1945, 3; Wingo, "It made the bricks vibrate," *San Francisco [CA] Examiner*, August 11, 1995, 18; Georgeson, "The Rape of San Francisco," *Real War*, 36.

6. Bodenweck, "City Went Crazy When WWII Ended," *San Francisco [CA] Examiner*, August 13, 1985, 9; Hyman, "Wild Night Greets End of War in S.F.," *San Francisco [CA] Examiner*, August 15, 1945, 1: "Hangover in S.F.," *Contra Costa Gazette*, August 15, 1945, 8; "Victory Day Noisy Here," *San Mateo [CA] Times*, August 15, 1945, 10.

7. "Victory Day Noisy Here," *San Mateo [CA] Times*, August 15, 1945, 10.

## Chapter Notes

It was reported that the sailor said "Birmington, Washington" but there is no such place in the state of Washington. The author has decided that the sailor actually responded, "Burlington, Washington."

8. Snyder, "Canteens, Centers Celebrate as Downtown S.F. Explodes in Jubilee," *San Francisco* [CA] *Examiner*, August 15, 1945, 18.

9. "Victory Baby," *San Francisco* [CA] *Examiner*, August 16, 1945, 5.

10. "Chican Describes Celebration in San Francisco," *The Chico* [CA] *Enterprise*, August 15, 1945, 3; Bodenweck, "City Went Crazy When WWII Ended," *San Francisco* [CA] *Examiner*, August 13, 1985, 9.

11. Snyder, "Canteens, Centers Celebrate as Downtown S.F. Explodes in Jubilee," *San Francisco* [CA] *Examiner*, August 15, 1945, 18.

12. Hartsell, "One big enthusiastic block party," *San Francisco* [CA] *Examiner*, August 11, 1995, 18.

13. "A Letter to Buddy," *San Francisco* [CA] *Examiner*, August 11, 1995, 18.

14. Simmons, *Keep the Spirit of '45 Alive*, http://spiritof45.org/storiesS0.aspx; "Chican Describes Celebration in San Francisco," *The Chico* [CA] *Enterprise*, August 15, 1945, 3.

15. Anderson (née Boyd) statement, *Keep the Spirit of '45 Alive*, http://spiritof45.org/storiesa0.aspx.

16. Navy—Together We Served, Ficalora, Anthony, "Service Reflections of a Navy Veteran," https://navy.togetherweserved.com/usn/voices/2017/151/Ficalora_voices.html; Bodenweck, "City Went Crazy When WWII Ended," *San Francisco* [CA] *Examiner*, August 13, 1985, 9; "Remembering V-J Day," *Mason Valley News*, Mason, NV, August 11, 1995, 16.

17. Hyman, "Wild Night Greets End of War in S.F.," *San Francisco* [CA] *Examiner*, August 15, 1945, 1.

18. Bodenweck, "City Went Crazy When WWII Ended," *San Francisco* [CA] *Examiner*, August 13, 1985, 9.

19. Rule statement, *Keep the Spirit of '45 Alive*, http://spiritof45.org/storiesr0.aspx.

20. Rule statement, *Keep the Spirit of '45 Alive*, http://spiritof45.org/storiesr0.aspx.

21. "3 Dead in S.F. Celebration," *San Mateo* [CA] *Times*, August 15, 1945, 10; Snyder, "Canteens, Centers Celebrate as Downtown S.F. Explodes in Jubilee," *San Francisco* [CA] *Examiner*, August 15, 1945, 18; "Hangover in S.F.," *Contra Costa Gazette*, Martinez, CA, August 15, 1945, 8; "San Francisco Stages Second Celebration; Crowds, Good Natured at First, Grow Rough," *San Francisco* [CA] *Examiner*, August 15, 1945, 4.

22. Snyder, "Canteens, Centers Celebrate as Downtown S.F. Explodes in Jubilee," *San Francisco* [CA] *Examiner*, August 15, 1945, 18; Hyman, "Wild Night Greets End of War in S.F.," *San Francisco* [CA] *Examiner*, August 15, 1945, C; Greene, "War Was Ended in Fun, Tragedy," *Greensboro* [NC] *Daily News*, August 14, 1965, 9.

23. Hyman, "Wild Night Greets End of War in S.F.," *San Francisco* [CA] *Examiner*, August 15, 1945, C.

24. Hyman, "Wild Night Greets End of War in S.F.," *San Francisco* [CA] *Examiner*, August 15, 1945, C; Caredio statement, *Keep the Spirit of '45 Alive*, http://spiritof45.org/storiesc0.aspx.

25. Hyman, "Wild Night Greets End of War in S.F.," *San Francisco* [CA] *Examiner*, August 15, 1945, C; "San Francisco Like a City Hit by Cyclone," *Palo Alto* [CA] *Times*, August 15, 1945, 2.

## Chapter 5

1. Wingo, "It made the bricks vibrate," *San Francisco* [CA] *Examiner*, August 11, 1995, 18; Greene, "War Was Ended in Fun, Tragedy," *Greensboro* [NC] *Daily News*, 9; Snyder, "Canteens, Centers Celebrate as Downtown S.F. Explodes in Jubilee," *San Francisco* [CA] *Examiner*, August 15, 1945, 18; "Hangover in S.F.," *Contra Costa Gazette*, Martinez, CA, August 15, 1945, 8.

2. Hyman, "Wild Night Greets End of War in S.F.," *San Francisco* [CA] *Examiner*, August 15, 1945, C; "Hangover in S.F.," *Contra Costa Gazette*, Martinez, CA, August 15, 1945, 8; "Millions of Firecrackers," *Buffalo* [NY] *Evening News*, August 15, 1945, 1.

3. "Throngs Give Peace Thanks," *San Francisco* [CA] *Examiner*, August 16, 1945, 5; "Victory Day Celebration on Noisy Side Here," *San Matea* [CA] *Times*, August 15, 1945, 1.

## Chapter Notes

4. Hyman, "Wild Night Greets End of War in S.F.," *San Francisco* [CA] *Examiner*, August 15, 1945, C.

5. Heagerty statement, *Keep the Spirit of '45 Alive*, http://spiritof45.org/storiesc0.aspx.

6. Wwdrkid, "VJ Day San Francisco Market Street, 1945," https://www.trainorders.com/discussion/read.php?11,1417808.

7. Snyder, "Canteens, Centers Celebrate as Downtown S.F. Explodes in Jubilee," *San Francisco* [CA] *Examiner*, August 15, 1945, 18; "Chican Describes Celebration in San Francisco," *The Chico* [CA] *Enterprise*, August 15, 1945, 3; Hyman, "Wild Night Greets End of War in S.F.," *San Francisco* [CA] *Examiner*, August 15, 1945, C.

8. Bacque, "It took 2 days to age 2 years," *Richmond* [VA] *Times-Dispatch*, September 3, 1995, 1.

9. Headlines in History, "August 15, 1945: The 75th Anniversary of V-J Day," *Fishwrap: The Official Blog of Newspapers*, https://blog.newspapers.com/august-15-1945-the-75th-anniversary-of-v-j-day/; Sullivan, "The Low Down," *San Francsico* [CA] *Examiner*, August 17, 1945, 22; Snyder, "Canteens, Centers Celebrate as Downtown S.F. Explodes in Jubilee," *San Francisco* [CA] *Examiner*, August 15, 1945, 18.

10. Heagerty statement, *Keep the Spirit of '45 Alive*, http://spiritof45.org/storiesc0.aspx; "Jubilee Soars in East Bay," *San Francisco* [CA] *Examiner*, August 15, 1945, 4.

11. Georgeson, "The Rape of San Francisco," *Real War*, 36; Greene, "War Was Ended in Fun, Tragedy," *Greensboro* [NC] *Daily News*, August 14, 1965, 9.

12. "Take Me Out—When the Family Car was a Streetcar in San Francisco," https://www.youtube.com/watch?v=TVIqQ0K-haI&t=5s.

13. "Soldiers, Sailors Civilians Burn Bond Booths," *The Ledger-Star*, Norfolk, VA, August 14, 1945, 8; "Stalled," *San Francisco* [CA] *Examiner*, August 15, 1945, 4; "Riot Jurors Ask Officials' Views," *Oakland* [CA] *Tribune*, August 22, 1945, 4.

14. Hyman, "Wild Night Greets End of War in S.F.," *San Francisco* [CA] *Examiner*, August 15, 1945, C; Wingo, "It made the bricks vibrate," *San Francisco* [CA] *Examiner*, August 11, 1995, 18.

15. Hartsell, "One big enthusiastic block party," *San Francisco* [CA] *Examiner*, August 11, 1995, 18.

16. LeBaron, "At Home, VJ Day Meant an End to the Waiting," *The Press Democrat*, Santa Rosa, CA, August 13, 1995, A2.

17. "A Letter to Buddy," *San Francisco* [CA] *Examiner*, August 11, 1995, 18.

18. Georgeson, "The Rape of San Francisco," *Real War*, 36.

19. Georgeson, "The Rape of San Francisco," *Real War*, 36.

20. Georgeson, "The Rape of San Francisco," *Real War*, 36.

21. Georgeson, "The Rape of San Francisco," *Real War*, 36.

22. Greene, "War Was Ended in Fun, Tragedy," *Greensboro* [NC] *Daily News*, August 14, 1965, 9; Georgeson, "The Rape of San Francisco," *Real War*, 36.

23. "Riot Jurors Ask Officials' Views," *Oakland* [CA] *Tribune*, August 22, 1945, 4; "Celebration Sequel," *San Francisco* [CA] *Examiner*, August 17, 1945, 16.

24. Bodenweck, "City Went Crazy When WWII Ended," *San Francisco* [CA] *Examiner*, August 13, 1985, 9.

25. Bodenweck, "City Went Crazy When WWII Ended," *San Francisco* [CA] *Examiner*, August 13, 1985, 9.

26. Bodenweck, "City Went Crazy When WWII Ended," *San Francisco* [CA] *Examiner*, August 13, 1985, 9.

27. Georgeson, "The Rape of San Francisco," *Real War*, 36.

28. Hyman, "Wild Night Greets End of War in S.F.," *San Francisco* [CA] *Examiner*, August 15, 1945, C; "3 Dead in S.F. Celebration," *San Mateo* [CA] *Times*, August 15, 1945, 1; Georgeson, "The Rape of San Francisco," *Real War*, 37.

29. Georgeson, "The Rape of San Francisco," *Real War*, 37.

## Chapter 6

1. Hyman, "Wild Night Greets End of War in S.F.," *San Francisco* [CA] *Examiner*, August 15, 1945, C; Snyder, "Canteens, Centers Celebrate as Downtown S.F. Explodes in Jubilee," *San Francisco* [CA] *Examiner*, August 15, 1945, 18.

2. "V-J Day Accidents Cost Lives of 7: Hundreds Injured in Bay Area Cities

## Chapter Notes

in Celebration," *Oakland* [CA] *Tribune*, August 15, 1945, 9.

3. Snyder, "Canteens, Centers Celebrate as Downtown S.F. Explodes in Jubilee," *San Francisco* [CA] *Examiner*, August 15, 1945, 18.

4. Snyder, "Canteens, Centers Celebrate as Downtown S.F. Explodes in Jubilee," *San Francisco* [CA] *Examiner*, August 15, 1945, 18; Bodenweck, "City Went Crazy When WWII Ended," *San Francisco* [CA] *Examiner*, August 13, 1985, 9.

5. Bodenweck, "City Went Crazy When WWII Ended," *San Francisco* [CA] *Examiner*, August 13, 1985, 9.

6. "Remembering V-J Day," *Mason Valley News*, Mason, NV, August 11, 1995, 16.

7. "V-J Strip Tease By S.F. Red Head," *San Mateo* [CA] *Times*, August 15, 1945, 2.

8. Clifford, "War's End Euphoria in San Francisco Turned to Riots," https://apnews.com/article/f53c9af440fb88498fe5d7d5ff3d7d59; Georgeson, "The Rape of San Francisco," *Real War*, 36.

9. "A Letter to Buddy," *San Francisco* [CA] *Examiner*, August 11, 1995, 18.

10. "Brown Balks Move to Quash Probe of Riot," *San Francisco* [CA] *Examiner*, August 23, 1945, 3; Ancestry.com, San Francisco Area Funeral Homes Records, Thompson, William James, https://www.ancestry.com/discoveryui-content/view/231449:2118?tid=&pid=&queryId=-fdf80550-2933-4563-9ace-4f2ca697eea1&_phsrc=sfc139&_phstart=successSource; Findagrave.com, Thompson, William James, William James "Sonny" Thompson (1924-1945)—Find a Grave Memorial.

11. "V-J Day Accidents Cost Lives of 7: Hundreds Injured in Bay Area Cities in Celebration," *Oakland* [CA] *Tribune*, August 15, 1945, p. 15; Ancestry.com, Prim, James W., https://www.ancestry.com/family-tree/person/tree/10671454/person/202549547981/facts?_phsrc=rBa5&_phstart=successSource; Findagrave.com, Prim, James W., https://www.findagrave.com/62566939/james-w-prim.

12. "V-J Day Accidents Cost Lives of 7: Hundreds Injured in Bay Area Cities in Celebration," *Oakland* [CA] *Tribune*, August 15, 1945, 15; "Celebration—Five Dead, 624 Injured," *San Francisco* [CA] *Examiner*, August 16, 1945, 11; "3 Killed, 468 injured in 5-Hour Row," *Oakland* [CA] *Tribune*, August 16, 1945, 2; "Liquor Store Ban Asked as Army, Navy, City Act in 'Peace' Riots," *San Francisco* [CA] *Examiner*, August 17, 1945, 12.

13. "Celebration—Five Dead, 624 Injured," *San Francisco* [CA] *Examiner*, August 16, 1945, 11; "V-J Day Accidents Cost of 7; Hundreds Injured in Bay Area Cities in Celebration," *Oakland* [CA] *Tribune*, August 15, 1945, 15.

14. "V-J Day Accidents Cost Lives of 7: Hundreds Injured in Bay Area Cities in Celebration," *Oakland* [CA] *Tribune*, August 15, 1945, 15; Morris, Estelle McArdle, https://www.findagrave.com/memorial/108021620/estelle-mcardle-morris.

15. "Lift Navy Ban on S.F. After Victory Riots," *Lodi* [CA] *News-Sentinel*, August 17, 1945, 6; "Liquor Store Ban Asked as Army, Navy, City Act in 'Peace' Riots," *San Francisco* [CA] *Examiner*, August 17, 1945, 12; "3 Killed, 468 Injured in 5-Hour Row," *Oakland* [CA] *Tribune*, August 16, 1945, 2; Findagrave.com, Gyorgy, Joseph Samuel, https://www.findagrave.com/memorial/106519640/joseph-samuel-gyorgy; Ancestry.com, Gyorgy, Joseph Samuel, https://www.ancestry.com/family-tree/person/tree/59671280/person/30255000854/facts.

16. Hyman, "San Francisco Stages Second Celebration; Crowds, Good Natured at First, Grow Rough," *San Francisco* [CA] *Examiner*, August 15, 1945, C; "Victory Day Noisy Here," *San Mateo* [CA] *Times*, August 15, 1945, 10.

17. Hyman, "San Francisco Stages Second Celebration; Crowds, Good Natured at First, Grow Rough," *San Francisco* [CA] *Examiner*, August 15, 1945, C; "V-J Day Accidents Cost Lives of 7; Hundreds Injured in Bay Area Cities in Celebrations," *Oakland* [CA] *Tribune*, August 15, 1945, 15.

18. Hyman, "San Francisco Stages Second Celebration; Crowds, Good Natured at First, Grow Rough," *San Francisco* [CA] *Examiner*, August 15, 1945, C; Georgeson, "The Rape of San Francisco," *Real War*, 37.

19. "Celebration—Five Dead, 624 Injured," *San Francisco* [CA] *Examiner*, August 16, 1945, 11; Ancestry.com, Krystal, Jack, https://www.ancestry.com/family-tree/person/tree/10456415/person/421821323/

## Chapter Notes

facts; "V-J Day Accidents Cost lives of 7: Hundreds Injured in Bay Area Cities in Celebration," *Oakland* [CA] *Tribune*, August 15, 1945, 15; Findagrave.com, Krystal, Jack, https://www.findagrave.com/memorial/209684076/jack-john-krystal.

20. "A Letter to Buddy," *San Francisco* [CA] *Examiner*, August 11, 1995, 18; Georgeson, "The Rape of San Francisco," *Real War*, 36.

21. Greene, "War Was Ended in Fun, Tragedy," *Greensboro* [NC] *Daily News*, August 14, 1965, 9; "S.F. Hails Victory!" *San Francisco* [CA] *Examiner*, August 15, 1945, 3.

22. Georgeson, "The Rape of San Francisco," *Real War*, 36.

23. "S.F. Rioters Smash Windows for Loot," *San Francisco* [CA] *Examiner*, August 16, 1945, 1; Georgeson, "The Rape of San Francisco," *Real War*, 37.

## Chapter 7

1. "Hangover in S.F.," *Contra Costa Gazette*, Martinez, CA, August 15, 1945, 8.
2. Georgeson, "The Rape of San Francisco," *Real War*, 37.
3. "A Letter to Buddy," *San Francisco* [CA] *Examiner*, August 11, 1995, 18.
4. "Stanford Daily Editorials—Features," *Stanford* [CA] *Daily*, August 17, 1945, 2.
5. Hyman, "San Francisco Stages Second Celebration; Crowds, Good Natured at First, Grow Rough," *San Francisco* [CA] *Examiner*, August 15, 1945, C; "Pacific Victory Holidays Proclaimed," *San Francisco* [CA] *Examiner*, August 15, 1945, 9.
6. "Chican Describes Celebration in San Francisco," *The Chico* [CA] *Enterprise*, August 15, 1945, 3; "V-J Day Accidents Cost Lives of 7," *Oakland* [CA] *Tribune*, August 15, 1945, 15; "Highway Officer Injured on Bridge," *San Francisco* [CA] *Examiner*, August 16, 1945, 5.
7. "V-J Day Accidents Cost Lives of 7," *Oakland* [CA] *Tribune*, August 15, 1945, 15.
8. Georgeson, "The Rape of San Francisco," *Real War*, 37.
9. Georgeson, "The Rape of San Francisco," *Real War*, 37.
10. Georgeson, "The Rape of San Francisco," *Real War*, 37
11. "Six Women Raped During S.F. Riot," *Bakersfield* [CA] *Californian*, August 22, 1945, 2; Clifford, "War's End Euphoria in San Francisco Turned to Riots," August 13, 1995, https://apnews.com/article/f53c9af440fb88498fe5d7d5ff3d7d59.
12. Georgeson, "The Rape of San Francisco," *Real War*, 37.
13. "Grand Jury Riot Probe Commends Authorities," *San Francisco* [CA] *Examiner*, August 30, 1945, 28.
14. Hackett, "San Francisco Celebration Turns Into Riot; State of Emergency Proclaimed," *Appeal Democrat*, Marysville, CA, August 16, 1945, 2; "Hangover in S.F.," *Contra Costa Gazette*, Martinez, CA, August 15, 1945, 8.
15. Clifford, "War's End Euphoria in San Francisco Turned to Riots," August 13, 1995, https://apnews.com/article/f53c9af440fb88498fe5d7d5ff3d7d59; Hackett, "Riot Squads of 3200 in S.F. Quell Mobs as Celebration becomes 'Orgy,'" *Santa Barbara* [CA] *News-Press*, August 16, 1945, 1; "Fete Turns Into Riot of Looters," *San Francisco* [CA] *Examiner*, August 16, 1945, 7.
16. Greene, "War Was Ended in Fun, Tragedy," *Greensboro* [NC] *Daily News*, August 14, 1965, 9.
17. "V-J Day Accidents Cost Lives of 7," *Oakland* [CA] *Tribune*, August 15, 1945, 15.
18. "V-J Day Accidents Cost Lives of 7," *Oakland* [CA] *Tribune*, August 15, 1945, 15; "Fete Turns Into Riot of Looters," *San Francisco* [CA] *Examiner*, August 16, 1945, 7.
19. "Fete Turns Into Riot of Looters," *San Francisco* [CA] *Examiner*, August 16, 1945, 7.
20. "Hangover in S.F.," *Contra Costa Gazette*, Martinez, CA, August 15, 1945, 8.

## Chapter 8

1. "Holiday," *Contra Costa Gazette*, Martinez, CA, August 15, 1945, 8; "Fete Turns into Riot of Looters," *San Francisco* [CA] *Examiner*, August 16, 1945, 7.
2. The Pacific War Online Encyclopedia, "Wright, Carleton Herbert," http://pwencycl.kgbudge.com/W/r/Wright_Carleton_H.htm; *Military Times*, "Hall of Valor:

## Chapter Notes

Carleton Herbert Wright," https://valor.militarytimes.com/recipient/recipient-21645/.

3. Hyman, "San Francisco Stages Second Celebration; Crowds, Good Natured at First, Grow Rough," *San Francisco* [CA] *Examiner*, August 15, 1945, C; "Victory Day Noisy Here," *San Mateo* [CA] *Times*, August 15, 1945, 10; "Liquor Store Ban Asked as Army Navy, City Act in 'Peace' Riots," *San Francisco* [CA] *Examiner*, August 17, 1945, 12.

4. "Three-Day Bay City Peace Riot Quelled," *Bakersfield* [CA] *Californian*, August 16, 1945, 2.

5. "Throngs Give Peace Thanks," *San Francisco* [CA] *Examiner*, August 16, 1945, 5.

6. "Fete Turns into Riot of Looters," *San Francisco* [CA] *Examiner*, August 16, 1945, 7.

7. "Filling Stations Again Hear Cry of 'Fill 'Er Up,'" *San Mateo* [CA] *Times*, August 15, 1945, 1; "Motorists Jam Gas Stations," *San Francisco* [CA] *Examiner*, August 16, 1945, 8.

8. "Victory Day Celebration on Noisy Side Here," *San Mateo* [CA] *Times*, August 15, 1945, 1; Fix, "The History of Gas Rationing Stickers," *Car Coach Reports*, January 2, 2014, https://carcoachreports.com/gas-rationing-gas-ration-stickers/; Sundin, "Make It Do—Gasoline Rationing in World War II," https://www.sarahsundin.com/make-it-do-gasoline-rationing-in-world-war-ii-2/.

9. "'Fill 'er Up,' Cry Happy Motorists," *Telegram-Tribune*, San Luis Obispo, CA, August 16, 1945, 1; "Motorists Jam Gas Stations," *San Francisco* [CA] *Examiner*, August 16, 1945, 8; Anderson, "The Human Side of It: Postwar Pleasure Drive," *Oakland* [CA] *Post-Enquirer*, August 25, 1945, 11.

10. Youtube.com, "V-J Day: San Francisco 1945," https://www.youtube.com/watch?v=LjPB9hjfjbg.

11. "Fete Turns into Riot of Looters," *San Francisco* [CA] *Examiner*, August 16, 1945, 7.

12. Hackett, "Riot Squads of 3200 in S.F. Quell Mobs as Celebration becomes 'Orgy,'" *Santa Barbara* [CA] *News-Press*, August 16, 1945, 1; "A Letter to Buddy," *San Francisco* [CA] *Examiner*, August 11, 1995, 18.

## Chapter 9

1. "Police Quell 3-Day S.F. 'Peace' Riot," *Bakersfield* [CA] *Californian*, August 16, 1945, 1, 2; Georgeson, "The Rape of San Francisco," *Real War*, 37; "Just Vandalism," *Contra Costa Gazette*, Martinez, CA, August 16, 1945, 5.

2. "S.F. Quiets Down; Toll: 11 Dead, 648 Persons Hurt," *Redwood City* [CA] *Tribune*, August 17, 1945, 2.

3. Georgeson, "The Rape of San Francisco," *Real War*, 37.

4. "Just Vandalism," *Contra Costa Gazette*, Martinez, CA, August 16, 1945, 5; "Navy Cancels Leaves as Aftermath of S.F. Riot," *Oakland* [CA] *Tribune*, August 16, 1945, 2; "3 Killed, 468 injured in 5-Hour Row," *Oakland* [CA] *Tribune*, August 16, 1945, 1; "S.F. Rioters Smash Windows for Loot," *San Francisco* [CA] *Examiner*, August 16, 1945, 1; "Fete Turns Into Riot of Looters," *San Francisco* [CA] *Examiner*, August 16, 1945, 7.

5. Editorial Page, "Where Responsibility Lies," *San Francisco* [CA] *Examiner*, August 17, 1945, 18; "Just Vandalism," *Contra Costa Gazette*, Martinez, CA, August 16, 1945, 5.

6. "Just Vandalism," *Contra Costa Gazette*, Martinez, CA, August 16, 1945, 5; "S.F. Rioters Smash Windows for Loot," *San Francisco* [CA] *Examiner*, August 16, 1945, 1; "Riot Squads Halt Tumult of S.F. Mob," *The Press Democrat*, Santa Rosa, CA, August 16, 1945, 3; "Dresses Torn Off Women," *The Press Democrat*, Santa Rosa, CA, August 16, 1945, 3.

7. "San Francisco Recalls War's-end Victory Riots," *The Belleville* [IL] *News Democrat*, August 14, 1995, 2; "Navy Cancels Leaves as Aftermath of S.F. Riot," *Oakland* [CA] *Tribune*, August 16, 1945, 2.

8. "3 Killed, 468 injured in 5-Hour Row," *Oakland* [CA] *Tribune*, August 16, 1945, 2; Hackett, "San Francisco Celebration Turns Into Riot; State of Emergency Proclaimed," *Appeal Democrat*, Marysville, CA, August 16, 1945, 2.

9. "3 Killed, 468 injured in 5-Hour Row," *Oakland* [CA] *Tribune*, August 16, 1945, 2; Hackett, "Riot Squads of 3200 in S.F. Quell Mobs as Celebration becomes 'Orgy,'" *Santa Barbara* [CA] *News-Press*, August 16, 1945, 1; "Just Vandalism," *Contra Costa*

## Chapter Notes

*Gazette*, Martinez, CA, August 16, 1945, 5; "Peace Crowds Riot in S.F.," *Redding* [CA] *Record Searchlight*, August 16, 1945, 1.

10. "3 Killed, 468 Injured in 5-Hour Row," *Oakland* [CA] *Tribune*, August 16, 1945, 2; "Four More Die in Celebration," *San Francisco* [CA] *Examiner*, August 16, 1945, 9.

11. "Four More Die in Celebration," *San Francisco* [CA] *Examiner*, August 16, 1945, 9.

12. "Liquor Store Ban Asked as RMY Navy, City Act in 'Peace' Riots," *San Francisco* [CA] *Examiner*, August 17, 1945, 12; "Two Rock Soldier Killed in Riot," *Petaluma* [CA] *Argus Courier*, August 17, 1945, 1; "Pvt. Wiliam Flaherty Killed in California," *Evening Herald*, Shenandoah, PA, August 18, 1945, 1; Ancestry.com—Flaherty, William E., https://www.ancestry.com/family-tree/person/tree/158246073/person/192076013720/facts?_phsrc=rBa23&_phstart=successSource; Findagrave.com, Flaherty, William, https://www.findagrave.com/memorial/25331200/william-flaherty.

13. "Lift Navy Ban on S.F. After Victory Riots," *Lodi* [CA] *News-Sentinel*, August 17, 1945, 6; "S.F. Guards Against More 'Celebrations,'" *Santa Barbara* [CA] *News-Press*, August 17, 1945, 1; Ancestry.com, Batchan, John Sutherland, San Francisco Area Funeral Home Records https://www.ancestry.com/search/collections/2118/records/340323?tid=&pid=&queryId=-abc33e22-4170-4541-89a3-80d18020 52b9&_phsrc=rBa31&_phstart=success Source; Georgeson, "The Rape of San Francisco," *Real War*, 37.

14. "Navy Cancels Leaves as Aftermath of S.F. Riot," *Oakland* [CA] *Tribune*, August 16, 1945, 2; "Fete Turns Into Riot of Looters," *San Francisco* [CA] *Examiner*, August 16, 1945, 7.

15. Hackett, "Riot Squads of 3200 in S.F. Quell Mobs as Celebration becomes 'Orgy,'" *Santa Barbara* [CA] *News-Press*, August 16, 1945, 1; "Navy Cancels Leaves as Aftermath of S.F. Riot," *Oakland* [CA] *Tribune*, August 16, 1945, 2; "Fete Turns Into Riot of Looters," *San Francisco* [CA] *Examiner*, August 16, 1945, 7.

16. "Police Quell Wild Rioting in Bay City," *The Modesto* [CA] *Bee and News-Herald*, August 16, 1945, 2; "Navy Cancels Leaves as Aftermath of S.F. Riot," *Oakland* [CA] *Tribune*, August 16, 1945, 2; Hackett, "Riot Squads of 3200 in S.F. Quell Mobs as Celebration becomes 'Orgy,'" *Santa Barbara* [CA] *News-Press*, August 16, 1945, 1; "Riot Squads Halt Tumult of S.F. Mob," *The Press Democrat*, Santa Rosa, CA, August 16, 1945, 3; "Dresses Torn Off Women," *The Press Democrat*, Santa Rosa, CA, August 16, 1945, 3.

17. "Police Quell Wild Rioting in Bay City," *The Modesto* [CA] *Bee and News-Herald*, August 16, 1945, 2; "Peace Crowds Riot in S.F.," *Redding* [CA] *Record Searchlight*, August 16, 1945, 1; "12 Dead as S.D. Riots End," *Herald-Examiner*, Los Angeles, CA, August 17, 1945, 2; "S.F. Quiets Down; Toll: 11 Dead, 648 Persons Hurt," *Redwood City* [CA] *Tribune*, August 17, 1945, 2.

18. "S.F. Rioters Smash Windows for Loot," *San Francisco* [CA] *Examiner*, August 16, 1945, 1, 7.

19. Hackett, "Riot Squads of 3200 in S.F. Quell Mobs as Celebration becomes 'Orgy,'" *Santa Barbara* [CA] *News-Press*, August 16, 1945, 1.

20. "Just Vandalism," *Contra Costa Gazette*, Martinez, CA, August 16, 1945, 5; "3 Killed, 468 Injured in 5-Hour Row," *Oakland* [CA] *Tribune*, August 16, 1945, 1; "Riot Squads Halt Tumult of S.F. Mob," *The Press Democrat*, Santa Rosa, CA, August 16, 1945, 1.

21. "Police Quell Wild Rioting in Bay City," *The Modesto* [CA] *Bee and News-Herald*, August 16, 1945, 2; "Navy Cancels Leaves as Aftermath of S.F. Riot," *Oakland* [CA] *Tribune*, August 16, 1945, 2; Georgeson, "The Rape of San Francisco," *Real War*, 37.

22. Hackett, "Riot Squads of 3200 in S.F. Quell Mobs as Celebration becomes 'Orgy,'" *Santa Barbara* [CA] *News-Press*, August 16, 1945, 1; "Riot Squads Halt Tumult of S.F. Mob," *The Press Democrat*, Santa Rosa, CA, August 16, 1945, 3; "Navy Cancels All Liberty in S.F. Celebration Riots," *The Fresno* [CA] *Bee*, August 16, 1945, 1.

23. "Rioting Celebrants in San Francisco," *Intelligencer Journal*, Lancaster, PA, August 16, 1945, 1.

## Chapter Notes

24. "Police Quell Wild Rioting in Bay City," *The Modesto [CA] Bee and News-Herald*, August 16, 1945, 2; "Navy Cancels Leaves as Aftermath of S.F. Riot," *Oakland [CA] Tribune*, August 16, 1945, 2.
25. "Navy Cancels Leaves as Aftermath of S.F. Riot," *Oakland [CA] Tribune*, August 16, 1945, 2.
26. "Police Quell Wild Rioting in Bay City," *The Modesto [CA] Bee and News-Herald*, August 16, 1945, 2; "Wild Night of Rioting in San Francisco," *Petaluma [CA] Argus Courier*, August 16, 1945, 1; "S.F. Rioters Smash Windows for Loot," *San Francisco [CA] Examiner*, August 16, 1945, 1.
27. "Riot Squads Halt Tumult of S.F. Mob," *The Press Democrat*, Santa Rosa, CA, August 16, 1945, 3; "Grand Jury Riot Probe Commends Authorities," *San Francisco [CA] Examiner*, August 30, 1945, 28.
28. "Navy Cancels Leaves as Aftermath of S.F. Riot," *Oakland [CA] Tribune*, August 16, 1945, 2.

## *Chapter 10*

1. Hackett, "Riot Squads of 3200 in S.F. Quell Mobs as Celebration becomes 'Orgy,'" *Santa Barbara [CA] News-Press*, August 16, 1945, 1.
2. "3 Killed, 468 Injured in 5-Hour Row," *Oakland [CA] Tribune*, August 16, 1945, 1, 2.
3. "Police Quell Wild Rioting in Bay City," *The Modesto [CA] Bee and News-Herald*, August 16, 1945, 2; Georgeson, "The Rape of San Francisco," *Real War*, 37; "3 Killed, 468 Injured in 5-Hour Row," *Oakland [CA] Tribune*, August 16, 1945, 1.
4. "A Letter to Buddy," *San Francisco [CA] Examiner*, August 11, 1995, 18.
5. Georgeson, "The Rape of San Francisco," *Real War*, 37.
6. "SF Celebration Turns Into Mild Rioting," *The Sacramento [CA] Union*, August 16, 1945, 2; "Wild Night of Rioting in San Francisco," *Petaluma [CA] Argos Courier*, August 16, 1945, 1; Georgeson, "The Rape of San Francisco," *Real War*, 37; Hartsell, "One big enthusiastic block party," *San Francisco [CA] Examiner*, August 11, 1995, 18; "A Letter to Buddy," *San Francisco [CA] Examiner*, August 11, 1995, 18; "City Attorney, District Attorney, Public Defender," *Report of the Grand Jury, San Francisco*, 12.
7. "Riot Jurors Ask Officials' Views," *Oakland [CA] Tribune*, August 22, 1945, 4; "A Letter to Buddy," *San Francisco [CA] Examiner*, August 11, 1995, 18.
8. "Police Quell Wild Rioting in Bay City," *The Modesto [CA] Bee and News-Herald*, August 16, 1945, 2.
9. "Navy Cancels Leaves as Aftermath of S.F. Riot," *Oakland [CA] Tribune*, August 16, 1945, 2; "Just Vandalism," *Contra Costa Gazette*, Martinez, CA, August 16, 1945, 5; Hackett, "Riot Squads of 3200 in S.F. Quell Mobs as Celebration becomes 'Orgy,'" *Santa Barbara [CA] News-Press*, August 16, 1945, 1; McDevitt, *The Naval History of Treasure Island*, 244.
10. "Liquor Store Ban Asked as Army, Navy, City Act in 'Peace' Riots," *San Francisco [CA] Examiner*, August 17, 1945, 12; Greene, "War Was Ended in Fun, Tragedy," *Greensboro [NC] Daily News*, August 14, 1965, 9; Findagrave.com, Tarkington, Bruce Keith, https://www.findagrave.com/memorial/3639765/3639765/bruce-keith-tarkington.
11. "S.F. Guards Against More 'Celebrations,'" *Santa Barbara [CA] News-Press*, August 17, 1945, 1; "Geiger Starts Attack Record," *San Francisco [CA] Examiner*, August 24, 1945, 3.
12. "Geiger Starts Attack Record," *San Francisco [CA] Examiner*, August 24, 1945, 3.
13. "Liquor Store Ban Asked as Army, Navy, City Act in 'Peace' Riots," *San Francisco [CA] Examiner*, August 17, 1945, 12.
14. "Fete Turns into Riot of Looters," *San Francisco [CA] Examiner*, August 16, 1945, 7; Hackett, "Riot Squads of 3200 in S.F. Quell Mobs as Celebration Becomes 'Orgy,'" *Santa Barbara [CA] News-Press*, August 16, 1945, 1.
15. "Lift Navy Ban on S.F. After Victory Riots," *Lodi [CA] News Sentinel*, August 17, 1945, 6; "3 Killed, 468 Injured in 5-Hour Row," *Oakland [CA] Tribune*, August 16, 1945, 1.
16. "3 Killed, 468 Injured in 5-Hour Row," *Oakland [CA] Tribune*, August 16, 1945, 1; "S.F. Quiets Down; Toll: 11 Dead,

648 Persons Hurt," *Redwood City* [CA] *Tribune*, August 17, 1945, 2; "Police Quell Wild Rioting in Bay City," *The Modesto* [CA] *Bee and News-Herald*, August 16, 1945, 2; "The Editor's Mail Box: The Riot," *San Francisco* [CA] *Examiner*, August 20, 1945, 10.

17. "Navy Orders All Sailors Off Streets," *The Press Democrat*, Santa Rosa, CA, August 17, 1945, 1; Georgeson, "The Rape of San Francisco," *Real War*, 37.

18. "Navy Cancels Leaves to Balk Outbreaks," *San Francisco* [CA] *Examiner*, August 17, 1945, 1.

19. "Lift Navy Ban on S.F. After Victory Riots," *Lodi* [CA] *News Sentinel*, August 17, 1945, 6; "Navy Cancels Leaves to Balk Outbreaks," *San Francisco* [CA] *Examiner*, August 17, 1945, 1.

20. "Lift Navy Ban on S.F. After Victory Riots," *Lodi* [CA] *News Sentinel*, August 17, 1945, 6; "S.F. Quiets Down; Toll: 11 Dead, 648 Persons Hurt," *Redwood City* [CA] *Tribune*, August 17, 1945, 2; "Liquor Store Ban Asked as Army, Navy, City Act in 'Peace' Riots," *San Francisco* [CA] *Examiner*, August 17, 1945, 12.

21. "Lift Navy Ban on S.F. After Victory Riots," *Lodi* [CA] *News Sentinel*, August 17, 1945, 6; "11 Die During Bay City Orgy; Women Raped," *Telegram-Tribune*, San Luis Obispo, CA, August 17, 1945, 5.

## Chapter 11

1. "Navy Cancels Leaves to Balk Outbreaks," *San Francsico* [CA] *Examiner*, August 17, 1945, 1; "11 Die During Bay City Orgy; Women Raped," *Telegram-Tribune*, San Luis Obispo, CA, August 17, 1945, 5.

2. SF.gov, "About the Civil Grand Jury," https://www.sf.gov/departments-civil-grand-jury-about.

3. National Governors Association, "California Gov. Edmund Gerald Brown," https://www.nga.org/governor/edmund-gerald-brown/.

4. "S.F. Quiets Down; Toll: 11 Dead, 648 Persons Hurt," *Redwood City* [CA] *Tribune*, August 17, 1945, 2; "Liquor Store Ban Asked as Army, Navy, City Act in 'Peace' Riots," *San Francisco* [CA] *Examiner*, August 17, 1945, 12; "Jurors to Get S.F. Riot Facts," *Oakland* [CA] *Tribune*, August 18, 1945, 3; "San Francisco Riots Cost Eleven Lives," *Oxnard* [CA] *Press-Courier*, August 18, 1945, 1; Editorial Page, "Where Responsibility Lies," *San Francisco* [CA] *Examiner*, August 17, 1945, 18.

5. Editorial Page, "Where Responsibility Lies," *San Francisco* [CA] *Examiner*, August 17, 1945, 18.; Anderson, "The Human Side of It: Drunken Sailors," *Oakland Post-Enquirer*, August 21, 1945, 20.

6. "Disgraceful Orgy," *The Sacramento* [CA] *Bee*, August 17, 1945, 20.

7. "Navy Cancels Leaves to Balk Outbreaks," *San Francisco* [CA] *Examiner*, August 17, 1945, 1, 12.

8. "Liquor Store Ban Asked as Army, Navy, City Act in 'Peace' Riots," *San Francisco* [CA] *Examiner*, August 17, 1945, 12.

9. "S.F. Rum Row Ired," *Contra Costa Gazette*, Martinez, CA, August 20, 1945, 3.

10. "S.F. Rum Row Ired," *Contra Costa Gazette*, Martinez, CA, August 20, 1945, 3.

11. "S.F. Rum Row Ired," *Contra Costa Gazette*, Martinez, CA, August 20, 1945, 3.

12. "Army Restrictions Are Removed in San Francisco," *The Modesto* [CA] *Bee and News-Herald*, August 18, 1945, 20; "Jury to Probe Peace Riot," *San Francisco* [CA] *Examiner*, August 20, 1945, 13.

13. "S.F. Quiets Down; Toll: 11 Dead, 648 Persons Hurt," *Redwood City* [CA] *Tribune*, August 17, 1945, 2; "Liquor Store Ban Asked as Army, Navy, City Act in 'Peace' Riots," *San Francisco* [CA] *Examiner*, August 17, 1945, 12; "Jurors to Get S.F. Riot Facts," *Oakland* [CA] *Tribune*, August 18, 1945, 3; "San Francisco Riots Cost Eleven Lives," *Oxnard* [CA] *Press-Courier*, August 18, 1945, 1; Editorial Page, "Where Responsibility Lies," *San Francisco* [CA] *Examiner*, August 17, 1945, 18.

14. "Army Restrictions Are Removed in San Francisco," *The Modesto* [CA] *Bee and News-Herald*, August 18, 1945, 20.

15. "Army Restrictions Are Removed in San Francisco," *The Modesto* [CA] *Bee and News-Herald*, August 18, 1945, 20; "Jurors to Get S.F. Riot Facts," *Oakland* [CA] *Tribune*, August 18, 1945, 3; "Grand Jury Quiz Seen of S.F.'s Victory Riots," *San Mateo* [CA] *Times*, August 18, 1945, 3; "S.F. Police Mobilize to Balk V-J Riots," *San Francisco* [CA] *Examiner*, September 1, 1945, 1.

## Chapter Notes

16. "The Editor's Mail Box: Lost to Our City," *San Francisco* [CA] *Examiner*, August 22, 1945, 10.

17. "Army Restrictions Are Removed in San Francisco," *The Modesto* [CA] *Bee and News-Herald*, August 18, 1945, 20; "Jurors to Get S.F. Riot Facts," *Oakland* [CA] *Tribune*, August 18, 1945, 3; "Navy Regrets Rioting in S.F.," *San Francisco* [CA] *Examiner*, August 19, 1945, 2.

18. "The Editor's Mail Box: Navy Men Shocked," *San Francisco* [CA] *Examiner*, September 4, 1945, 10.

19. "Letters to the Editor from Post-Enquirer Readers: An Apology," *Oakland* [CA] *Post-Enquirer*, August 21, 1945, 20.

20. "Letters to the Editor from Post-Enquirer Readers: Clowning Commandos," *Oakland* [CA] *Post-Enquirer*, August 24, 1945, 22.

21. "The Editor's Mail Box: Kick Back," *San Francisco* [CA] *Examiner*, August 29, 1945, 16.

22. "The Editor's Mail Box: Placing the Blame," *San Francisco* [CA] *Examiner*, September 5, 1945, 16.

## Chapter 12

1. "S.F. Grand Jury to Probe Riots," *Long Beach* [CA] *Independent*, August 20, 1945, 16; "Grand Jury to Open Riot Probe Tomorrow," *San Francisco* [CA] *Examiner*, August 20, 1945, 1.

2. "S.F. Grand Jury to Probe Riots," *Long Beach* [CA] *Independent*, August 20, 1945, 16.

3. "Admiral May Be Asked to Explain Bay Peace Riots," *Riverside* [CA] *Enterprise*, August 20, 1945, 2, Courtesy The Press-Enterprise/SCNG.

4. "S.F. Rum Stores in Row," *Oakland* [CA] *Post-Enquirer*, August 20, 1945, 4; "Admiral May Be Asked to Explain Bay Peace Riots," *Riverside* [CA] *Enterprise*, August 20, 1945, 2, Courtesy The Press-Enterprise/SCNG.

5. "The Editor's Mail Box: Where to Go," *San Francisco* [CA] *Examiner*, August 20, 1945, 10; "Grand Jury to Sift S.F. Peace Riot," *Oakland* [CA] *Tribune*, August 20, 1945, 13.

6. "The Forum," *Oakland* [CA] *Tribune*, August 21, 1945, 28.

7. Anderson, "The Human Side of It: Drunken Sailors," *Oakland* [CA] *Post-Enquirer*, August 21, 1945, 20.

8. "The Editor's Mail Box: The Riot," *San Francisco* [CA] *Examiner*, August 20, 1945, 10.

9. "The Forum," *Oakland* [CA] *Tribune*, August 21, 1945, 28.

10. "Jury to Probe Peace Riot," *San Francisco* [CA] *Examiner*, August 20, 1945, 13.

11. "Jury to Probe Peace Riot," *San Francisco* [CA] *Examiner*, August 20, 1945, 13.

12. "Grand Jury to Sift S.F. Peace Riots," *Oakland* [CA] *Tribune*, August 20, 1945, 13; "S.F. Rum Stores in Row," *Oakland* [CA] *Post-Enquirer*, August 20, 1945, 4; "Jury to Probe Peace Riot," *San Francisco* [CA] *Examiner*, August 20, 1945, 13; "Liquor Dealers Hit S.F. Curb," *The Tribune-Sun*, San Diego, CA, August 20, 1945, 3.

13. "S.F. Return to Norman Schedules," *Oakland* [CA] *Tribune*, August 21, 1945, 7; "'Riot' Liquor Ban Ends; Quiz Opens Tonight," *San Francisco* [CA] *Examiner*, August 21, 1945, 1; "Package Liquor Stores Hit Two Hour Sale Rule," *San Francisco* [CA] *Examiner*, August 21, 1945, 5; "Liquor Stores in S.F. Return to Normal Schedules," *Oakland* [CA] *Tribune*, August 21, 1945, 7.

14. "Package Liquor Stores Hit Two Hour Sale Rule," *San Francisco* [CA] *Examiner*, August 21, 1945, 5.

## Chapter 13

1. "Jury Will Probe Riots," *Hanford* [CA] *Sentinel*, August 21, 1945, 3.

2. "Liquor Stores in S.F. Return to Normal Schedules," *Oakland* [CA] *Tribune*, August 21, 1945, 7; "Package Liquor Stores Hit Two Hour Sale Rule," *San Francisco* [CA] *Examiner*, August 21, 1945, 5.

3. "Brown Balks Move to Quash Probe of Riot," *San Francisco* [CA] *Examiner*, August 23, 1945, 3; Findagrave.com, Thompson, William James, https://www.findagrave.com/memorial/65282517/william-james-thompson; Ancestry.com—Thompson, William James, https://www.ancestry.com/family-tree/person/tree/65624967/person/44378696208/facts?_phsrc=KiH25&_phstart=successSource.

## Chapter Notes

4. "Riot Jurors Ask Officials' Views," *Oakland* [CA] *Tribune*, August 22, 1945, 4.
5. "Riot Jurors Ask Officials' Views," *Oakland* [CA] *Tribune*, August 22, 1945, 4.
6. "Six Women Raped During S.F. Riot," *Bakersfield* [CA] *Californian*, August 22, 1945, 2; "1059 Injured in S. F. Peace Day Riots," *Petaluma* [CA] *Argus Courier*, August 22, 1945, 1.
7. "Six Women Raped During S.F. Riot," *Bakersfield* [CA] *Californian*, August 22, 1945, 2; "Six Women Raped During Riots in San Francisco," *Corona* [CA] *Daily Independent*, August 22, 1945, 1; "1059 Injured in S. F. Peace Day Riots," *Petaluma* [CA] *Argus Courier*, August 22, 1945, 1.
8. "Riot Jurors Ask Officials' Views," *Oakland* [CA] *Tribune*, August 22, 1945, 4; "Bay City Peace Riot Hurt 1,059," *Medford* [OR] *Mail Tribune*, August 22, 1945, 1.
9. "S.F. Junior Chamber Seeks Halt on Probe," *Lodi* [CA] *News Sentinel*, August 23, 1945, 3; "Prosecutor Will Not Drop Probe of S.F. Rioting," *The Modesto* [CA] *Bee and News-Herald*, August 23, 1945, 16; "Brown Balks Move to Quash Probe of Riot," *San Francisco* [CA] *Examiner*, August 23, 1945, 3.
10. "S.F. Junior Chamber Seeks Halt on Probe," *Lodi* [CA] *News Sentinel*, August 23, 1945, 3; "Prosecutor Will Not Drop Probe of S.F. Rioting," *The Modesto* [CA] *Bee and News-Herald*, August 23, 1945, 16.
11. "S.F. Junior Chamber Seeks Halt on Probe," *Lodi* [CA] *News Sentinel*, August 23, 1945, 3; "Prosecutor Will Not Drop Probe of S.F. Rioting," *The Modesto* [CA] *Bee and News-Herald*, August 23, 1945, 16.

## Chapter 14

1. "Churches Back Probe of Riot," *San Francisco* [CA] *Examiner*, August 24, 1945, 3.
2. "The Editor's Mail Box: Placing the Blame," *San Francisco* [CA] *Examiner*, August 23, 1945, 16.
3. "The Editor's Mail Box: Placing the Blame," *San Francisco* [CA] *Examiner*, August 23, 1945, 16.
4. Findagrave.com, Pfister, Hans Herbert, https://www.findagrave.com/memorial/95600246/hans-herbert-pfister; Ancestry.com, Pfister, Hans Herbert, U.S., Headstone Applications for Military Veterans, 1861–1985, https://www.ancestry.com/search/collections/2375/records/878151.
5. "The Forum: From Sailor's Sister," *Oakland* [CA] *Tribune*, August 25, 1945, 16.
6. "Well Done, San Diego," *The Tribune-News*, San Diego, CA, August 23, 1945, 22.
7. "Well Done, San Diego," *The Tribune-News*, San Diego, CA, August 23, 1945, 22.
8. "All Absolved in S.F. Riots," *San Francisco* [CA] *Examiner*, August 29, 1945, 12.
9. "More Police Essential!" *San Francisco* [CA] *Examiner*, August 22, 1945, 10; "Thorough Probe of S.F. Police Need Set by Board," *San Francisco* [CA] *Examiner*, August 26, 1945, 3.
10. "Jury Will Fix Blame in Riots," *San Francisco* [CA] *Examiner*, August 27, 1945, 5; "Grand Jury Will Fix Blame for S.F. Victory Riots," *Oakland* [CA] *Tribune*, August 28, 1945, 17.
11. "Jury Will Fix Blame in Riots," *San Francisco* [CA] *Examiner*, August 27, 1945, 5.

## Chapter 15

1. "All Absolved in S.F. Riots," *Oakland* [CA] *Tribune*, August 29, 1945, 12; "Victory Riot Inquiry Ended," *San Francisco* [CA] *Examiner*, August 29, 1945, 3.
2. "All Absolved in S.F. Riots," *Oakland* [CA] *Tribune*, August 29, 1945, 12; "Grand Jury Riot Probe Commends Authorities," *San Francisco* [CA] *Examiner*, August 30, 1945, 28.
3. "Grand Jury Riot Probe Commends Authorities," *San Francisco* [CA] *Examiner*, August 30, 1945, 28.
4. "Grand Jury Riot Probe Commends Authorities," *San Francisco* [CA] *Examiner*, August 30, 1945, 28.
5. "All Absolved in S.F. Riots," *Oakland* [CA] *Tribune*, August 29, 1945, 12; "Grand Jury Riot Probe Commends Authorities," *San Francisco* [CA] *Examiner*, August 30, 1945, 28.
6. "Grand Jury Riot Probe Commends Authorities," *San Francisco* [CA] *Examiner*, August 30, 1945, 28.
7. "Grand Jury Riot Probe Commends Authorities," *San Francisco* [CA] *Examiner*, August 30, 1945, 28.

## Chapter Notes

8. "All Absolved in S.F. Riots," *Oakland* [CA] *Tribune*, August 29, 1945, 12; "'Frisco Jurors Absolve Rioters," *Springfield* [OH] *Daily News*, August 29, 1945, 1.

9. "Victory Riot Inquiry Ended," *San Francisco* [CA] *Examiner*, August 29, 1945, 3.

10. "All Absolved in S.F. Riots," *Oakland* [CA] *Tribune*, August 29, 1945, 12; "'Frisco Jurors Absolve Rioters," *Springfield* [OH] *Daily News*, August 29, 1945, 1.

11. "Police Department, Coroner, Liquor Permits, Morals," *Report of the Grand Jury, San Francisco*, 16; "Traffic," *Report of the Grand Jury, San Francisco*, 39.

12. "All Absolved in S.F. Riots," *Oakland* [CA] *Tribune*, August 29, 1945, 12; "'Frisco Jurors Absolve Rioters," *Springfield* [OH] *Daily News*, August 29, 1945, 1; "Victory Riot Inquiry Ended," *San Francisco* [CA] *Examiner*, August 29, 1945, 3.

13. "All Absolved in S.F. Riots," *Oakland* [CA] *Tribune*, August 29, 1945, 12; "S.F. Peace Riots Blamed Upon GIs," *The Press Democrat*, Santa Rosa, CA, August 30, 1945, 1.

14. "Extraordinary Conclusion," *Redwood City* [CA] *Tribune*, September 1, 1945, 2.

15. Editorial, "The investigations…," *The Bakersfield* [CA] *Californian*, September 1, 1945, 12; National Security Agency/Central Security Service, "Doing it Until We Got it Right: A Short History of the Pearl Harbor Investigations," https://www.nsa.gov/Press-Room/News-Highlights/Article/Article/3609901/doing-it-until-we-got-it-right-a-short-history-of-the-pearl-harbor-investigatio/#:~:text=In%20 1946%2C%20the%20committee's%20 findings,seen%20the%20end%20of%20 it.%E2%80%9D.

16. "Riot Jurors Ask Officials' Views," *Oakland* [CA] *Tribune*, August 22, 1945, 4.

## Chapter 16

1. "S.F. Police Mobilize to Balk V-J Riots," *San Francisco* [CA] *Examiner*, September 1, 1945, 1; "No Liquor Sales on V-J Day," *Alameda* [CA] *Times-Star*, September 1, 1945, 1.

2. "No Liquor Sales on V-J Day," *Alameda* [CA] *Times-Star*, September 1, 1945, 1.

3. "Lapham Warns Against New Peace Rioting," *San Francisco* [CA] *Examiner*, September 2, 1945, 1.

4. "No Liquor Sales on V-J Day," *Alameda* [CA] *Times-Star*, September 1, 1945, 1.

5. "S.F. Police Mobilize To Balk V-J Riots," *San Francisco* [CA] *Examiner*, September 1, 1945, 1; "No Liquor Sales on V-J Day," *Alameda* [CA] *Times-Star*, September 1, 1945, 1; "Grand Jury Riot Probe Commends Authorities," *San Francisco* [CA] *Examiner*, August 30, 1945, 28.

6. "S.F. Police Mobilize To Balk V-J Riots," *San Francisco* [CA] *Examiner*, September 1, 1945, 1, 6; "No Liquor Sales on V-J Day," *Alameda* [CA] *Times-Star*, September 1, 1945, 1.

7. "S.F. Officers Prepare To Avert Riots," *The Modesto* [CA] *Bee and News-Herald*, September 1, 1945, 1; "No Liquor Sales on V-J Day," *Alameda* [CA] *Times-Star*, September 1, 1945, 1.

8. The American Presidency Project, "Radio Address to the American People After the Signing of the Terms of Unconditional Surrender by Japan," https://www.presidency.ucsb.edu/documents/radio-address-the-american-people-after-the-signing-the-terms-unconditional-surrender.

9. "San Francisco Bars Closed, Police Alerted," *Press-Telegram*, Long Beach, CA, September 2, 1945, 1.

10. "San Francisco Closed UP Tight By Police," *The Chico* [CA] *Enterprise*, September 9, 1945, 1, 3; "Quiet V-J Celebration Here Anticlimax to 'Victory Riots,'" *San Francisco* [CA] *Examiner*, September 3, 1945, 9; "S.F. Quiet in V-J Day Observance," *San Mateo* [CA] *Times*, September 3, 1945, 3.

11. "S.F. Is Quiet," *The Fresno* [CA] *Bee*, September 2, 1945, 2; "Four Arrested Over Weekend," *Santa Cruz* [CA] *Sentinel-News*, September 4, 1945, 1.

12. "Oakland V-J Day Quiet," *The Oakland* [CA] *Post-Enquirer*, September 3, 1945, 6.

13. "Quiet V-J Celebration Here Anticlimax to 'Victory Riots,'" *San Francisco* [CA] *Examiner*, September 3, 1945, 9.

14. "Oakland V-J Day Quiet," *The Oakland* [CA] *Post-Enquirer*, September 3, 1945, 6.

## Chapter Notes

15. "CIO Threatens Strike for Shorter Work Day," *San Francisco* [CA] *Examiner*, September 4, 1945, 1.

16. "Labor Day Rites in Bay Area," *Alameda* [CA] *Times-Star*, September 3, 1945, 1; "Old Fashioned Labor Day to Be Celebrated," *San Francisco* [CA] *Examiner*, September 2, 1945, 7; "C.I.O. To Demand Shorter Work Week To Spread Jobs," *Oakland* [CA] *Tribune*, September 4, 1945, 10.

17. "Mishaps Few in Oakland Area," *Oakland* [CA] *Tribune*, September 4, 1945, 10.

## Chapter 17

1. "The Day's News in Brief: Skaneateles, N.Y.," *Alameda* [CA] *Times-Star*, September 3, 1945, 1.

2. McManus, *Fire and Fortitude*, 117, 155, 460; "Yamashita Enters U.S. Lines for Surrender," *San Francisco* [CA] *Examiner*, September 3, 1945, 1.

3. "Wainwright Coming Home," *Oakland* [CA] *Tribune*, September 4, 1945, 1; "Wainwright on Way to S.F. by Plane; May Arrive Today," *San Francisco* [CA] *Examiner*, September 4, 1945, 1; "Wainwright Due Back in U.S. Sunday, Wife Says," *Pasadena* [CA] *Independent*, September 5, 1945, 22.

4. "Wainwright to Lead S.F. Parade," *Oakland* [CA] *Tribune*, September 6, 1945, 3; "Victory March Details Given; 20,000 Parade," *San Francisco* [CA] *Examiner*, September 6, 1945, 26.

5. "Wainwright to Lead S.F. Parade," *Oakland* [CA] *Tribune*, September 6, 1945, 3; "Victory March Details Given; 20,000 Parade," *San Francisco* [CA] *Examiner*, September 6, 1945, 26; "S.F. Gives Wainwright Thunderous Ovation," *San Francisco* [CA] *Examiner*, September 10, 1945, 3.

6. "Victory March Details Given; 20,000 Parade," *San Francisco* [CA] *Examiner*, September 6, 1945, 26; "Wainwright to Lead Parade in S.F. celebration Sunday," *San Francisco* [CA] *Examiner*, September 7, 1945, 1; "Hundreds of Planes to Roar Salute As 20,000 Parade Here Sunday," *San Francisco* [CA] *Examiner*, September 7, 1945, 7.

7. Johnson, "Bataan's Defender Hailed," *Dayton* [OH] *Herald*, September 10, 1945, 1; Hyer, "S.F. Welcomes Wainwright," *San Francisco* [CA] *Examiner*, September 10, 1945, 1.

8. Johnson, "Bataan's Defender Hailed," *Dayton* [OH] *Herald*, September 10, 1945, 1.

9. Hyer, "S.F. Welcomes Wainwright," *San Francisco* [CA] *Examiner*, September 10, 1945, 1; "Vast Throngs Greet Gen. Wainwright as He Lands in San Francisco," *The Boston* [MA] *Daily Globe*, September 10, 1945, 8; Johnson, "Bataan's Defender Hailed," *Dayton* [OH] *Herald*, September 10, 1945, 1.

10. Hyer, "S.F. Gives Wainwright Thunderous Ovation," *San Francisco* [CA] *Examiner*, September 10, 1945, 3.

11. Hyer, "S.F. Welcomes Wainwright," *San Francisco* [CA] *Examiner*, September 10, 1945, 1; Hyer, "S.F. Gives Wainwright Thunderous Ovation," *San Francisco* [CA] *Examiner*, September 10, 1945, 3; Johnson, "Bataan's Defender Hailed," *Dayton* [OH] *Herald*, September 10, 1945, 1.

12. Hyer, "S.F. Gives Wainwright Thunderous Ovation," *San Francisco* [CA] *Examiner*, September 10, 1945, 3; "Vast Throngs Greet Gen. Wainwright as He Lands in San Francisco," *The Boston* [MA] *Daily Globe*, September 10, 1945, 8; Johnson, "Bataan's Defender Hailed," *Dayton* [OH] *Herald*, September 10, 1945, 1.

13. Hyer, "S.F. Gives Wainwright Thunderous Ovation," *San Francisco* [CA] *Examiner*, September 10, 1945, 3; Johnson, "Bataan's Defender Hailed," *Dayton* [OH] *Herald*, September 10, 1945, 1.

14. "Vast Throngs Greet Gen. Wainwright as He Lands in San Francisco," *The Boston* [MA] *Daily Globe*, September 10, 1945, 8.

15. "15 Casualties During Parade," *San Francisco* [CA] *Examiner*, September 10, 1945, 3.

16. "Saratoga Comes Home," *Hayward* [CA] *Review*, September 14, 1945, 1; Greene, "War Was Ended in Fun, Tragedy," *Greensboro* [NC] *Daily News*, August 14, 1965, 9.

17. Bodenweck, "City Went Crazy When WWII Ended," *San Francisco* [CA] *Examiner*, August 13, 1985, 9; Siegel, "All Things Considered: Recalling an American Riot on V-J Day," August 15, 2005, https://www.npr.org/2005/08/15/4800963/recalling-an-american-riot-on-v-j-day.

## Chapter Notes

18. "Grand Jury to Sift S.F. Peace Riot," *Oakland* [CA] *Tribune*, August 20, 1945, 13.
19. Georgeson, "The Rape of San Francisco," *Real War*, 35.
20. Georgeson, "The Rape of San Francisco," *Real War*, 35.

## Chapter 18

1. Siegel, "All Things Considered: Recalling an American Riot of V.J. Day," https://www.npr.org/2005/08/15/4800963/recalling-an-american-riot-on-v-j-day; History News Network, "The dark side of V-J Day: The worst riot in San Francisco's history," https://www.historynewsnetwork.org/article/the-dark-side-of-v-j-day-the-worst-riot-in-san-fra.
2. "Monroe Riots Eggs Police Head," *Wisconsin State Journal*, Madison, WI, August 15, 1945, 10; "Monroe Joyful," *Monroe* [WI] *Evening Times*, August 15, 1945, 1.
3. "New Bedford Men Deny Inciting Riot," *The Boston* [MA] *Evening Globe*, August 17, 1945, 14; "Guardsmen Quell New Bedford Riot," *San Francisco* [CA] *Examiner*, August 17, 1945, 12; "Night Riot in New Bedford," *Springfield* [MA] *Daily News*, August 17, 1945, 7.
4. "Combat Veterans Observe Victory," *Monroe* [LA] *Morning World*, August 15, 1945, 8.
5. Bernstein, "Even Rain Ignored By Cheering Crowd Exceeding 100,000," *Buffalo* [NY] *Courier Express*, August 15, 1945, 1; Meddoff, "Victory Prayers Follow City's Wild Rejoicing," *Buffalo* [NY] *Evening News*, August 15, 1945, 1.
6. "State Observance Noisy, Harmless," *Monroe* [WI] *Evening Times*, August 15, 1945, 1.
7. "500,000 Here Celebrate Peace with Noise and Merrymaking," *The Evening Star*, Washington, DC, August 15, 1945, 1.
8. Potter, "Whoopee-Bent Mob Jams City," *The Pittsburgh* [PA] *Press*, August 15, 1945, 1.
9. Potter, "Whoopee-Bent Mob Jams City," *The Pittsburgh* [PA] *Press*, August 15, 1945, 1; "Liquor and Beer Sale Stopped by Governor," *Pittsburgh* [PA] *Post-Gazette*, August 15, 1945, 1.
10. Potter, "Whoopee-Bent Mob Jams City," *The Pittsburgh* [PA] *Press*, August 15, 1945, 1; Jewell, "Riotous Scenes Follow Official End of Fighting," *Pittsburgh* [PA] *Post-Gazette*, August 15, 1945, 1.
11. Linscott, "Boston Becomes Bedlam of Jubilant Demonstrators," *The Boston* [MA] *Daily Globe*, August 15, 1945, 1.
12. "Crowds Joyously Celebrate End of the War Into Morning Hours," *St. Louis* [MO] *Post-Dispatch*, August 15, 1945, 1.
13. "Baltimore Cuts Loose with Bang as 200,000 Celebrate End of War," *The Sun*, Baltimore, MD, August 15, 1945, 18.
14. "Baltimore Cuts Loose with Bang as 200,000 Celebrate End of War," *The Sun*, Baltimore, MD, August 15, 1945, 4, 18.
15. Loveland, "Cleveland Boils Over," *The Plain Dealer*, Cleveland, OH, August 15, 1945, 1.
16. "L.A. Celebration Spares Property," *Telegram-Tribune*, San Luis Obispo, CA, August 15, 1945, 8; "No Damage to Property in L.A.," *Santa Barbara* [CA] *News-Press*, August 15, 1945, 2.
17. Pooler, "City Greets End with Wildest Day," *Detroit* [MI] *Free Press*, August 15, 1945, 1; "Detroit Sidelights," *Detroit* [MI] *Free Press*, August 15, 1945, 3.
18. "1 Dead, over 100 Injured in Victory Celebrations," *The Philadelphia* [PA] *Inquirer*, August 15, 1945, 4.
19. "Police Battle Victory Rioters," *The Philadelphia* [PA] *Inquirer*, August 15, 1945, 4.
20. "Joyous Bedlam Loosed in City," *Chicago* [IL] *Tribune*, August 15, 1945, 1; "Opening of Bars Is Signal for 2d Peace Outburst," *Chicago* [IL] *Tribune*, August 16, 1945, 10.
21. Gotthart, "2 Million Blow Off Lid in N.Y. Riot of Noise," *Chicago* [IL] *Tribune*, August 15, 1945, 3.
22. Berman, "More from the Scene of That Famous V-J Day Kiss in Times Square," https://www.life.com/history/v-j-day-kiss-times-square/.
23. Clifford, "V-J festivities in San Francisco turned into nights of hell," *Record Searchlight*, Redding, CA, August 14, 1995, 3.
24. Linscott, "Boston Becomes Bedlam of Jubilant Demonstrators," *The Boston* [MA] *Daily Globe*, August 15, 1945, 1.

# Bibliography

## Internet Sources

The American Presidency Project, "Radio Address to the American People After the Signing of the Terms of Unconditional Surrender by Japan," https://www.presidency.ucsb.edu/documents/radio-address-the-american-people-after-the-signing-the-terms-unconditional-surrender.

Ancestry.com, Batchan, John Sutherland, San Francisco Area Funeral Home Records, https://www.ancestry.com/search/collections/2118/records/340323?tid=&pid=&queryId=abc33e22-4170-4541-89a3-80d1802052b9&_phsrc=rBa31&_phstart=successSource.

———, Flaherty, San Francisco Area Funeral Home Records, https://www.ancestry.com/discoveryui-content/view/340792:2118?ssrc=pt&tid=158246073&pid=192076013720.

———, Gyorgy, Joseph Samuel, https://www.ancestry.com/family-tree/person/tree/59671280/person/30255000854/facts.

———, Krystal, Jack, https://www.ancestry.com/family-tree/person/tree/10456415/person/55967011/facts.

———, Pfister, Hans Herbert, U.S., Headstone Applications for Military Veterans, 1861–1985, https://www.ancestry.com/search/collections/2375/records/878151.

———. Prim, James W., https://www.ancestry.com/family-tree/person/tree/10671454/person/202549547981/facts?_phsrc=rBa5&_phstart=successSource.

———. Thompson, William James, https://www.ancestry.com/family-tree/person/tree/65624967/person/44378696208/facts?_phsrc=KiH25&_phstart=successSource.

Bay Area Census, San Francisco County, 1940, http://www.bayareacensus.ca.gov/counties/SanFranciscoCounty40.htm.

Berman, Eliza, "More from the Scene of That Famous V-J Day Kiss in Times Square," https://www.life.com/history/v-j-day-kiss-times-square/.

Bonnett, Wayne, *Build Ships! San Francisco Bay Wartime Shipbuilding Photographs*, excerpted in National Park Service, "World War II Shipbuilding in the San Francisco Bay Area," https://www.nps.gov/articles/000/world-war-ii-shipbuilding-in-the-san-francisco-bay-area.htm.

Canadian War Museum, "Canada and the War: The Halifax VE Day Riots, 7–8 May 1945," https://www.warmuseum.ca/cwm/exhibitions/newspapers/canadawar/halifax_e.html.

*Car Coach Reports*, January 2, 2014, https://carcoachreports.com/gas-rationing-gas-ration-stickers/.

Clifford, James O., "War's End Euphoria in San Francisco Turned to Riots," August 13, 1995. https://apnews.com/article/f53c9af440fb88498fe5d7d5ff3d7d59.

Findagrave.com, Gyorgy, Joseph Samuel, https://www.findagrave.com/memorial/106519640/joseph-samuel-gyorgy.

———, Krystal, Jack, https://www.findagrave.com/memorial/209684076/jack-john-krystal.

———, Morris, Estelle McArdle, https://www.findagrave.com/memorial/108021620/estelle-mcardle-morris.

———, Pfister, Hans Herbert, https://

# Bibliography

www.findagrave.com/memorial/95600246/hans-herbert-pfister.

———, Tarkington, Bruce Keith, https://www.findagrave.com/memorial/3639765/3639765/bruce-keith-tarkington.

———, Thompson, William James, https://www.findagrave.com/memorial/65282517/william-james-thompson.

Fix, Lauren, "The History of Gas Rationing Stickers," Found SF: The San Francisco Digital History Archive, "A guide to the Roger D. Lapham photograph collection, 1892–1956," https://oac.cdlib.org/findaid/ark:/13030/c8jm2c1f/admin/.

———, "Mayor Roger Lapham," https://www.foundsf.org/index.php?title=Mayor_Roger_Lapham.

Harry S Truman Library and Museum, "The President's News Conference," https://www.trumanlibrary.gov/library/public-papers/100/presidents-news-conference.

Headlines in History, *Fishwrap: The Official Blog of Newspapers*, https://blog.newspapers.com/august-15-1945-the-75th-anniversary-of-v-j-day/.

History News Network, "The dark side of V-J Day: The worst riot in San Francisco's history," https://www.historynewsnetwork.org/article/the-dark-side-of-v-j-day-the-worst-riot-in-san-fra.

*Keep the Spirit of '45 Alive*, http://spiritof45.org/home0.aspx.

Market Street Railway Museum, "Jubilation—and riots—on Market Street 75 years ago," https://www.streetcar.org/jubilation-and-riots-on-market-street-75-years-ago/.

Martini, John A., "Seacoast Defense: Fortress San Francisco," https://www.nps.gov/articles/000/seacoast-defense-fortress-san-francisco.htm.

*Military Times*, "Hall of Valor: Carleton Herbert Wright," https://valor.militarytimes.com/recipient/recipient-21645/.

Museum of the City of San Francisco, "San Francisco Police Dept. World War II Years," https://sfmuseum.org/sfpd/sfpd6.html.

National Governors Association, "California Gov. Edmund Gerald Brown," https://www.nga.org/governor/edmund-gerald-brown/.

National Park Service, "Fort Mason Historic District," https://www.nps.gov/places/fort-mason-historic-district.htm.

———, "Travel World War II Sites in the San Francisco Bay Area," https://www.nps.gov/subjects/travelbayareawwii/stories.htm#:~:text=The%20San%20Francisco%20Bay%20Area's,world's%20largest%20combined%20shipbuilding%20complex.

National Security Agency/Central Security Service, "Doing It Until We Got It Right: A Short History of the Pearl Harbor Investigations," https://www.nsa.gov/Press-Room/News-Highlights/Article/Article/3609901/doing-it-until-we-got-it-right-a-short-history-of-the-pearl-harbor-investigatio/#:~:text=In%201946%2C%20the%20committee's%20findings,seen%20the%20end%20of%20it.%E2%80%9D.

Navy—Together We Served, Ficalora, Anthony, "Service Reflections of a Navy Veteran," https://navy.togetherweserved.com/usn/voices/2017/151/Ficalora_voices.html.

Online Archive of California, "A guide to the Roger D. Lapham photograph collection, 1892–1956," https://oac.cdlib.org/findaid/ark:/13030/c8jm2c1f/admin/.

The Pacific War Online Encyclopedia, "Wright, Carleton Herbert," http://pwencycl.kgbudge.com/W/r/Wright_Carleton_H.htm.

SF.gov, "About the Civil Grand Jury," https://www.sf.gov/departments-civil-grand-jury-about.

Siegel, Robert, "All Things Considered: Recalling an American Riot on V-J Day," National Public Radio, August 15, 2005, https://www.npr.org/2005/08/15/4800963/recalling-an-american-riot-on-v-j-day.

Sundin, Sarah, "Make It Do—Gasoline Rationing in World War II," https://www.sarahsundin.com/make-it-do-gasoline-rationing-in-world-war-ii-2/.

"Take Me Out—When the Family Car was a Streetcar in San Francisco," https://www.youtube.com/watch?v=TVIqQ0K-haI&t=5s.

Wwdrkid, "VJ Day San Francisco Market

## Bibliography

Street, 1945." https://www.trainorders.com/discussion/read.php?11,1417808.

YouTube.com, "V-J Day: San Francisco 1945." https://www.youtube.com/watch?v=LjPB9hjfjbg.

## Identified Newspaper Writers

(Few newspaper reporters were identified as the writer of articles in 1945. Most were submitted simply as either AP [Associated Press] or UP [United Press] articles.)

Bacque, Peter, "It Took 2 Days to Age 2 Years," *Richmond* [VA] *Times-Dispatch*, September 3, 1995, 1.

Bernstein, Manuel, "Even Rain Ignored by Cheering Crowd Exceeding 100,000," *Buffalo* [NY] *Courier Express*, August 15, 1945, 1.

Bodenweck, Bill, "City Went Crazy When WWII Ended," *San Francisco* [CA] *Examiner*, August 13, 1985, 9.

Burns, Eugene, "Gleeful, Wild S. F. Uproar Recalls Pearl Harbor Horror," *The Fresno* [CA] *Bee*, August 14, 1945.

Clifford, James O., "V-J festivities in San Francisco turned into nights of hell," *Record Searchlight*, Redding, CA, August 14, 1995, 3.

Dailey, Jack, "SF Blows Its Top as Japs Surrender," *Hayward* [CA] *Review*, August 14, 1945, 2.

Gotthart, Charles, "2 Million Blow Off Lid in N.Y. Riot of Noise," *Chicago* [IL] *Tribune*, August 15, 1945, 3.

Greene, Davis S., "War Was Ended in Fun, Tragedy," *Greensboro* [NC] *Daily News*, August 14, 1965, 9.

Hackett, Hennen, "Riot Squads of 3200 in S.F. Quell Mobs as Celebration becomes 'Orgy,'" *Santa Barbara* [CA] *News-Press*, August 16, 1945, 1.

———. "San Francisco Celebration Turns Into Riot; State of Emergency Proclaimed," *Appeal Democrat*, Marysville, CA, August 16, 1945, 2.

Hartsell, Lynn, "One big enthusiastic block party," *San Francisco* [CA] *Examiner*, August 11, 1995, 18.

Hyer, Richard V., "S.F. Gives Wainwright Thunderous Ovation," *San Francisco* [CA] *Examiner*, September 10, 1945, 3.

———, "S.F. Welcomes Wainwright," *San Francisco* [CA] *Examiner*, September 10, 1945, 1.

Hyman, Alvin D., "San Francisco Stages Second Celebration; Crowds, Good Natured at First, Grow Rough," *San Francisco* [CA] *Examiner*, August 15, 1945, C.

———. "Wild Night Greets End of War in S.F.," *San Francisco* [CA] *Examiner*, August 15, 1945, 1.

Jewell, Ingrid, "Riotous Scenes Follow Official End of Fighting," *Pittsburgh* [PA] *Pittsburgh Post-Gazette*, August 15, 1945, 1.

LeBaron, Gaye, "At Home, VJ Day Meant an End to the Waiting," *The Press Democrat*, Santa Rosa, CA, August 13, 1995, A2.

Linscott, Seymour R., "Boston Becomes Bedlam of Jubilant Demonstrators," *The Boston* [MA] *Daily Globe*, August 15, 1945, 1.

Loveland, Roelif, "Cleveland Boils Over," *The Plain Dealer*, Cleveland, OH, August 15, 1945, 1.

Meddoff, Jack, "Victory Prayers Follow City's Wild Rejoicing," *Buffalo* [NY] *Evening News*, August 15, 1945, 1.

Morgan, Joe W., "Joyous Nation is Premature," *Anaheim* [CA] *Bulletin*, August 14, 1945.

Pooler, James S., "City Greets End With Wildest Day," *The Detroit* [MI] *Free Press*, August 15, 1945, 1.

Potter, Chester, "Whoopee-Bent Mob Jams City," *The Pittsburgh* [PA] *Press*, August 15, 1945, 1.

Snyder, Bernardine, "Canteens, Centers Celebrate as Downtown S.F. Explodes in Jubilee," *San Francisco* [CA] *Examiner*, August 15, 1945, 18.

Sullivan, Prescott, "The Low Down," *San Francisco* [CA] *Examiner*, August 17, 1945, 22.

Wingo, Josette Dermody, "It made the bricks vibrate," *San Francisco* [CA] *Examiner*, August 11, 1995, 18.

## Newspapers

*Alameda Times-Star*, Alameda, CA, September 1 and 3, 1945.

*Anaheim* [CA] *Bulletin*, August 14, 1945.

*Anderson* [IN] *Daily Bulletin*, August 14, 1945.

# Bibliography

Bakersfield [CA] *Californian*, August 16, 22, 1945; and September 1, 1945.
Bangor [ME] *Daily News*, October 14, 1942.
The Belleville [IL] *News Democrat*, August 14, 1995.
The Boston [MA] *Daily Globe*, September 10, 1945.
The Boston [MA] *Evening Globe*, August 17, 1945.
Buffalo [NY] *Courier Express*, August 15, 1945.
Buffalo [NY] *Evening News*, August 15, 1945.
Chicago [IL] *Tribune*, August 15 and 16, 1945.
The Chico [CA] *Enterprise*, August 13, 15, 1945; September 9, 1945.
*Contra Costa Gazette*, Martinez, CA, August 15, 16, and 20, 1945.
Corona [CA] *Daily Independent*, August 22, 1945.
Dayton [OH] *Journal*, September 10, 1945.
Detroit [MI] *Free Press*, August 15, 1945.
*Evening Herald*, Shenandoah, PA, August 18, 1945.
*Evening Star*, Washington, DC, August 15, 1945.
The Fresno [CA] *Bee*, August 14, 16, 1945; September 2, 1945.
Grand Forks [ND] *Herald*, August 15, 1945.
Greensboro [NC] *Daily News*, August 14, 1965.
Hanford [CA] *Sentinel*, August 21, 1945.
The Hayward [CA] *Review*, August 14, 1945; September 14, 1945.
*Herald-Examiner*, Los Angeles, CA, August 17, 1945.
*Imperial Valley Press*, El Centro, CA, August 16, 1945.
*Intelligencer Journal*, Lancaster, PA, August 16, 1945.
The *Ledger-Star*, Norfolk, VA, August 14, 1945.
Lodi [CA] *News-Sentinel*, August 17 and 23, 1945.
Long Beach [CA] *Independent*, August 20, 1945.
Mandan [ND] *Daily Pioneer*, August 14, 1945.
*Mason Valley News*, Mason, NV, August 11, 1995.
Medford [OR] *Mail Tribune*, August 22, 1945.
The Modesto [CA] *Bee and News-Herald*, August 14, 16, 18, 23, 1945; September 1, 1945.

Monroe [LA] *Morning World*, August 15, 1945.
Monroe [WI] *Evening Times*, August 15, 1945.
New Orleans [LA] *States*, August 14, 1945.
Norfolk [VA] *Ledger-Dispatch*, August 13, 1945.
Oakland [CA] *Post-Enquirer*, August 14, 17, 20, 21, 24, 25, 1945; September 3, 1945.
Oakland [CA] *Tribune*, May 9, 10, August 12, 13, 14, 15, 16, 18, 20, 21, 22, 25, 28, 29, 1945; September 4, 6, 1945.
*Oregon Daily Journal*, Portland, OR, August 14, 1945.
Oroville [CA] *Mercury-Register*, August 20, 1945.
Oxnard [CA] *Press-Courier*, August 18, 1945.
Palo Alto [CA] *Times*, August 15, 1945.
Pasadena [CA] *Independent*, September 5, 1945.
Pauls Valley [OK] *Democrat*, August 23, 1945.
Petaluma [CA] *Argus-Courier*, August 16, 17, and 22, 1945.
The Philadelphia [PA] *Inquirer*, August 15, 1945.
Pittsburgh [PA] *Post-Gazette*, August 15, 1945.
The *Plain Dealer*, Cleveland, OH, August 15, 1945.
The *Press Democrat*, Santa Rosa, CA, August 16, 17, and 30, 1945.
*Press-Telegram*, Long Beach, CA, September 2, 1945.
Redding [CA] *Record Searchlight*, August 16, 1945.
Redwood City [CA] *Tribune*, August 17, September 1, 1945.
Richmond [VA] *Times-Dispatch*, September 3, 1995.
Riverside [CA] *Enterprise*, August 20, 1945. Courtesy *The Press-Enterprise/SCNG*.
Rushville [IN] *Republican*, August 13, 1945.
The Sacramento [CA] *Bee*, August 17, 1945.
The Sacramento [CA] *Union*, August 17, 1945.
St. Louis [MO] *Post-Dispatch*, August 15, 1945.
St. Louis [MO] *Star-Times*, August 14, 1945.
San Francisco [CA] *Examiner*, May 8, 9, 10, 1945; August 10, 11, 13, 14, 15, 16, 17, 19,

## Bibliography

20, 21, 22, 23, 24, 26, 27, 29, 30, 1945; September 1, 2, 3, 4, 5, 6, 7, 10, 1945; August 13, 1985; August 11, 1995.

*San Mateo* [CA] *Times*, August 11, 13, 14, 15, 18, 1945; September 3, 1945.

*Santa Barbara* [CA] *News-Press*, August 15, 16, and 17, 1945.

*Santa Cruz* [CA] *Sentinel-News*, May 8 and September 4, 1945.

*The Sioux Center* [IA] *News*, November 18, 1943.

*Springfield* [MA] *Daily News*, August 17, 1945.

*Springfield* [OH] *Daily News*, August 29, 1945

*Stanford* [CA] *Daily*, August 17, 1945.

*The Sun*, Baltimore, MD, August 15, 1945.

*Telegram-Tribune*, San Luis Obispo, CA, August 15. 16, and 17, 1945.

*The Tensas Gazette*, St. Joseph, LA, October 16, 1943.

*The Tribune-News*, San Diego, CA, August 23, 1945.

*Ukiah* [CA] *Republican Press*, August 22, 1945.

*The Vallejo* [CA] *News-Chronicle*, August 10, 13, 1945.

*Wilmington* [CA] *Press-Journal*, August 11, 1945.

*Wisconsin State Journal*, Madison, WI, August 15, 1945.

*The Wynnewood* [OK] *Gazette*, August 23, 1945.

## Books and Magazines

California, Grand Jury, *Report of the Grand Jury, San Francisco*, Vol. 1945–46, Grand Jury, San Francisco, CA, 1953.

Garvey, John, and the California Center for Military History, *Images of America: San Francisco in World War II*, Arcadia, Charleston, SC, 2007.

Georgeson, Sidney, "The Rape of San Francisco," *Real War*, Vol. 2, No. 3, November 1958.

Hopkins, William B., *The Pacific War: The Strategy, Politics, and Players That Won the War*, Zenith Press, Minneapolis, 2008.

Lockwood, Kim, *VJ Day: The End of WWII in the Pacific*, Wilkinson, Melbourne, Australia, 2015.

McDevitt, E.A., ed., *The Naval History of Treasure Island*, U.S. Naval Training and Distribution Center, San Francisco, 1946.

McManus, John C., *Fire and Fortitude: The US Army in the Pacific War, 1941–1943*, Dutton Caliber, New York, 2019.

_____, *To the End of the Earth: The US Army and the Downfall of Japan, 1945*, Dutton Caliber, New York, 2023.

Wardlow, Chester, *United States Army in World War II: The Technical Services—The Transportation Corps: Responsibilities, Organization, and Operations*, Center of Military History United States Army, Washington, DC, 1999.

# Index

Numbers in ***bold italics*** indicate pages with illustrations

Admission Day Monument  39, ***40***, ***49***, 50
Albert Samuel Clock  72–73
Albuquerque, NM  27
Anderson, A.E.  14, 85, 86, 96

Baltimore, MD  135–36
Batchan, John Sutherland  70–71
Bodenweck, Bill  11, 22, 31, 33–34, 45–46
bonfires  ***23***, 24, 27, 37, 46–47, 48, 52, 55
Boston, MA  133–34, 138
Bowen, Al  49
Boyd, Florence  33
Brown, Edmund G. "Pat"  78, 82, 84, 88, 94–95, 99–100, 102, 103, 106–7, 109, 113, 128; background 85; Civil Grand Jury 100–1, 108
Buffalo, NY  130–31

Caredio, Bob  35
Chicago, IL  27, 30, 138
Chinatown  14, 26, 37, 63, 76
Civic Center  21–22, 65, 118, 120, 122
Cleveland, OH  136

deaths  50–51, 52, 53, 70–71, 79, 100, 104–5
Detroit, MI  137
Dullea, Charles  7, 9, 11, 13, 26, 28, 35, 72, 74, 75, 80, 82, 88, 94, 99, 101, 106, 107, 109, 114, 116, 117, 120; background 10; Civil Grand Jury testimony 108; criticism of Naval personnel 81, 96, 97, 105; invokes Riot Act 73; issues General Order No. 80 89, 115; praised by Civil Grand Jury 111; responsibility 127, 136, 141, 142

Eisenstaedt, Alfred  30, 139

Ficalora, Anthony  33
firecrackers  14, 32, 37, 46, 60, 63
Flaherty, William E.  70

Fracchia, Charles  20, 127, 129
Frederickson, Robert  50, 69

Geiger, Jacob Casson  79–80, 101
Georgeson, Sidney  11, 17, 30, 41, 44, 45, 46, 47, 50, 52, 53, 54, 55, 57–59, 67, 73, 77, 81, 127–28
Getchell, Bonnie  48–49
Greene, Davis S.  6–7, 17, 20, 22, 35, 37, 41, 45, 53, 60, 79, 126
Gyorgy, Samuel  52

Hackett, Hennen  59, 66, 73, 76
Halifax, Nova Scotia, Canada VE-Day Riot  9, 110, 141
Harris, Bernard A.  40
Hartsell, Lynn  10, 32, 43
Heagerty, Dave  30, 38, 39, 41
Hennigan, Virginia  24, 30, 31
Hoffman, Phil  41–42
Houser, Frederick F.  56, 133, 136, 140
Hyman, Alvin D.  30, 33, 35, 39, 43, 46, 48, 52, 56

Jones, Samuel J.  86, 97–98

Krystal, Jack  54

Lapham, Roger D.  8, 10, 13, 28, 56, 82, 83, 84, 101, 106, 107, 113–14, 120, 135, 136; August 16 press conference 80; background 9; Civil Grand Jury testimony 108; liquor enforcement meeting 82–83; military meeting 98; responsibility 140, 141, 142; on Victory Parade 126
Leiser, Peggy  43
looting  26, 43, 46, 46, 53–54, 56, 59, 67, 69, 71–72, 74, 77, 100
Los Angeles, CA  27, 89, 120, 136–37

*Index*

Marshall, Larry 42, 67, 82, 100
Milwaukee, WI 130
molestation/rape of women 1, 44–45, 48–49, 57, 58, 69–70, 79–80, 82, 101, 110, 111
Monroe, WI 129
Mooney, Charles David 51
Morgan, Joe W. 18, 20, 26
Morris, Estelle McArdle 51–52

New Beford, MA 129
New Orleans, LA 130
New York, NY 4, 13, 15, 27, 28, 30, 138–39

Oakland, CA 5, 14, 15, 19, 20, 26, 39, 41, 48, 56–7, 60, 63, 70, 76, 90, 91, 105, 117
O'Callahan, Joseph T. 38

Payne, Bill 33
Pepsi Cola Center for Service Men and Women 33, 43, 50
Pfister, Hans Herbert 51, 104–5
Philadelphia, PA 70, 137–38
Pittsburgh, PA 132–33
Potsdam Declaration 3, 10, 13, 16, 18, 27, 29
Prim, James W. 51

Ramirez, Raymond Joseph 70
rape *see* molestation/rape of women
Reilly, George R. 11, 13–14, 82, 97–98, 101, 102, 111, 114; Civil Grand Jury testimony 110
Roos Brothers Store 23–24
Rule, Betty 34

Sacramento, CA 11, 28, 56, 86, 114, 140, 141
St. Louis, MO 27, 28, 134–35
Salt Lake City, UT 27

Scobie, Gustave H. 70
Simmons, Bud 6, 32–33
Snyder, Bernadine 31, 41, 48
State Board of Equalization 7, 11, 13, 35, 53, 63, 82, 86, 97, 98, 101, 107, 110, 111, 114
streetcars/trolley, destruction of 24, 41–42, 43–44, 56, 63, 78, 100

Tarkington, Bruce Keith 51, 79
Taylor, Lloyd 59, 100–1
Thompson, William James "Sonny" 50–51, 100
Treasure Island U.S. Naval Training and Distribution Center 4, *5*, 8, 10, *19*, 51, 62, 70, 79, 100, 124, 126, 135, 141, 142
Truman, Harry S 7, 8, 14, 26, 28, 30, 31, 34, 35, 48, 51, 56, 60, 63, 66, 71, 77, 90, 106, 111, 115, 117, 126, 128, 130, 131, 132, 133, 136, 138, 140, 141; Japanese signing announcement 116; VJ-Day announcement 29

Wainwright, Jonathan M. 119, 120, ***121***, 122–25, 126, 143
Warren, Earl 28, 56, 112, 120, 124; responsibility 133, 136, 140
Washington, DC 14, 15, 27, 28, 29, 30, 56, 62, 64, 116, 125, 131–32
Williams, Daniel Burdette 51
Wingo, Josette Dermody 30, 37, 43, 77
Wright, Carleton H. 65, 73, 81, 88, 94, 99, 101, 102, 113; background 62; cancellation of leave 76–7; Grand Civil Jury 95, 107, 108–9; liquor enforcement meeting 82; responsibility 141, 142

Zlokovich, V.M. 45, 100

**168**

www.ingramcontent.com/pod-product-compliance
Ingram Content Group UK Ltd.
Pitfield, Milton Keynes, MK11 3LW, UK
UKHW041938210426
5322IPUK00016B/246